MODERN BUSINESS CORRESPONDENCE

fourth edition

A Text-Workbook for Colleges

which → proper noun
that

Marjorie Hunsinger, Ph.D.

Donna C. McComas

GREGG DIVISION/McGraw-Hill Book Company
New York   St. Louis   Dallas   San Francisco   Auckland   Bogotá   Düsseldorf
Johannesburg   London   Madrid   Mexico   Montreal   New Delhi   Panama   Paris
São Paulo   Singapore   Sydney   Tokyo   Toronto

Marjorie Hunsinger has taught business correspondence at several colleges and universities, including Michigan State University, Fairmont State College, and the University of Louisville. Professor Hunsinger has also taught business subjects in several high schools and has written various professional articles for publication. She received her Ph.D. from the University of Pittsburgh.

Donna C. McComas received her B.S. and M.S. in Education at Arkansas State University, and she is currently completing her Ed.D. in Business Education and Curriculum Instruction at Memphis State University.

Sponsoring Editor: Joseph Tinervia
Senior Editing Manager: Elizabeth Huffman
Book Editors: Joan Jesurun and Timothy Perrin
Production Supervisor: Frank Bellantoni
Art Director: Frank Medina
Design Supervisor: Karen Miño
Designer: Richard Stalzer

Library of Congress Cataloging in Publication Data

Hunsinger, Marjorie.
  Modern business correspondence.

  Includes index.
  1. Commercial correspondence.   I.   McComas, Donna C., joint author.   II.   Title.
HF5726.H8   1979   651.7'5'0711   78-24107
ISBN 0-07-031275-3

MODERN BUSINESS CORRESPONDENCE, Fourth Edition

    4 5 6 7 8 9 0   WCWC   8 8 7 6 5 4 3 2 1

Letters, memorandums, and reports are the primary means of sending and receiving written information in business. These forms of communication permit an exchange of ideas, facts, recommendations, and proposals. Without this exchange, modern businesses could not exist. Because the exchange of written communications is vital to business, the ability to write letters, memorandums, and reports can often shape your success as a business worker.

The primary objective of *Modern Business Correspondence, Fourth Edition,* is to help you develop the ability to write successful business letters, memorandums, and informal reports. The materials have been carefully developed to present the fundamentals of business writing logically, clearly, and completely. The topics covered in the previous edition of the text-workbook have been expanded and reorganized to ensure coverage of all essential subjects and have been updated to reflect current accepted business practices. New examples and exercises have been added throughout the book.

Modern Business Correspondence, Fourth Edition, consists of a text-workbook and an instructor's manual, which includes a set of tests.

THE TEXT-WORKBOOK

The text-workbook has been designed so that it keeps students involved in a natural learning process from the beginning of the course to the end. The book includes a text section, a workbook section, and a reference section.

Text Section. The text divides the elements of business writing into four major parts. Part 1 (Units 1-5) is concerned with the appearance of business correspondence. Part 2 (Units 6-10) introduces the student to the general principles of good writing, including how to plan and outline correspondence. Part 3 (Units 11-20) offers the student the opportunity to apply the principles presented in Part 2 to specific types of business letters. Finally, Part 4 (Unit 21) presents the principles of writing business reports.

Workbook Section. The workbook section contains exercises correlated with the units in the text section. Each worksheet gives the student immediate practice in applying the principles studied in a particular unit. Together, the worksheets give the student comprehensive practice in handling realistic communication problems.

Reference Section. This section provides a concise, illustrated summary of the rules of grammar, punctuation, capitalization, number expression, abbreviation usage, word division, and spelling. It supplements the text discussion of these topics and gives the student a convenient source of information to use throughout the course.

THE INSTRUCTOR'S GUIDE AND KEY

The *Instructor's Guide and Key* presents unit-by-unit teaching suggestions, the key to the worksheets, and other aids for the instructor.

The Tests. The *Instructor's Guide and Key* also contains four tests—one for each of the four parts of the text-workbook. These tests make it convenient to evaluate the student's progress at regular intervals throughout the course.

Marjorie Hunsinger
Donna C. McComas

contents

Introduction

Business firms cannot function without communication; and they cannot function properly without effective communication. Although much corporate communication is accomplished through talking and listening, much more—information, directives, and inquiries—must be put in writing in the form of letters, memos, and reports.

Millions of business messages are written and read every day. For each company, the volume of correspondence and its high cost increase the need for people who possess good communication skills. The skill of writing must be learned, and the purpose of this text is to help you learn to write letters, memos, and reports that facilitate business, not frustrate it.

Business letters are involved in about 90 percent of all business transactions today; and they will continue to be the major form of written business communication for many years.

ADVANTAGES OF THE BUSINESS LETTER

The business letter has several advantages over other types of business communication. For one thing, it is frequently much less expensive than a personal visit or a telephone call. And, of course, a letter will get into an office when a telephone call may not be accepted. Also, the business letter provides a written record of a transaction, one that may be legally acceptable as a binding contract or as evidence.

Business letters are confidential, since they are usually read in privacy. The reader will most likely be able to concentrate on the message without interrup-

tion. Therefore, material that might be unsuitable for a telephone conversation can be communicated in a letter (especially if the envelope is marked "Confidential").

DISADVANTAGES OF THE BUSINESS LETTER

The business letter also has several disadvantages. Cost is perhaps the primary one. To produce the average letter now costs about $6, and this figure is constantly rising. Actually, the cost of paper, envelope, and postage is negligible; the most expensive element is time. Considered in the total cost of producing a letter are the following:

1. The time of the writer or dictator.

2. The time of the secretary if he or she took dictation directly or the proportionate cost of the dictating machine (and belt or tape) if one was used.

3. The time the secretary took to type the letter and get it signed.

4. The time used in preparing the envelope, folding and inserting the letter, stamping it, and delivering it to the post office.

5. The time and supplies involved in filing the copies.

Much effort is exerted today to reduce the time it takes people to produce effective business letters. Steps taken to save time will save money.

Poor business letters are costly and damaging. A second or even third letter made necessary by bad writing not only increases the cost greatly but also has a disastrous effect on the reader's impression of both the writer and the company.

THE IMPORTANCE OF LETTER-WRITING ABILITY

What can the ability to write good business letters mean to you? It can make it much easier to get a job, especially that important first job after you finish school. Employers will usually choose the applicant who demonstrates skill as a business communicator. Presenting yourself well in writing means that you will be able to project a favorable image of your company as well as promote successful business operations.

Once you have that first job, you will discover that keeping the job and getting promotions and raises often depend upon your ability to communicate clearly in writing. Maintaining the flow of written information is essential to business operations. Your communication skills can have a significant impact on those operations both inside and outside the company.

You will also find that the techniques presented in this book can be applied to your personal business affairs. Everyone must write business letters in dealing with retailers, banks, insurance companies, and other businesses. Letter-writing skill facilitates effective communication in all aspects of life.

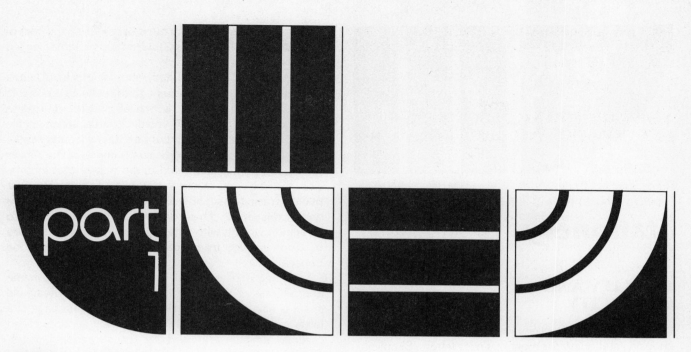

The Appearance of Business Letters

The total effect that the letter has on the reader determines whether the letter has achieved its purpose. And this total effect is produced as a result of the appearance, style, tone, mechanics, organization, and other features of the letter. In the first five units of this text we will be concerned with the mechanics of producing good letters.

The focus of the letter should be on the reader. You should be as helpful, pleasant, and courteous to the reader as possible. You will learn that the appearance of the letter, an appropriate tone, and a natural, informal writing style are very important elements of successful business correspondence.

Basically, the "rule" about the appearance of a letter is: Anything that draws the reader's attention away from the content of the letter and makes him or her aware of its physical qualities hinders it from doing its job.

Sometimes, of course, the appearance of a letter shouts for attention, as in certain direct mail letters and sales letters. In all other business correspondence, however, as soon as the reader becomes aware of how the letter looks—the stationery, the format, or the typing—he or she is no longer paying attention to the message of the letter. This inattention can be disastrous, because the reader may neither receive your message nor respond to it in the way you would like.

A business letter is like a person; the reader forms an initial impression from its appearance just as he or she does when meeting people. With letters, as with people, that first impression carries over for quite some time. What the physical appearance of a letter should do, without calling attention to itself, is to give the reader an initial subconscious impression of normalcy and businesslike attitude. The reader will then be in the right frame of mind to receive your message.

In Units 1 through 5 you will find most of what you need to know to produce letters that are practically guaranteed a pleasant reception. You will profit by studying these units carefully—they are basic to your understanding of the mechanics of letter writing. As you begin to master the mechanics, you will be able to clear up any misconceptions you may have and develop your ability to produce a letter that makes a good first impression.

The first thing that begins to build a letter's "image" is the stationery.

Stationery

QUALITY AND SIMPLICITY

Quality and simplicity are the major factors in choosing stationery for most business letters. Simplicity means the opposite of *eye-catching*—you do *not* want your stationery to catch the reader's eye and detract from the message. Since the cost of the paper and envelope is only a small fraction of the total cost of a letter, it is dangerous to compromise quality by using cheap paper and envelopes. The loss of status in the eyes of the reader cannot be easily compensated.

CHOOSING PAPER

Bond paper is used almost universally today for business stationery. It is generally available in three weights: 16-pound, 20-pound, and 24-pound bond. (Weight is figured as the weight of four reams of 8½- by 11-inch paper.) Bond paper is generally available in 25 percent "rag," which refers to the amount of rag lint in the paper. The higher the rag content, the higher the quality (and the price) of the paper.

With the inexpensive 16-pound bond paper, a typist can make as many as ten carbon copies. Because two or three sheets and an envelope of 16-pound bond usually weigh less than an ounce, this lightweight paper is often used in offices sending a good deal of mail overseas. On the other hand, disadvantages of 16-pound bond make it a poor choice for everyday business stationery. It is flimsy to the touch, often leaves an impression of cheapness, and generally seems to be "wrong" even to undiscerning readers. It also tends to be somewhat transparent, and one typed sheet on top of another can be difficult to read. Ordinarily, stay away from 16-pound bond, unless you are willing to risk having your business letters look and feel "cheap."

At the other end of the scale is 24-pound bond—rich, thick, heavy—and expensive! Other drawbacks to 24-pound bond are these: It is so thick that only a few carbon copies can be made; it tends to fill up a file drawer rapidly; and its weight brings two or three sheets

and an envelope to over an ounce, increasing the cost of postage. It is also hard to fold neatly; it looks jagged along the fold line.

The standard-weight stationery for business use is 20-pound bond. It is light enough to make a reasonable number of carbons, it is mailable without excess postage, and it takes up relatively little space in file drawers. It usually is not transparent, and it folds neatly.

You are probably familiar with some of the newer plasticized papers marketed under names that emphasize the ease of erasing mistakes. The quality that makes erasing easy, however, also makes these papers quite transparent. These easily erasable papers tend to be light in weight, with a hard finish. In general, they are different enough from good-quality bond paper to be noticeable.

"Letterhead" refers to the printed company name and address at the top of the sheet of paper; the whole sheet is also called a letterhead. Only the first page of a letter carries the letterhead. Plain sheets of paper called "second sheets" are used for the succeeding pages. Don't make the common mistake of choosing a good rag-content 20-pound bond for letterhead paper but an inferior paper for the second sheets. Use paper of exactly the same weight, quality, and size for both.

Size of Paper

The *standard size* of a business letterhead is 8½ by 11 inches (a metric size called A4 measures 210 by 297 millimeters). There are other sizes of paper in use, such as the *baronial size,* which measures 5½ by 8½ inches (metric size A5: 148 by 210 millimeters). Its small size makes it immediately noticeable to a reader, but this size also tends to be hard to find in a file drawer. Other sizes of letterheads include *monarch* (7¼ by 10½ inches), which is often used by executives; *official* (8 by 10½ inches); and *legal size* (8½ by 13 inches). There are no metric equivalents for monarch, official, and legal-size stationery.

Since you want your stationery to do its job without flagging the reader's attention, you'll be wise to use standard 8½- by 11-inch 20-pound bond paper.

Color of Stationery

Just as 8½ by 11 inches is the standard size, white is the standard color. In fact, tinted stationery may be a little startling when it comes across your desk in the morning mail! Some firms, such as cosmetics manufacturers, fashion houses, and beauty salons may benefit from the eye-catching effect of tinted stationery. But if you want to impress your reader subconsciously that everything is normal and businesslike, use only white stationery.

If you do use blue, green, or some other color of

stationery, be prepared to pay the price. First of all, your letters are going to attract attention. Second, you will spend more money for tinted paper than for white, both for letterheads and second sheets and for envelopes. Third, you will probably want a colored ribbon to match your colored paper, and it not only costs more than the standard black but also is not often readily available. Three suitable color combinations are dark blue type on pale blue paper, dark green type on light green paper, and dark brown type on buff or cream-colored paper. Finally, it is more difficult to correct errors on tinted paper.

Letterhead Design

Business letterheads of several years ago were elaborately and excessively decorated. The company name was bannered across the top like a circus poster, the names of all the officers of the company with their titles marched down the left margin, a list of products spread across the bottom, and in the middle often appeared a faint impression of "our founder" or "our factory."

Today letterhead design tends toward the simple and uncluttered. In the most-used layout, the essential information is simply placed at the top in a neat, uncrowded fashion. Occasionally a line or two is added at the bottom of the page to list a company's products or the locations of its factories. Type styles also tend to be simple, moderately bold, and spaced out (expanded). If a trademark or logotype (company symbol) is used, it no longer dominates the letterhead. The use of embossed rather than simply printed logotypes has been increasing in the past few years.

Although a letterhead is often printed in black alone, printing in one color other than black and printing in black plus another color have increased in use.

The primary purpose of a printed letterhead is to tell your reader quickly how to address a reply to you. The letterhead therefore gives the name of the company, its address, and often the telephone number. The ZIP Code must always be given; and when a telephone number is used, the area code should also be given. The company logotype may be used and, less often, a line or a few words identifying the type of business.

A letterhead should reflect a company's personality, its "image." A lawyer or a CPA is likely to select a sedate style of type with just his or her name, address, and phone number printed at the top of the sheet. An advertising agency may have a very different style, as it seeks to convey an image of creativity and imagination. In any case, planning a company letterhead should be done by a professional designer, an advertising agency, or a good printer.

You can see some examples of modern letterheads on pages 14 and 15 of Unit 3.

ENVELOPES

If you've settled on 8½- by 11-inch letterhead, your choice of envelope size is simple: *No. 10* is the name of the standard size of envelope for standard letterheads. If you have chosen a different-size letterhead, you must select envelopes to fit it.

Envelopes, like second sheets, should match letterheads in color and quality of paper. Usually a company orders envelopes at the same time as letterheads and second sheets, to be sure that all three will match.

The return address is printed in the upper left-hand corner of the face of the envelope. It should follow the form, style, and color of the letterhead.

Since window envelopes have traditionally been used to mail bills, they are rarely used for letters. Even though they represent a saving in time and money (the letter is folded so that the inside address shows through the window), they create an unnecessary hazard when a reader approaches your letter as if he or she were about to read a bill!

OTHER STATIONERY

Stationery other than letterheads and envelopes includes interoffice memorandums, invoices, business cards, order forms, and other special types. If possible, the company's identification on these should match its letterhead in style and color. Uniform stationery, especially if it carries the logotype, helps reinforce the company's identity and thus acts as part of the overall advertising and marketing effort. It also builds morale by helping branch offices feel they belong to the parent organization.

ASSIGNMENT: To make sure you understand the importance of stationery to the appearance of a letter, complete Sections A and B of the Worksheet for Unit 1.

The Parts of a Letter

Since the initial impression a reader receives is strongly affected by the appearance of the letter, the arrangement of the parts of a business letter on the letterhead is important. Is the letter placed for good balance on the page? Are punctuation and indention consistent? The arrangement of the letter parts on the letterhead is called the "format" or "letter style," which is the subject of Unit 3. This unit reviews the letter parts.

THE HEADING

On a printed letterhead, the name and address of your company serve as the heading. But for your personal business letters, do not use your company's letterhead. Instead, use a plain sheet of bond paper and type your heading information.

In place of the printed letterhead, type your full address on two lines. For standard stationery begin it on line 13 and at the center of the page. Then type the date on the next line. From the date line, space down four lines and type the inside address.

> 3804 Edgewood Street
> Dayton, Ohio 45407
> September 10, 1978

Another style gaining in popularity is to place the address directly below the typed name following the signature at the end of the letter.

> Sincerely yours,
>
> *Bill J. Farrell*
>
> Bill J. Farrell
> 1232 E. Temperance Road
> Temperance, MI 48182

Placing the address following the signature has become acceptable because it seems more logical.

THE DATE

When you use a letterhead, type the date at the left margin or begin at the center of the page (depending on the letter style). It should be at least a triple space below the letterhead and about four lines above the inside address, according to the policy of your company or the length of the letter. (See Unit 3 for more about placement.)

When typing the date, do not use an abbreviated style, such as *5/12/78*. This may mean *May 12, 1978* to you, but to a military person or a European it means *December 5, 1978*.

Don't abbreviate the month, either in the date or in the body of the letter. Typing *Feb.* may save a little time, but *February* looks better to a reader. Do not use *th, st, nd,* or *d* after the date: *May 12, 1978* is clear and acceptable. Note that the comma must be inserted before the year. In the rare instances where the form is reversed, such as *12 May 1978* (European or military usage), the comma is omitted.

THE INSIDE ADDRESS

The inside address contains the reader's full name and address, including the name of his or her company. The inside address is essential in order to identify to whom the letter should go, since a letter and its envelope may be separated after opening. The inside address indicates that the letter is a business letter.

> Ms. Evelyn T. Trask
> Manager, Personnel Relations
> Cooper & Helms, Inc.
> 12 Berkeley Drive
> Bethel, NC 27812

In addition to the reader's full name and address and the name of her company, the inside address above includes a courtesy title (*Ms.*) and a job title.

Names and Titles of Persons

The one important rule about people's names and titles is: Spell them right! A person will surely notice that his or her name or title is misspelled or given incorrectly. Here are some pointers.

1. Always write the name exactly as the owner prefers, as he or she writes it. Be sure to spell it correctly. Watch out for the variations in the spelling of many names, such as *Philip, Phillip; Jean, Jeanne, Gene; Alan, Allan, Allen; Joan, Joanne, JoAnn; Stuart, Stewart; and Lewis, Louis.*

Do not abbreviate a person's name unless the abbreviation appears in his or her signature. For example, write out *William* unless the person to whom you are writing signs *Wm.*

Follow the owner's preference in the use of initials. If a middle initial is used, such as *James R. Cook*, or *Sally G. Rice*, do not address him as *James Cook* or her as *Sally Rice*.

2. Use a courtesy title with the name of every person to whom you write, with one exception: If you do not know whether the addressee is a man or a woman, omit the courtesy title.

If the person has no special title—such as *Doctor, Reverend, Professor*—use *Miss, Mrs., Ms.,* or *Mr.* If you do not know whether a woman to whom you are writing prefers *Miss, Mrs.,* or *Ms.,* address her as *Ms.*

Do not use two titles that mean the same. For instance, *Dr. J. K. Rainey, M.D.,* is redundant, since *Dr.* and *M.D.* mean the same thing. Use only one of them.

The honorary titles *Reverend* and *Honorable* should be spelled out and preceded by *The—The Honorable Lee F. Garrison.* In inside addresses, such titles should always be followed by either a given name or a title—for example, *The Reverend Frederick W. Donahue* (NOT: *The Reverend Donahue*) or *The Reverend Mr. Donahue.*

3. If the person has a business or an executive title, use the title in the inside address—*Mr. Thomas N. Cross, Vice President; Dr. Hugh M. Brown, Dean of Students;* or *Ms. Sharon Delaney, Office Manager.*

4. Where possible, the lines in the inside address should be fairly equal in length. If the addressee's name is shorter than the firm name, type the title on the line with the name, preceded by a comma.

> Mr. Ronald O'Connor, President
> O'Connor Construction Company
> 7431 Berclair Road
> Cleveland, Ohio 44115

If the firm name is short, you may type the addressee's title on the second line, preceding the firm name, with a comma after it.

> Mrs. Jeanne Hummelstein
> Manager, Jeanne's Interiors

If the addressee's title is of such length that it would seriously unbalance the address, type the title alone on the second line.

> Dr. Benjamin H. Sinclair
> Supervising Resident Physician
> Park Memorial Hospital

For the company name, follow the style used in the addressee's letterhead. If abbreviations are used in the addressee's letterhead, they should be used in the inside address of your letter. For instance, if a letterhead shows *Cooper & Helms, Inc.,* then use the ampersand (&) and *Inc.* in the inside address. If the words *and, Company,* and *Incorporated* are spelled out in a letterhead, then spell them out in the inside address.

Use the official name in the inside address—for example, *Remington Rand* (no hyphen); *Harley-Davidson, Inc.* (hyphen, comma); *Sears, Roebuck & Co.* (comma after *Sears*); *McGraw-Hill Book Company* (hyphen); *Hoffman Ltd.* (no comma); *Clairol Inc.* (no comma). Use *The* as the first word in a company name only if it is part of the official name, as in *The Wig Castle.*

Street Addresses

The following styles are standard for street addresses:

1. Write house numbers without a prefix—*2058 Waring Road* (NOT: *No. 2058 Waring Road* or *#2058 Waring Road*).

2. Write *street, avenue,* and similar designations in full unless you *must* abbreviate to save space. When you do abbreviate, use the correct forms: *Ave.* for *Avenue; Blvd.* for *Boulevard; Hts.* for *Heights; N.* for *North; Pl.* for *Place; Rd.* for *Road; S.* for *South; Sq.* for *Square;* and *St.* for *Street.*

3. For easy reading, spell out street names from *First* through *Tenth: 850 Third Street.* Use figures for numbers from *11th* on: *1155 47th Street.* Omit the ordinals *st, d,* and *th* when a word like *North* or *South* separates the two numbers: *206 North 32 Street.*

4. In street names write out *North, South, East, West, Southeast, Northwest,* and the like, to avoid misreading, unless it is necessary to abbreviate to save space.

5. Type abbreviations for sections of a city this way: *5971 Central Avenue, N.E.* (note comma).

6. If *and* appears in a street address, write it out: *Jackson Avenue and Perkins Road.*

Cities, States, and ZIP Codes

In writing the city, state, and ZIP Code, follow these recommendations.

1. Always write the city, state, and ZIP Code on one line.

2. Do not abbreviate the name of the city unless it is customarily written with an abbreviation. For example, *St. Louis* and *St. Paul* should be written with the word *Saint* abbreviated.

3. Write the name of the state in full, or use the two-letter abbreviation recommended by the U.S. Postal Service and written without periods or space between the letters. A list of state names and two-letter abbreviations is given below.

4. Do not use a comma between the state and the ZIP Code, but leave one space between them.

> Empire Music Shop   Dr. Erica Daniels
> 2303 Monroe   3795 Graceland Drive
> Columbus, GA 31905   Dallas, Texas 75248

5. The Post Office recommends that the ZIP Code be used on all letters in order to speed up the mail; refer to the ZIP Code Directory in your office to obtain the correct number for areas you are not familiar with.

ABBREVIATIONS OF STATE NAMES AND CANADIAN PROVINCES

Alabama	AL	North Carolina	NC
Alaska	AK	North Dakota	ND
Arizona	AZ	Ohio	OH
Arkansas	AR	Oklahoma	OK
California	CA	Oregon	OR
Canal Zone	CZ	Pennsylvania	PA
Colorado	CO	Puerto Rico	PR
Connecticut	CT	Rhode Island	RI
Delaware	DE	South Carolina	SC
District of		South Dakota	SD
Columbia	DC	Tennessee	TN
Florida	FL	Texas	TX
Georgia	GA	Utah	UT
Guam	GU	Vermont	VT
Hawaii	HI	Virgin Islands	VI
Idaho	ID	Virginia	VA
Illinois	IL	Washington	WA
Indiana	IN	West Virginia	WV
Iowa	IA	Wisconsin	WI
Kansas	KS	Wyoming	WY
Kentucky	KY		
Louisiana	LA	Alberta	AB
Maine	ME	British Columbia	BC
Maryland	MD	Labrador	LB
Massachusetts	MA	Manitoba	MB
Michigan	MI	New Brunswick	NB
Minnesota	MN	Newfoundland	NF
Mississippi	MS	Northwest	
Missouri	MO	Territories	NT
Montana	MT	Nova Scotia	NS
Nebraska	NE	Ontario	ON
Nevada	NV	Prince Edward	
New Hampshire	NH	Island	PE
New Jersey	NJ	Quebec	PQ
New Mexico	NM	Saskatchewan	SK
New York	NY	Yukon Territory	YT

THE ATTENTION LINE

In theory, using an attention line on the envelope and in the inside address signals that the letter is company business and should be handled by someone else if the addressee is absent. But any letter coming into an office is assumed to be company business unless it is marked "Personal" or "Confidential."

To address a letter to

DuBois Chemicals
3030 Covington Pike
Chattanooga, TN 37407
Attention Mr. John Stewart

is not really different from one addressed to

Mr. John Stewart
DuBois Chemicals
3030 Covington Pike
Chattanooga, TN 37407

And a letter addressed to

Farnsworth and Associates Inc.
2598 Lakeshore Drive
New Orleans, LA 70122
ATTENTION ADVERTISING MANAGER

is hardly much different from one addressed to

Advertising Manager
Farnsworth and Associates Inc.
2598 Lakeshore Drive
New Orleans, LA 70122

In actual practice you will usually find that when you think you should use an attention line, you can just as well insert the title or name in the inside address in the normal manner.

A variation of the attention line, however, is useful when you write to a large company. For instance, if you are writing to a company with whom you have a credit account to inform them that you have changed your address, you can speed things up by indicating the nature of your business on the envelope. A letter addressed simply to *Goldsmith's Department Store* would be opened first at a central mailroom and read before it could be routed to the right person or department. If, however, you put "Change of Address" on the front of the envelope in the upper left-hand corner below your return address, your letter will go to the right person without delay.

If you do use an attention line, there are several acceptable styles. If you include the person's name and title in the attention line, you may arrange them on one or two lines. If you do not know the name of the person, you may refer to him or her by title, or you may use the name of a particular department.

Attention Mr. Kenneth Mitchell

ATTENTION SALES MANAGER

Since the attention line is part of the inside address, it is typed a double space below the city, state, and ZIP Code line. (A double space is also left between the attention line and the salutation.) The attention line should start at the left margin of the letter. It may be typed in all capital letters or in initial caps and underscored (notice the examples above).

Remember that using an attention line does not change the salutation. If a letter is addressed to a company, the salutation that is most commonly used is *Gentlemen*.

Hatcher Carpet Company Inc.
3163 Bellbrook Drive
Lake Worth, Florida 33461

ATTENTION MR. KENNETH MITCHELL

Gentlemen:

Note also that a courtesy title should precede the name in the attention line.

THE SALUTATION

The salutation is the greeting to the reader and helps set the tone of the letter. *Gentlemen, Ladies,* or *Ladies and Gentlemen* is acceptable in greeting a company and *Dear Mr. McGhee* in greeting a person named *Travis McGhee*. If the reader is a personal friend, however, *Dear Travis* is acceptable.

In typing salutations for business letters, you will find the following suggestions helpful:

1. Use a double space above and below the salutation.

2. Abbreviate the titles *Mr., Mrs., Ms.,* and *Dr.* Spell out titles such as *Professor, Reverend,* and *Major*.

3. Capitalize the first word and any noun or title in a salutation: *Dear Sir; My dear Miss Phillips; Dear Father Whitaker; Dear Senator Bryant*.

4. Below are the salutations most used in business letters.

For a business firm or other organization, the most often used salutation is *Gentlemen,* even when the organization is composed of both women and men. However, because of the masculine bias of the terms *Gentlemen* and *Sirs,* you might consider using the salutation *Ladies and Gentlemen* or *Gentlemen and Ladies*. (The older form, *Dear Sirs,* is seldom used in American business letters.)

For an individual, use *Dear Mr. Jordan* or *Dear Miss Haynes*. If you know the person's title but not his or her name, write *Dear Sir* or *Dear Madam*. The more formal versions are *My dear Mr. Jordan; My dear Miss Haynes; Sir;* or *Madam*.

Efforts of executives to move away from conventional salutations toward a friendly, personal touch in their business letters have led to two trends which are slowly growing in popularity.

One trend is to omit the salutation and complimentary closing (as illustrated in the simplified letter, page 15). This omission saves time and, in the opinion of some, eliminates phrases that have grown meaningless through overuse. But others think it makes the letter seem blunt and a little discourteous.

Another trend is to use unusual salutations, sometimes called "salutopenings," which start letters in a friendly, conversational way. These are used most often in sales promotion letters but are also used in other informal business letters. Among the common salutopenings are the familiar greetings: *Good morning, Mr. Carnes; Hello, Mr. Gibson; Merry Christmas, Miss Foley*. A letter may also start right out with the message. The reader's name is then inserted in the first sentence.

Mr. Edward L. Caruthers
4960 Darlington Drive
Toledo, OH 43606

Thank you, Mr. Caruthers, for the chance to tell you about the wide variety of Kiser products.

THE SUBJECT LINE

A subject line enables your reader to grasp the content of the letter quickly. In one glance he or she can see what the letter is about. Since the subject line is part of the body of the letter, it is typed a double space below the salutation and is followed by a double space before the first paragraph of the message. The subject line may be typed in capital and small letters and underscored, or it may be typed all in capitals. It may be centered, begun at the left margin, or indented (if the letter has indented paragraphs), depending on the letter style that you are using.

Miss Karen S. Whitaker
Norris Health Foods, Inc.
4704 Woodridge Drive
St. Louis, MO 63122

Dear Miss Whitaker:

Subject: Federal Regulations on Food Labeling

The word *Subject* may be omitted. *Re* and *In re* are used only for legal correspondence. The subject line replaces the salutation in the simplified letter style (see page 15).

Mr. Robert W. Bell Jr.
Scotsman Ice Systems
2089 Lynnfield Road
Pueblo, CO 81005

Dear Mr. Bell:

SERVICE CALLS ON ICE DISPENSERS

THE MESSAGE

Since you understand how important the appearance of the body of the letter is, you should observe these principles in typing the message.

1. Keep the left margin of the letter even. The right margin should be as nearly even as practical without dividing too many words.

2. Start the body of the letter a double space below the salutation; or if no salutation is used, begin the message a double space below the last line of the inside address.

3. Single space all business letters. (Double-spacing is acceptable only in extremely short letters. Whenever you must double space, be sure to indent all paragraphs.)

4. Always double space between paragraphs in single-spaced letters.

5. Either indent or block single-spaced paragraphs, according to the letter style you are using (see Unit 3). If you indent paragraphs, the first line usually begins five spaces in from the left margin. Seven-space, eight-space, or ten-space indentions are sometimes used.

THE COMPLIMENTARY CLOSING

The complimentary closing should match the salutation in its degree of formality. If you have greeted your reader with *Dear Jack,* you will probably close with *Sincerely.* Here are some typical closings:

FORMAL: Yours truly,
Respectfully yours,
Yours very truly,
Very truly yours,

INFORMAL: Sincerely yours,
Cordially yours,
Sincerely,
Cordially,

The more formal closings are disappearing from use, and the more informal closings are increasing in popularity for general usage.

Remember the following points when typing a complimentary closing:

1. Capitalize only the first word.

2. Place a comma after the complimentary closing unless you are using open punctuation (in the open punctuation style, omit both the colon following the salutation and the comma following the complimentary closing).

3. Start the complimentary closing at the center of the page, a double space below the body of the letter, unless you are using the full-blocked style (see Unit 3). With this style, start the closing at the left margin.

THE COMPANY SIGNATURE

Some business firms (and individuals) prefer that the name of the company (typed in all capitals) follow the closing to indicate that the company—not the writer—is legally responsible for the message. In this case the firm name is typed a double space below the closing.

Sincerely yours,

VIP LIMOUSINE SERVICE

THE WRITER'S IDENTIFICATION

The handwritten signature of the writer appears immediately below the complimentary closing or the typed company name, if used. Three blank lines are allowed for the signature, below which is then typed the writer's identification, consisting of his or her typed name, title or department, or both.

Sincerely yours,

LYONS PRINTING COMPANY

Victor Lyons

Victor Lyons
President

Cordially yours,

James P. Vinson

James P. Vinson
Vice President, Marketing

It is important to type the name of the writer so that the reader may easily address a reply to him or her.

A man ordinarily does not use a courtesy title before either his handwritten signature or his typed name. However, if he has a name which could also be a woman's name, or if he uses initials, he should include *Mr.* in his signature to avoid confusion.

A woman should use a courtesy title unless she has a special title such as *M.D.* or *Ph.D.* She has a choice of the following appropriate forms:

Marcia Rogers
Ms. Marcia Rogers

Elizabeth Clay
Elizabeth Clay, Ph.D.

(miss) Carla Fernandez
Carla Fernandez

(mrs.) Ruth Ann Morgan
Ruth Ann Morgan

Laura V. Watson
Mrs. Laura V. Watson

REFERENCE INITIALS

The initials of the dictator and the transcriber are usually typed at the left margin a double space below the last line in the signature section. In an attempt to streamline letter form and produce letters faster, many business writers prefer to omit the dictator's initials if the dictator is identified in the signature.

The identification data may be typed in various ways. Occasionally numbers instead of initials are used to identify dictators and transcribers. If the dictator's name or initials are included, they always precede the transcriber's initials.

Some popular styles are:

GRP:EMS   LVM/dc
FBGray:rm   Celia Brown/b
nyb (typist's initials only)

ENCLOSURE NOTATION

An enclosure is indicated by the word *Enclosure* or the abbreviation *Enc.* typed on the line below the identifying initials. If there is more than one enclosure, the number is usually indicated.

Enclosure   Check enclosed
2 Enc.   Enclosures:
                     1. Catalog
Enclosures 2   2. Reply card

Since the enclosure notation is usually the last thing typed, it helps remind the secretary to put the enclosure in the envelope.

CARBON COPY NOTATION

If you wish the addressee of the letter to know you are sending a carbon copy to someone, type a carbon copy notation one line below the identifying initials. Use one of the following styles:

cc Ms. B. E. Wright   cc: J & B Marine
CC Mr. Talbert   cc: Vincent Stevenson
                             Elton Parks

If you do not want the addressee to know you are sending a carbon to someone, type the notation *bcc* (for *blind carbon copy*) at the upper left of each blind carbon copy and your file copy *only.* The *bcc* notation does *not* appear on the original copy.

bcc C. Mills   bcc: Tony Barker
                             Peter Bettina

POSTSCRIPT

Since postscripts are unusual in business letters, the reader pays more attention to them, spends more time reading them, and reads them more carefully than the body of the letter. Therefore, a postscript can be used to give strong emphasis to an important idea that has been deliberately positioned in this strategic spot.

A postscript may also represent an afterthought, something remembered after the letter has been written. This usage may indicate poor planning and organization.

Restrict your use of postscripts, then, to occasions when you wish to take advantage of their attention-getting qualities. Sales letters often make good use of postscripts, especially to prompt someone to send in an

order. Sometimes you can take the sting out of a bad-news letter or make a routine letter more friendly by adding a handwritten postscript, especially if you know your reader personally. Like all such devices, though, postscripts lose their effectiveness if overused.

If you type a postscript on a business letter, start it a double space below the reference notations. Treat it as you did the other paragraphs in the letter; that is, indent it if the other paragraphs are indented.

Type *PS.* or *PS:* and leave two spaces before the first word of the postscript.

PS: Mail the coupon today!

PS.   Remember—we meet at seven o'clock.

You may also omit the abbreviation *PS.* At the end of your letter, the postscript might appear this way:

VOW:jc

For long-distance phone orders, just call collect (901) 372-4578.

SECOND-PAGE HEADING

If a letter is more than one page in length, each page after the letterhead should have a heading giving the name of the addressee, the page number, and the date.

Start the second-page heading one inch from the top edge of the paper (on line seven) at the left margin. Leave two blank lines between the heading and the first line of the body. The following are two acceptable forms:

Mr. Jason P. Rafferty
Page 2
January 17, 1978

Dr. Julia Andrews   2   May 14, 1978

In typing second pages, remember these suggestions for attractive placement and easy reading.

1. Carry at least two lines of the body of the letter to the second page; do not type only the closing lines of the letter on the second page.

2. If a paragraph is divided at the end of a page, leave at least two lines at the bottom of the first page, and carry at least two lines to the top of the second page. Do not divide a paragraph containing fewer than four lines.

3. Never hyphenate the last word on a page.

4. If the letter continues on a third page, the bottom margin of the second page should be the same as the bottom margin of the first page.

ASSIGNMENT: Complete Sections A, B, and C of the Worksheet for Unit 2, correcting errors in arrangement and style of letter parts.

unit 3

Correspondence Styles

LETTERS

Choosing the right format for your letter is another step in creating the desired first impression on a reader. The letter style or format you select says much about your personality or that of your company. A traditional letter style, such as the semiblocked, indicates a solid, well-established company; but to younger people, at least, it may appear to be a little old-fashioned. A very informal style, such as the simplified letter, appears creative and fresh; but to older people it may seem too unconventional.

Some companies have letterheads designed specifically to complement one letter style. Of course, all employees must use that style. If there is no "rule," executives may choose whichever letter style they prefer. If you choose the letter style, be sure to consider the letterhead. Select a style that will make your letters look pleasing and balanced.

The two leading styles—which together are used in more than 75 percent of the business letters typed today—are the blocked and semiblocked. Two other styles, somewhat less popular, are the full-blocked and the simplified letters. Each of these styles is illustrated on the following pages.

The newest style is the simplified letter, designed by the Administrative Management Society. It is not only a letter style but a plan to produce better letters at less cost by simplifying the format and content. Although it is streamlined and timesaving, the simplified letter has not been widely adopted, perhaps because it seems rather brusque and impersonal (the salutation and complimentary closing are omitted). It is possible in the simplified letter to indicate friendship and create goodwill, but it requires care.

As you look at the four letter styles, study both the format and the content of each letter, since the body describes the characteristics of the particular style. You will, of course, form your own opinions and your own preferences.

Standard punctuation, consisting of a colon follow-

ing the salutation and a comma following the complimentary closing, is illustrated in the blocked, semiblocked, and full-blocked sample letters.

Once you choose the letter style, you must type the letter properly. Unit 5 will help you with the details of typing letters and envelopes, good placement, accuracy, and neatness.

ASSIGNMENT: To make sure you understand the various letter styles, complete Section A of the Worksheet for this unit.

POSTAL CARDS

For short messages, postal cards are quick and easy to prepare and cost less than a letter. They save the time of folding, sealing, and stamping, and the cost of first-class mailing. Postal cards may be used for some announcements and notices.

Double postal cards may be used when a reply is needed. One card is typed as a regular postal card; the other card is addressed to the sender and is usually a quick-check form for the addressee to fill out. The cards are perforated or stapled together.

When typing on a postal card (which was recently changed by the U.S. Postal Service from 5½ by 3¼ inches to 5½ by 3½ inches):

1. Set the margins five spaces from left and right edges.

2. On the address side, begin on line 12 from the top, about 2 inches in from the left edge.

```
Mrs. Natalie Zanetta
1656 Rosewood Drive
East Lansing, MI 48823



                    Mr. John R. Quincy
                    423 Lauderdale Road
                    Ann Arbor, MI 48103
```

```
                              October 20, 19--

Dear Member:

The monthly meeting of the Michigan State University
Alumni Association will be held in the University
Center, Room 111G, MSU campus, on Wednesday,
November 8, at 7:30 p.m.

                    Sincerely,

                    Natalie Zanetta

                    Mrs. Natalie Zanetta
                    Secretary
```

3. On the message side, begin the date on line 3 from the top edge, at the center point.

4. Because the address is on the reverse side of the card, you may omit the inside address on the message side. Type the salutation a double space below the date, at the left margin (the salutation may be omitted).

5. Begin the message on the second line below the salutation.

6. Type the closing lines a double space below the last line of the message, starting at the center (the complimentary closing, handwritten signature, and reference initials may be omitted to save space).

ASSIGNMENT: Practice typing postal cards in Section B of the Worksheet for Unit 3.

INTEROFFICE CORRESPONDENCE

Written communications within a business organization are called interoffice memorandums. They are not typed on company letterhead, nor do they require the formality of an inside address, salutation, or complimentary closing.

Many companies provide special printed memorandum forms. Such forms may be either full sheets (8½ by 11 inches) or half sheets (8½ by 5½ inches) for brief messages. (One disadvantage of the half sheet is that it may easily be overlooked in a file folder.) The printed memo forms provide the standard headings *To, From, Subject,* and *Date,* so that the typist simply inserts the information after each heading (see the memo form below). When typing on printed forms, set the left margin even with the inserts following the printed heading; then set the right margin the same number of spaces from the right edge of the paper.

Begin typing the body on the third line below the last heading. Do not indent paragraphs. Double space between paragraphs.

If no printed forms are available, memos may be typed on plain sheets in the style preferred by the company. When typed on plain paper, to save space and to save time in adjusting margins, memos are usually typed with standard margins of about 1 inch. A two-page memo typed on plain paper is illustrated on page 16.

ASSIGNMENT: Complete Section C of the Worksheet for this unit.

MEMORANDUM

Date: November 5, 19--

To: All Typists

From: Training Director

Subject: Names and Initials on Interoffice Memos

Follow the writer's preference in the use of his or her name at the end of an interoffice memo. Some writers prefer to sign their names or initials. Some like their names typed at the bottom; others like only their initials typed at the bottom when their names appear at the top after the heading "From."

If the writer prefers to have his or her signature at the bottom, type the name on the fourth line below the body. If the memo is not to be signed, type the writer's name, initials, or title (whichever he or she prefers) a double space below the body of the memo.

David Harrison

jl

On a printed memo form such as this one, the standard headings *To, From, Subject,* and *Date* are included so that the typist simply inserts the appropriate information after each heading. This memo is typed on a half sheet (8½ by 5½ inches).

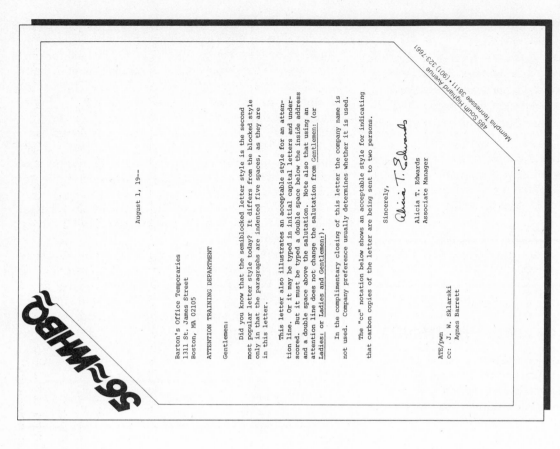

Supporters of the **semiblocked style** say (1) it gives the best-looking arrangement of all letter styles; (2) it pleases the more conservative reader; (3) paragraph indentions make reading somewhat easier; and (4) readers like the indentions so familiar in handwriting and print.

Critics say that it slows the typist, who must set several tab stops.

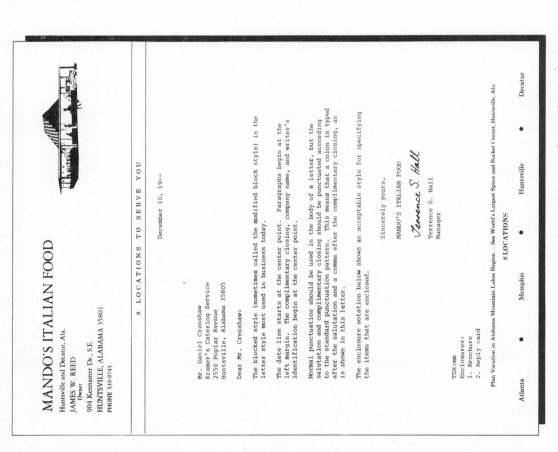

Those who like the **blocked style** say that it looks well balanced, neat, and businesslike; it is relatively fast to type; and it is fairly conservative.

Those who do not like it say that readers miss the indented paragraphs familiar in handwriting and print.

IBM

International Business Machines Corporation   Parson's Pond Drive
Franklin Lakes, New Jersey 07417
201/848-1900

October 9, 19--

Mrs. Marion Haywood
3296 Park Forest Road
Belleville, IL 62225

Dear Mrs. Haywood:

Subject: Form of a Full-Blocked Letter

This letter is set up in the full-blocked style, in which all lines begin at the left margin. Many business firms use the full-blocked style for their correspondence, because it is faster to type than any of the other letter styles except the simplified; and it is considered very modern.

If a subject line is used, it may be typed as shown here. The word Subject may be omitted, or the entire line may be typed in capital letters. The subject line must always be typed a double space below the salutation since it is considered part of the body of the letter. In the full-blocked style, the subject line must begin at the left margin, as it does here.

As you can see, the full-blocked letter has a good appearance. Using this style eliminates many extra typing strokes and motions and therefore helps to increase letter production rates.

Sincerely,

INTERNATIONAL BUSINESS MACHINES CORPORATION

Christopher Scott
Christopher Scott
Vice President, Sales

CS/jm

National Wildlife Federation

1412 16TH ST., N.W., WASHINGTON, D.C. 20036   Phone 202—797-6800

March 1, 19--

Mr. James J. Stallman
P.O. Box 230
Cherry Hill, New Jersey 08034

SIMPLIFIED LETTER

You are looking at a sample of the simplified letter style, Mr. Stallman. This style was introduced by the Administrative Management Society several years ago.

As its name implies, the simplified letter streamlines the traditional letter format. It uses the full-blocked style. A subject line is typed in all capitals with a triple space (two blank lines) above and below.

The salutation and complimentary closing are omitted. The signer's name and title are typed in all capital letters four blank lines below the body of the letter. Reference initials are not used.

The tone of the letter is brisk but friendly. Note that the addressee's name is used at least in the first sentence and often elsewhere in the body.

The simplified letter is certainly efficient to produce, Mr. Stallman, but some object that it doesn't look like a letter and that it seems impersonal.

Grace Martin
GRACE MARTIN - OFFICE MANAGER

Courtesy IBM

People who like the **full-blocked style** say it is fast to set up and type because it does not require setting tab stops; it looks efficient and businesslike.

Critics say it is a bit crowded.

The Administrative Management Society urges typists to use the **simplified letter style** because it saves time, eliminates meaningless salutations and closings, and is practical and efficient.

Critics say it lacks warmth and friendliness, seems blunt, and is too unconventional.

MEMORANDUM

DATE: April 25, 19--

TO: All Employees

FROM: Tom Hughes

SUBJECT: Virginia Central Credit Union Membership

We have been studying the possibility of the employees of Business
Service Industries either forming or becoming affiliated with a
credit union.

From our research we have found that our company is too small to
have its own credit union. However, we have learned of a credit
union formed about one year ago known as the Virginia Central Credit
Union. We have investigated this credit union thoroughly and found
it to be reputable, growing, and able to supply full services to its
members. BSI is eligible to become part of VCCU.

Attached is a list of the services offered by the credit union and
an information sheet on what a credit union does. You may wish to
know the following things which are not included on the attached
material.

1. A Norfolk office will open on June 1; however, until that time
    you may make withdrawals from your account by phone and receive
    a check within the next two days.

2. In addition to the savings account, a checking account will be
    available. The credit union will pay 5½ percent interest on the
    monthly balance of your checking account. This is a feature
    which is not available in most credit unions.

3. Signature loans may be repaid up to 42 months; other loans, such
    as new-car and personal loans exceeding $2,500, may be repaid
    over 48 months.

4. There is no ceiling on the maximum amount you may borrow. The
    amount of money in your savings account has no relationship to
    the amount you may borrow.

5. You are allowed to choose the number of months on any loan that
    you make up to the maximum, with the right of prepayment.

6. All weekly deposits, loans, and repayments will be handled
    through the payroll department.

All Employees   2   April 25, 19--

All employees are invited to join VCCU. Membership in the credit
union is on an individual basis. You are under no obligation to join.

Please look over the information and call or see me if you wish
further explanation and the forms to fill out to become a member.
I would like to hear from you as soon as possible.

                                        T. H.

/km
Enclosures

This two-page memo is typed on plain stationery, not on a printed memo form.
Note the second-page heading.

Correct English Usage

Just as you will want to choose a letterhead and a style that will not distract your reader's attention from the content of your message, you will also want your language to be unobtrusive. Unfortunately, even people whose own grammar, spelling, and punctuation are far from perfect and who see few errors of their own are quick to spot every mistake someone else makes. Why? Because most of us are accustomed to reading books, magazines, and other materials that were carefully edited and proofread before they were published; we are therefore accustomed to reading near-perfect English. Thus a letter that contains a language-usage error doesn't "sound right" to the reader. And as soon as the reader notices something out of the ordinary, he or she is no longer paying full attention to your message. The result is that your letter does not fulfill its purpose.

Very few people appear to be indifferent to flaws in the business letters they receive; the vast majority react to sloppily written letters with either irritation or amusement. With the odds very much against you, then, why take a chance? The reader who is irritated by your poor English usage will probably immediately conclude, "If this person hasn't mastered even the basics of English grammar, how can he possibly have anything important to say to me?" Is a reader who is irritated and skeptical going to be receptive to what you say? No. And is the reader who finds your mistakes amusing likely to do what you want? Perhaps—after he or she stops laughing.

GETTING RID OF BASIC ERRORS IN ENGLISH USAGE

What is good English, and what are the rules of good English? The "rules" are conventions or general agreements among the users of English as to how the language should be used to achieve certain goals under various circumstances. Journalists, novelists, poets, business writers—all use English for different purposes and under different circumstances. No one set of "rules" is completely acceptable to all writers and speakers. Our discussion will therefore be limited to the conventions of good English for business communication—the level of usage adhered to by the majority of skilled writers and speakers in the business world.

Carelessness is a major contributor to grammatical errors in writing. Frankly, it is much easier to be a sloppy writer than it is to be a careful writer. But once you accept sloppiness in your writing, it soon becomes a habit—a habit you will find very hard to break. The best (and most difficult) procedure is to develop the habit of giving careful attention to all aspects of your writing.

No one is a "born writer." We have to learn how to express ourselves on paper through practice and understanding. Usually, the more we write, the better we write. Understanding is a matter of realizing what is involved in writing, how the process works, and how to make it work for us.

How do you know what is correct, or standard, English usage? Reading, listening, writing, speaking, studying and practicing the rules of grammar—all these have helped and will continue to help you develop a "feel" for correct English usage, an ability to know almost instinctively whether or not something is correct. The ability to recite the rules of grammar, punctuation, and so on, will not necessarily give you the ability to write without making errors. It is much more important for you to develop your language sense to the point where you can instantly recognize your own errors and then turn to a reliable reference manual or English handbook for the rules you need to apply to correct your mistakes.

You will find a brief summary of grammar, punctuation, and other rules in the Reference Section at the end of this text, but you may wish to buy and use one of the many comprehensive English-usage handbooks that are available. And, like every other writer—even the most competent one—you will want to own and make constant use of an up-to-date, reliable dictionary.

In summary, then, you must be the first and severest judge of your own writing. If you think that once you get ahead in the business world, someone else—a secretary or a proofreader—will take care of your "mechanical errors," you are misleading yourself. Stenographers who can write without making language-usage errors will be promoted to executive secretaries, who perform many other duties besides taking and transcribing dictation. On the other hand, business workers who repeatedly make errors in their writing and do not correct them will soon find themselves sliding down the job ladder to positions where they will neither have nor need a secretary. Without a doubt, the ability to handle the English language competently is the first, surest, and quickest step up the ladder to success.

If you want to find the basic English faults in your writing and if you want to learn to write clearly, coherently, and effectively, you have already taken the biggest step toward achieving your goal. To help you further, this unit presents the four most common types of errors that most of us make in our writing: errors in agreement, errors with pronouns, misplaced modifiers, and troubles with commas. In addition, this unit discusses a fifth category, miscellaneous errors. Most of the examples in this book appeared in business letters or in student letters.

ERRORS IN AGREEMENT

Do Your Verbs Agree With Their Subjects?

Most writers know that a singular verb should be used with a singular subject and a plural verb with a plural subject. Yet lack of agreement of a verb with its subject is one of the most common grammatical errors in business letters. As you read the following examples, pay particular attention to sentence construction as it affects subject-verb agreement.

When the Subject Follows the Verb

Standing outside the door *were* Ms. Warren and Mr. Kitterman.
NOT: Standing outside the door *was* Ms. Warren and Mr. Kitterman.

Here the subject *Ms. Warren and Mr. Kitterman* follows the verb *were*. Although the word *door* is in the position where you would expect to find the subject, *door* is not the subject. Watch for sentences that have subjects *following* verbs.

When Words Separate the Subject From the Verb

The annual report, consisting of 26 pages, *gives* complete details of the firm's financial status.
NOT: The annual report, consisting of 26 pages, *give* complete details of the firm's financial status.

Report, not *pages,* is the subject of the sentence. Without the phrase *consisting of 26 pages,* the choice of *gives* is clearly correct. But with this phrase separating the subject from the verb, the sentence can trick you into making a mistake.

The distribution center as well as the branch offices *is* included in the reorganization plan.
NOT: The distribution center as well as the branch offices *are* included in the reorganization plan.

Center, a singular noun, is the subject; it requires the singular verb *is.*

The reservations form along with the tickets *is* to be collected in the lobby.
NOT: The reservations form along with the tickets *are* to be collected in the lobby.

Here again the separation of the subject from its verb blurred their relationship in the writer's mind. As you can see, the subject is the singular noun *form;* it requires the singular verb *is.*

When a Compound Subject Is Used

Neatness and an attractive appearance *have* a positive effect on the image a secretary wishes to convey.
NOT: Neatness and an attractive appearance *has* a positive effect on the image a secretary wishes to convey.

Neatness and *appearance* are singular when they are used individually, but that *and* between them makes them a compound subject. Compound subjects like this one are plural, and they require plural verbs.

When "You," "There," "That," or a Similar Word Introduces the Sentence or Clause

You, not Hank, *are* scheduled to meet with the board next Monday.
NOT: You, not Hank, *is* scheduled to meet with the board next Monday.

It was his opinion that there *were* too many deductions.
NOT: It was his opinion that there *was* too many deductions.

There *are* several pages that contain illustrations.
NOT: There *is* several pages that contains illustrations.

Remember that the subject of the sentence is not necessarily the word immediately preceding the verb.

When Collective Nouns Are Used

A collective noun is one that denotes a group of persons or things even though the noun is singular in form; for example, *committee, audience, staff,* and *department.* Such a noun may take either a singular verb or a plural verb, depending upon the meaning it expresses in the sentence. (See page 131, G-3-b, item 4, of the Reference Section.)

The number of business opportunities in the Northeast and the Northwest *is* increasing.
NOT: The number of business opportunities in the Northeast and the Northwest *are* increasing.

The staff *anticipates* an early-morning rush.
NOT: The staff *anticipate* an early-morning rush.

In the first example *number* refers to a group of opportunities as a single unit, not as individual opportunities. In the second example, *staff* refers to a group of people who are in collective agreement; therefore, *staff* requires a singular verb. If you determine the function of a collective noun when you are writing or proofreading, you will soon be able to identify it quickly as singular or plural and match it to the proper verb form.

When a Contraction Is Used

Contractions are useful in writing, for they help keep your writing conversational in tone. Many writers have trouble with them, though, especially with *hasn't* and *haven't* and with *doesn't* and *don't.*

He *doesn't* believe that we will meet the deadline.
NOT: He *don't* believe that we will meet the deadline.

The promotions *haven't* been made public yet.
NOT: The promotions *hasn't* been made public yet.

Confusion in using contractions usually stems from forgetting that they are contractions, not separate words by themselves. *Doesn't* is the contraction of *does not; don't,* of *do not;* and so on. People who would not write or say "He *do not* believe that we will meet the deadline" often write or say "He *don't* believe that we will meet the deadline." Like so much else in grammar and writing, choosing the proper contraction is largely a matter of thinking about what you're doing.

Are the Tenses of Your Verbs Consistent?

Sometimes the events you are narrating require a change of tense within a sentence: "We completed the report this morning and plan to submit copies to the officers tomorrow." When the sequence of events is clear, the reader will follow such changes in tense easily. More often in business writing, however, tense and mood should not change, especially within sentences and within paragraphs.

We *checked* your records and *found* that your payments are two months overdue.
NOT: We *checked* your records and *find* that your payments are two months overdue.

Please *write* us immediately so that we *may* plan the conference.
NOT: Please *write* us immediately so that we *might* plan the conference.

When you switch tense or mood without having a reason for doing so, your reader may notice the change immediately because the continuity of thought may be interrupted or destroyed.

Do You Avoid Shifting Your Point of View in Sentences?

It's important that you maintain the same point of view throughout a sentence. A shift usually results in an awkward or ambiguous sentence, and communication suffers accordingly.

From Active to Passive Voice (and Vice Versa)

We *invite* all employees to join the credit union, and the company *encourages* them to join.
NOT: We *invite* all employees to join the credit union, and they *are encouraged* by the company to join.

We *received* your letter yesterday and *will ship* your order immediately.
NOT: Your letter *was received* yesterday, and we *will ship* your order immediately.

From a Personal to an Impersonal Subject (and Vice Versa)

Even though it is usually better to admit our mistakes, *we find* it easy to place the blame on someone else.
NOT: Even though it is usually better to admit our mistakes, *one finds* it easy to place the blame on someone else.

Occasionally *everyone* makes a mistake that *he or she* cannot correct easily.
NOT: Occasionally *everyone* makes a mistake that *you* cannot correct easily.

If *you* try to walk in another's shoes, *you* usually *find* them to be uncomfortable at best.
NOT: If *you* try to walk in another's shoes, *one* usually *finds* them to be uncomfortable at best.

Are Similar Parts Parallel in Construction?

Parts of a sentence are "parallel" when they are similar in construction. When similar parts are not treated in a similar manner, the result is an awkward sentence. Lack of balance in sentence construction indicates either that the writer hasn't taken the time to think out each sentence or that the writer both thinks and writes in a sloppy manner. The following examples indicate four ways in which parallelism—as well as meaning—is often lost.

Change From an Infinitive to a Participle (and Vice Versa)

His objective is *to advertise* the position immediately and *to fill* it as quickly as possible.
NOT: His objective is *to advertise* the position immediately and *filling* it as quickly as possible.

Your duties will consist of *supervising* the executive committee and *directing* the affairs of the club.
NOT: Your duties will consist of *supervising* the executive committee and *to direct* the affairs of the club.

Change From a Dependent Clause to a Dependent Phrase (and Vice Versa)

May I have lists of the agenda items and of the names of the participants for each meeting.
NOT: May I have lists of the agenda items and who will participate in each meeting.

Change in a Series of Items

Dr. Bowen's lectures are *entertaining, informative,* and *interesting* to many types of people.
NOT: Dr. Bowen's lectures are *entertaining, informative,* and *of interest* to many types of people.

Omission of a Word or Words Needed to Show Parallelism

The fall workshop will begin *in* and continue through September.
NOT: The fall workshop will begin and continue through September.

The commission that the Stevens Corporation pays is higher than *that of* my company.
NOT: The commission that the Stevens Corporation pays is higher than my company.

She has no appreciation *of* or confidence in Louise's hard work.
NOT: She has no appreciation or confidence in Louise's hard work.

ASSIGNMENT: Correcting the errors in agreement in Section A of the Worksheet for Unit 4 will give you valuable practice in spotting such errors and help check what you have learned about the principles of agreement presented in this unit.

ERRORS WITH PRONOUNS

Most writers make heavy use of pronouns. Since you will find pronouns helpful, you should learn to use them correctly. Often, misusing a pronoun results in a funny sentence. But it isn't funny when a misused pronoun causes your reader to laugh at you or fail to understand what you're saying. The most common errors in the use of pronouns are discussed below. It will pay you to study them carefully—and to avoid them in your writing.

Are All Antecedents Clear? Does Each Pronoun Agree With Its Antecedent?

Two common errors in agreement are the use of pronouns that have unclear antecedents and the use of pronouns that do not agree with their antecedents.

The Pronoun Whose Antecedent Is Not Clearly Identified

The graph shows the different levels of television viewing by months. *The levels* represent percentages of prime-time viewing.
NOT: The graph shows the different levels of television viewing by months. *They* represent percentages of prime-time viewing.

The franchise agreement should be carefully checked. *Franchise agreements* sometimes have restrictions you do not expect.
NOT: The franchise agreement should be carefully checked. *They* sometimes have restrictions you do not expect.

The Pronoun That Refers to a Sentence or a Clause Rather Than to a Single Word

Please stop in to see me while you are in Boston; *your visit* will prove worthwhile.
NOT: Please stop in to see me while you are in Boston; *it* will prove worthwhile.

If you plan to pay by mail, please send *your payment* today.
NOT: If you plan to pay by mail, please send *it* today.

The Pronoun That Disagrees With Its Antecedent in Number

Either Ms. Jerrell or Mrs. Baker will lose *her* job.
NOT: Either Ms. Jerrell or Mrs. Baker will lose *their* job. (The use of *either-or* is strictly singular—only *one* person will lose her job.)

Everyone who did not attend last month's meeting should pay *his or her* dues tonight.
NOT: Everyone who did not attend last month's meeting should pay *their* dues tonight. (*Everyone* is singular, but *their* is plural. *His or her* is singular.)

Do You Use the Correct Case for All Pronouns?

In its early history (before 1200), the English language included complete sets of endings for use with nouns. These endings clearly indicated whether the nouns were being used in sentences as subjects, objects, indirect objects, possessives, and so on. Today most of these endings have been lost. Now we rely on the position of a noun in a sentence as the primary indicator of the function it performs. About the only relics that still remain are the 's we use to indicate possession and the s or es we use to show plurality.

However, the pronouns that we use today still have different forms or endings to indicate person, number, gender, and case. For example, if we were saying what Sal Martino is doing, we could say, "He is taking his work home with him." All three pronoun forms are third person, singular, and masculine; however, *he* is the nominative case, *his* is possessive case, and *him* is objective case. Errors in the use of the correct case forms are quite common.

When the Pronoun Is the Subject of a Verb

A pronoun that is the subject of a verb must be in the nominative case. The nominative case personal pronouns are *I, we, you, he, she, it,* and *they.*

You know as well as *he* that your account is long past due.
NOT: You know as well as *him* that your account is long past due. (*You* is the subject of the verb *know*, and *he* is the subject of the understood verb *knows:* You know that your account is long past due, as well as he knows. . . . The phrase *as well as* makes it clear that both *you* and *he* are subjects.)

When the Pronoun Is the Object of a Verb or a Preposition, the Subject of an Infinitive, or an Indirect Object

The objective case personal pronouns are *me, us, you, him, her, it,* and *them.* When the pronoun is the direct or indirect object of a verb, the object of a preposition, or the subject of an infinitive, it must be in the objective case.

If you need help, just ask *him* or *me.* (*Him* and *me* are both objects of the verb *ask.*)
NOT: If you need help, just ask him or *I.*

A seminar in human relations is being planned for *us* secretaries. (*Us* is the object of the preposition *for.*)
NOT: A seminar in human relations is being planned for *we* secretaries.

Jim decided to go with *her* and *me.* (*Her* and *me* are objects of the preposition *with.*)
NOT: Jim decided to go with *she* and *I.*

When the Pronoun Precedes a Gerund

Of course, the possessive case shows possession. The possessive pronoun forms are *my, mine, our, ours, your, yours, his, her, hers, its, their,* and *theirs.*

His signing the lease represented a major step in the transaction.
NOT: *Him* signing the lease represented a major step in the transaction.

I appreciate *your* asking my opinion of the proposal.
NOT: I appreciate *you* asking my opinion of the proposal.

Do You Distinguish Between Possessive Pronouns and Contractions?

The most common error in choosing between possessive pronouns and contractions is confusing the pronoun *its* and the contraction *it's.* Also frequent are mixups between *your* and *you're, their* and *they're,* and *whose* and *who's.* The easiest way to keep them straight is to remember that the contractions represent *two* words; substitute the two words for the contraction. If the two words make sense, then the contraction is correct; if they do not, then the possessive form is correct. The following sentences illustrate correct usage.

It's a pleasure to welcome you to ADP Company.

The reference manual serves *its* purpose well.

Who's going to the board meeting?

Whose turn is it to make the coffee?

The secretaries had *their* work finished by 4 p.m.

Ms. Tanner and Ms. Galbraith confessed that *they're* thinking of resigning.

You're taking the job because it is a step up the ladder to success.

You should give *your* full attention to *your* work.

Are You Cautious in the Use of "Myself"?

Never as the Subject

Susan and *I* were the only witnesses to the accident.
NOT: Susan and *myself* were the only witnesses to the accident.

For Emphasis Only When "I" or "Me" Is Expressed

I *myself* was to blame for the misunderstanding.
NOT: *Myself* was to blame for the misunderstanding.

I will complete the job *myself.*

For Reference to the Subject

I consider *myself* the leading candidate.

ASSIGNMENT: Turn to Section B of the Worksheet for Unit 4 to see if you can use pronouns correctly in different situations.

MISPLACED MODIFIERS

Since English sentences rely heavily on the positions of the words and phrases to indicate meanings, it is necessary that modifiers clearly relate to the words they modify. A misplaced modifier is one that appears to modify the wrong word or phrase and thus changes or obscures the meaning of a sentence. A good way to avoid misplaced modifiers and at the same time make your writing clearer is to place modifiers as near as possible to the word or words they modify.

Misplaced Adverbs That May Confuse the Meaning

I tried all day to write a good letter.
NOT: I tried to write a good letter all day.

He had only one chance.
NOT: He only had one chance.

Friday's sale will feature these colored plastic seat covers.
NOT: Friday's sale will feature these plastic colored seat covers. (What color is "plastic color"?)

Misplaced Modifiers That May Amuse (but Distract) Your Reader

The discipline committee met in the board room to discuss the possible suspension of two students.
NOT: The discipline committee met to discuss the possible suspension of two students in the board room.

The man in the elevator said rain is forecast for today.
NOT: The man said rain is forecast for today in the elevator.

Did you see a woman with brown hair driving a black car?
NOT: Did you see a woman driving a black car with brown hair?

Do You Avoid Awkwardness by Skillful Placement of Modifiers?

Misplaced modifiers often result in split infinitives. Splitting an infinitive is not necessarily bad. In your writing, you may use a split infinitive to emphasize the modifying word if the result is not awkward.

For Emphasis

Our braces are designed to *correctly* support your weight. (By splitting the infinitive *to support,* the writer stresses the correctness of the support given.)

Miss Mendez was able to *easily* fit the design to our particular needs. (By splitting the infinitive *to fit,* the writer stresses the ease of adaptation.)

Awkward

She decided not to visit the exhibit.
NOT: She decided to not visit the exhibit.

Jim always seems to be cheerful.
NOT: Jim seems to always be cheerful.

Do You Avoid Dangling Modifiers?

A dangling modifier is an introductory phrase or clause that should modify the subject of a sentence but doesn't. It is usually a participial phrase that has an "ing" word in it. When the reader automatically attaches the dangling modifier to the subject of the sentence, the result is often ridiculous! By the time the reader untangles the meaning, you've lost his or her attention. Perhaps you've also lost the reader's belief in you and what you're saying. To correct a dangling modifier, either replace it with a clause or recast the sentence so as to give it the right noun or pronoun to modify.

After examining the encyclopedia in your home, you may return it if you are not completely satisfied.
NOT: After being examined in your home, you may return the encyclopedia if you are not completely satisfied.

After you eat dinner at an exotic restaurant, your guide will escort you on a tour of fabulous Chinatown.
NOT: After eating your dinner at an exotic restaurant, your guide will escort you on a tour of fabulous China-town.

To get the most value for your money, you should complete and return the enclosed coupon today.
NOT: To get the most value for your money, the enclosed coupon should be completed and returned today.

ASSIGNMENT: Section C of the Worksheet for Unit 4 will give you practice in placing (and replacing) modifiers *effectively.*

TROUBLES WITH COMMAS

Writers generally have more trouble with commas than with any other punctuation mark. A comma frequently fogs the meaning of a sentence when it is out of place or otherwise misused. Commas are misused in three ways: they are inserted where they don't belong; they are omitted where they are needed; or they are shifted to a wrong position in a sentence. In each case the result is usually damaging.

When you speak, you intersperse what you say with pauses of varying lengths. Your pauses between syllables (the major elements in words) are almost imperceptible. Between words themselves the pauses (represented in writing by spaces between words) are more noticeable. Longer pauses occur in speech between the elements of a sentence (commas), slightly longer ones between major elements (colons and semicolons), and the longest of all between sentences (periods, question marks, and exclamation points). In writing, we use punctuation to guide the reader in understanding the message. Punctuation is essential to communicating.

When you are not sure how to use commas in a sentence, try saying the sentence aloud as naturally as you can, listening for the pauses you put in without thinking about them. A noticeable pause probably means a comma is needed. Of course, this is hardly a foolproof guide to comma placement. But it may guide you correctly most of the time. And it doesn't cost you anything to try it—cautiously!

Omission of One of a Pair of Commas

A more recent policy, even more comprehensive, is now being marketed.
NOT: A more recent policy even more comprehensive, is now being marketed.

Rosemary Fitzgerald, editorial assistant, called while you were out of the office.
NOT: Rosemary Fitzgerald, editorial assistant called while you were out of the office.

Tom vacationed in Las Vegas, Nevada, last week.
NOT: Tom vacationed in Las Vegas, Nevada last week.

The next meeting will be on Monday, December 8, at 7 p.m.
NOT: The next meeting will be on Monday, December 8 at 7 p.m.

Omission of Commas With Introductory or Explanatory Clauses and With Participial Phrases

After you have reviewed the enclosed brochure, we are sure you will want to visit Terra Alta Lake Resort.
NOT: After you have reviewed the enclosed brochure we are sure you will want to visit Terra Alta Lake Resort.

The advertising manager, hoping to win approval for the new plan, attached a detailed report.
NOT: The advertising manager hoping to win approval for the new plan attached a detailed report. (Without the commas, do you tend to read "the new plan attached"?)

Omission of Commas When Needed to Make a Series of Words or Phrases Explicit

Items are charged to the following accounts: Personnel Services, Current Expense, Repairs and Alterations, Reserve for Depreciation, and New Equipment.
NOT: Items are charged to the following accounts: Personnel Services, Current Expense, Repairs and Alterations, Reserve for Depreciation and New Equipment. (The comma after *Depreciation* makes it clear that *New Equipment* is a separate account.)

Inserting a Comma Between a Subject and Its Verb

Two essential qualities are honesty and intelligence.
NOT: Two essential qualities, are honesty and intelligence.

Analyzing the data and presenting recommendations by May 2 will be difficult.
NOT: Analyzing the data and presenting recommendations by May 2, will be difficult.

Inserting a Comma Before a Clause Used as Object of a Verb

He agreed that the athletic facilities must be expanded.
NOT: He agreed, that the athletic facilities must be expanded.

The parties discussed how they could come to a satisfactory agreement.
NOT: The parties discussed, how they could come to a satisfactory agreement.

Inserting Commas That Set Off Restrictive Modifiers

Here are the names of the persons who have passed the test.
NOT: Here are the names of the persons, who have passed the test.

The applicant who I believe is best qualified is Miss Kelly.
NOT: The applicant, who I believe is best qualified, is Miss Kelly.

The extra copies that were lying on my desk are missing.
NOT: The extra copies, that were lying on my desk, are missing.

Inserting a Comma With No Reason for Its Use

We typed the notices and prepared them for mailing.
NOT: We typed the notices, and prepared them for mailing. (*And* here joins the parts of a compound predicate, not of a compound sentence.)

He submitted a complete and concise report.
NOT: He submitted a complete, and concise report. (*And* here joins two adjectives, not two parts of a compound sentence.)

Thank you for your request for information about our sprinkler systems.
NOT: Thank you for your request, for information about our sprinkler systems.

Jack was asked to complete the study and to present his findings as soon as possible.
NOT: Jack was asked to complete the study, and to present his findings as soon as possible.

It is a pleasure, Mrs. Garrett, to welcome you to our organization.
NOT: It is a pleasure, Mrs. Garrett, to welcome you, to our organization.

Interrupting the Thought of a Sentence With Misplaced Commas

Mr. Johnson canceled his appointment for today, but he said he would make another appointment soon.
NOT: Mr. Johnson canceled his appointment for today but, he said he would make another appointment soon.

The most important, and also the most frequently discussed, topic was the discount rate.
NOT: The most important, and also the most frequently discussed topic, was the discount rate.

ASSIGNMENT: In Section D of the Worksheet for this unit, you are to distinguish between essential and nonessential commas.

MISCELLANEOUS ERRORS

The errors described below often occur in business letters. They are the grammatical mistakes that make readers lose faith in letters—and in the people who write the letters. Go over the errors carefully. Are any of them mistakes you make? If so, learn to recognize and to avoid them.

Prepositions and Conjunctions

He is behaving *like* a child.
NOT: He is behaving *as* a child.

Julia locked the doors at 5 p.m., *as* she had been instructed to do.
NOT: Julia locked the doors at 5 p.m., *like* she had been instructed to do.

The new building is quite different *from* the old one.
NOT: The new building is quite different *than* the old one.

Try *to* meet me in the lobby at two o'clock.
NOT: Try *and* meet me in the lobby at two o'clock.

Adverbs, Adjectives, and Articles

The president feels *bad* about the change and even looks *bad* because of worry over it.
NOT: The president feels *badly* about the change and even looks *badly*....
(*Feels badly* means one's sense of touch is impaired; *looks badly* means one's sight is impaired; *feels bad*

means one feels ill or regrets something; *looks bad* means one's appearance is below par.)

Jan and Sue work *well* together.
NOT: Jan and Sue work *good* together.

We had *fewer* bad debts last year than we had the year before.
NOT: We had *less* bad debts last year than we had the year before.

This kind of information is very useful.
NOT: *These* kind of information is very useful.

Words Essential for Clarity

Last month's net sales were less than *net sales for* any other month this year.
NOT: Last month's net sales were less than any other month this year.

The proceeds from this fund-raising dinner probably will be as much *as* or more than the proceeds from any previous fund-raising event.
NOT: The proceeds from this fund-raising dinner will probably be as much or more than the proceeds from any previous fund-raising event.

Superb customer service always has *been* and always will be Mallory's primary objective.
NOT: Superb customer service always has and always will be Mallory's primary objective.

Double Subjects, Double Negatives, Other Doublets, and Redundancies

Style Nos. 3910 and 4480, scheduled for January delivery, will not arrive until March.
NOT: Style Nos. 3910 and 4480, scheduled for January delivery, *these* will not arrive until March.

I ask each of you to make a generous contribution.
NOT: I ask each *and every one* of you to make a generous contribution.

We have only a few rooms ready for occupancy.
NOT: We *don't have but* a few rooms ready for occupancy.

You may wish to refer to page 18.
NOT: You may wish to refer *back* to page 18.

Misspellings

Misspelling is perhaps the most prevalent as well as the most irksome smog that can cloud up your letters. Here are three simple suggestions to help you type letters free from misspellings: (1) check each word carefully; (2) when in doubt, consult a dictionary; (3) keep an up-to-date list of your personal spelling demons and memorize the correct spelling of each word on your list.

To discover some of your own spelling problems, you might check the pairs of similar words often

confused, on page 36 of Unit 6, and the following words that many people find troublesome:

absence	excellent	persuade
accommodate	experience	preceding
acknowledgment	explanation	prescription
advantageous	extension	privilege
approximately	February	professor
beneficial	finally	pronunciation
business	guarantee	quantity
column	license	questionnaire
commitment	loyalty	receipt
committee	maintenance	receive
conscientious	manufacturer	recognize
conscious	miscellaneous	recommend
convenience	occasionally	restaurant
defendant	occurred	schedule
definitely	omitted	separate
dependent	pamphlet	similar
description	parallel	sincerely
development	partially	subpoena
disappoint	patience	thoroughly
dissatisfied	perform	through
embarrass	perhaps	together
emphasize	personnel	transferred

Numbers

If you are in doubt about accepted practice in writing numbers, turn to the discussion of numbers in the Reference Section (page 140). Also study the sentences below. Be sure you are not guilty of any of the glaring errors made by letter writers who are confused about using figures or words for numbers.

I noticed two enclosures had been left out.
NOT: I noticed 2 enclosures had been left out.

The cost of each item is $1.75.
NOT: The cost of each item is one dollar and seventy-five cents.

The order consisted of 5 boxes of paper clips, 5 boxes of rubber bands, 25 pencils, and 25 pens.
NOT: The order consisted of five boxes of paper clips, five boxes of rubber bands, 25 pencils, and 25 pens.

He read exactly one-half of the novel in two hours.
NOT: He read exactly ½ of the novel in 2 hours.

Bill is 6½ feet tall.
NOT: Bill is 6 and one-half feet tall.

The meeting is scheduled for 7:30 p.m.
NOT: The meeting is scheduled for seven-thirty p.m.

Abbreviations

You know, of course, that abbreviations—even accepted abbreviations—should generally be avoided in business letters. However, some abbreviations (*a.m.* and *p.m.*, for example) are never spelled out in business letters, memos, and reports. Consult the Reference Section (page 141) for more facts about the use of abbreviations. Then scan the examples below to prevent such standout errors from creeping into your letters.

> The enclosures included a deed, an abstract of title, *and* a check.
> **NOT**: The enclosures included a deed, an abstract of title, & a check.

> Will you refer my request to *Professor* Henderson tomorrow?
> **NOT**: Will you refer my request to *Prof.* Henderson tomorrow?

> We received your letter on *November 3.*
> **NOT**: We received your letter on *Nov. 3.*

> Check *No.* 41582 was issued to Mr. Dennis L. Bailey on June 30.
> **NOT**: Check *Number* 41582 was issued to Mr. Dennis L. Bailey on June 30.

Apostrophes

> He reluctantly accepted the *secretary's* resignation.
> **NOT**: He reluctantly accepted the *secretaries* resignation.

> The store advertises both *men's* and *women's* clothing.
> **NOT**: The store advertises both *mens'* and *womens'* clothing.

> She was offered two *weeks'* vacation with pay but took only a week's vacation.
> **NOT**: She was offered two *weeks* vacation with pay but took only a *weeks'* vacation.

Hyphens, Capitals, and Quotation Marks

Used inaccurately or lavishly, hyphens, capital letters, and quotation marks call attention to themselves and thus detract from ease of reading.

> **TYPE**: ahead, through, didn't, solved.
> **NOT**: . . . a-head, thr-ough, did-n't, sol-ved. (Do not divide one-syllable words or contractions.)

> I took several courses in *English* literature in high school but only one *history* course.
> **NOT**: I took several courses in *english* literature in high school but only one *History* course.

> The *president* told us about the possible merger with another company.
> **NOT**: The *President* told us about the possible merger with another company.

> Leo wrote: "We will not change our decision under any circumstances."
> **NOT**: Leo wrote: We will not change our decision "under any circumstances."

> Leo said his decision was final.
> **NOT**: Leo said "his decision was final."

Review pages 138 through 142 in the Reference Section for the correct uses of hyphens, capitals, and quotation marks.

ASSIGNMENT: Section E of the Worksheet for Unit 4 will help you see how well you can avoid miscellaneous errors.

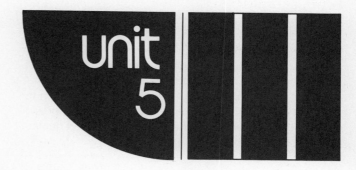

The Final Touches

If your letter is to make a good impression on the reader, careful attention to details is essential. As you look over a letter for the last time and prepare it for mailing, you want it to give you the image of a careful, professional writer, not a careless amateur.

Consider the carelessly typed letter (shown on page 26) that Jay Karnes received from McGoof Airlines. Do you think that Jay is likely to fly with McGoof?

THE LAST LOOK

Go over the general appearance of your letter. Is it neat? Is it well arranged and well placed on appropriate stationery? Have you used a single letter style throughout?

As you review the letter, you find that it is often too late to make improvements. The final touch to an immaculate, attractively arranged, correct letter should begin when the typing begins.

If you type your own letters, you alone are responsible for the final touch. It is up to you to make sure that your good typing techniques, careful handling, and pride in the finished product justify the time and money invested in composing the message. Watch details carefully so that you do not detract from the message of the letter by calling attention to its sloppy appearance.

What are the most important details to keep in mind? If you were to examine a hundred letters selected at random—those that might be sent or received by a business firm on any one day—you would probably find the answer. The flaws contained in typical letters suggest that your letter will make a better impression if you pay careful attention to:

Typing quality
Placement
Accuracy
Neatness
Envelopes

Typing Quality

You know, of course, that a letter should look fresh, crisp, and neat. But have you considered that one or more of the typing faults discussed here may keep a letter from reaching this standard?

Use a Good-Quality Ribbon. One common fault is typing with a worn-out ribbon. The standard color for a typewriter ribbon is black. Good-quality black typewriter ribbons are smear-proof, quick-drying, and nonfading. Stationery stores or office supply companies have ribbons in a wide range of fabrics and grades—and for almost any typewriter. While the new carbon and correctable film ribbons are of a higher quality than fabric ribbons, they are also more expensive and are not reusable. But they noticeably improve the appearance of the type print.

Avoid Uneven Stroking. Most offices today have electric typewriters, which make it possible to turn out high-quality work with minimum fatigue. A standard electric typewriter generally solves the problems of poor rhythm and uneven stroking, which result in light-and-dark variations and other irregularities in type so common when the manual typewriter is used. However, in itself an electric typewriter is no guarantee against uneven stroking; a poor typist will produce poorer typing on an electric typewriter than a good typist will.

McGOOF AIRLINES
1290 Airways
Neverle, Wisconsin 54961

Tel. (608) 321-4589

February 13, 19--

Mr. Jay Karnes
550 Johnson Drive
Duluth, Minn.

Dear Student

Last year over 10,000 students travaled on McGoof Airlines. Serving 6 states - Wisconsin, Michigan, Iowa, Indiana, Minesota, and Illinois, McGoof offers you a special rate which you can obtain by joining the McGoof Travel Club. Your membership card which you can order by returning the enclosed card only costs $5.

You will like McGoof airlines because of our convient air schedules and exellent personnel service. Meals or snacks are served on all frights.

With your membership card, flying may be the least expensive way for your to travel to your home, to other colleges, to visit with friends, or to on vacation. Flying is also the safest way to travel: in 16 years of operation, we have had only one fetality.

So won't you return the card with your $5 today. You will be gald you did.

Yours sincerly,

Jim Nivens

Jim Nivens

JN;me

The writer of this letter paid no attention to details—and made a very poor impression on the reader.

Even electric machines are sensitive to the people who type on them.

Correct Errors Neatly. Only an absolute perfectionist expects a letter to be typed without any errors at all, but every error should be neatly corrected. Until about ten years ago, one of the measures of an expert typist was how well he or she could erase mistakes and type·over the erasures so that they could not be detected. A great deal of attention was given to using exactly the right eraser for each kind of paper, using light, even strokes, and so on.

Today few typists erase their mistakes. Almost all of them use a white-out product, either a paper coated with chalk or a liquid, to cover up mistakes so that the corrections can be typed over them.

The liquid product is essentially a quick-drying white paint. The typist paints over an error, waits until the liquid has dried, then types the item correctly over the dried liquid.

The paper product looks like strips of white carbon paper. After typing a wrong letter, the typist backspaces to it, places the white-out tape behind the ribbon, and types the wrong letter again to make it nearly invisible. The correct letter is then typed over the whited-out mistake.

The newest device is a correction ribbon which may be part of the regular ribbon, or it may be a separate ribbon. The typist merely switches the ribbon position, backspaces, and types the correction.

These procedures are much faster than erasing, do not demand the practice and acquired skill that unnoticeable erasures require, and are therefore less expensive. To make almost perfect corrections, though, be sure to choose a liquid that matches the tone of your paper, and be sure that the white chalk product will not rub off easily, revealing the error.

Although these products are quick and easy, some employers prefer that their typists erase.

Do Not Strike Over a Letter. A strikeover in a business letter is an almost unforgivable error. It brands the writer as careless about the appearance of the letter. As students of typewriting usually learn quickly, a strikeover is as noticeable as an uncorrected error. *Never* try to correct a typing misstroke by striking over it with another character.

Keep Keys Clean. The keys of a typewriter must be kept clean. If they fill up with ribbon-ink deposits, they cannot make a sharp impression against the typewriter platen. As a result, the characters—especially the *e* and *o*—become messy and blurred. To prevent indistinct type impressions, clean the keys of the machine at least once a week if you use it regularly (clean the keys more often just after putting a new fabric ribbon on). Always clean the keys before and after typing mimeograph stencils. To prevent dark streaks on your letters from a dirty platen or paper bail, make sure that these machine parts are cleaned occasionally.

If your typewriter is equipped with a "one-time"

carbon or film ribbon, you will not have to clean your keys as often, but you must still keep the rest of your machine clean to keep it operating reliably and neatly.

Keep the Right Margin Even. Guard against a right margin that looks too ragged, a fault that often makes business letters look out of balance. Take a moment to glance at the right margin of this paragraph:

```
     We certainly appreciate the attractive
booklets on "How to Make Friends by
Telephone."  The clever writing style
and illustrations make the tips on placing
and answering telephone calls interesting to
read and easy to remember.  These tips
will be even more useful to us when
we take the office jobs for which we are
now preparing.
```

Do you agree that this paragraph is expertly typed and looks fine except for the ragged right margin? A right margin as sawtoothed as this can spoil the appearance of an otherwise attractive letter. Now, notice the improvement in the looks of the letter when the right margin is evened up a little.

```
     We certainly appreciate the attractive
booklets on "How to Make Friends by Telephone."
The clever writing style and illustrations make
the tips on placing and answering telephone
calls interesting to read and easy to remember.
These tips will be even more useful to us when
we take the office jobs for which we are now
preparing.
```

The right margin is still not perfectly even, nor need it be. It is no longer extremely zigzagged and therefore does not disturb the balanced appearance. In this paragraph it was easy to eliminate the unpleasant effect of a too-jagged margin by watching the copy and breaking lines at the proper places.

Often you will find that the only effective way to avoid a ragged right margin is to divide some of the longer words at the ends of a few lines. But use common sense in dividing words at the ends of lines in your letters. Don't think of divided words as the lazy way out or as a cure for all the ills of ragged margins. Words incorrectly divided or too many divided words can be just as disastrous to the looks of your letter as a jagged margin. Here are three principles that will help you with word division:

1. Divide words *only* between their syllables.

	cer-tify	dis-honest	cen-tral
NOT:	cert-ify	dish-onest	cent-ral

You can usually recognize each syllable when you pronounce the word slowly and distinctly. If in doubt, consult your dictionary.

2. Avoid divisions even between syllables unless they enhance the appearance and do not detract from the ease of reading your letter.

3. Do not hyphenate words at the ends of more than two consecutive lines.

If you need more help with word division, turn to Dividing Words on page 141 of the Reference Section.

Placement

Make sure that all the letter parts are in their proper places (see Units 2 and 3). Attractive arrangement is just as important to the appearance of your letter as clear, clean typing. Unless a letter has good form, it will not make the best possible impression on the reader.

Perhaps the most noticeable flaw in business letters is unbalanced placement. All of us quickly see something is wrong when we look at a letter that is unusually high or unusually low on the page or that has one side margin much wider than the other.

To give your reader that important good first impression, the letter must be placed attractively on the page. Like many other business skills, learning to place a letter attractively requires both knowledge and practice.

Follow the Standard Letter Placement Guide

While you are developing good judgment, you will find it useful to follow the standard letter-placement guide shown here. The guide, of course, is only approximate. Naturally, you will not count the actual number of words in a letter or waste time measuring and backspacing to get the margins exact to the last space.

The comparison of a well-balanced letter to a picture in a frame is still a reliable standard against which to judge a letter. To make your letters "picture perfect" means that the bottom margin should be slightly wider than the side margins and that both side margins should be the same. The letterhead usually determines the top margin. If you are typing on a plain sheet, however, you should make the top margin approximately the same as the bottom margin. The letters on pages 14-15 illustrate good placement.

Use the Standard-Line Plan

Another placement guide is the standard-line plan. As its name indicates, this plan requires that the same line length be used for all letters of ordinary length. For standard stationery, use a 50-space line for pica type and a 60-space line for elite type. Adjustments for variations in length are then made by altering the top and bottom margins, the space between the date line and the inside address, and the space between the elements of the complimentary closing.

The standard-line plan saves typing time and money because it eliminates the need to reset the margins for a long letter and then a short one. Since this plan is so widely accepted, the less pleasing appearance is no longer so important an objection to its use.

Does your letter meet the picture-frame test? Or if you used the standard-line plan, were your adjustments for letter length made successfully? If you used the letter-placement guide, is the overall effect pleasing? If not, what should you do?

Again, prevention is better (and faster) than cure. The time to check for placement is before you finish (or even start) typing the letter. If it is too short, you can stretch it; if it is too long, shorten it. How? By making any or all of the following adjustments.

To stretch a short letter:

1. Lower the date line.
2. Move the margins in to shorten the typing line.
3. Allow extra space between the date and inside address.
4. Allow up to six blank lines for the writer's signature.
5. Type the title on the line below the writer's name.

To shorten a long letter:

1. Raise the date line.
2. Move the margins a few spaces toward the edges (in no case leave less than 1-inch margins).
3. Allow less space between the date and inside address.
4. Allow less space for the writer's signature.

STANDARD LETTER-PLACEMENT GUIDE

Letter Factor	Short	Average	Long
Words in the body	Under 100	100-200	Over 200
Position of date	Line 15	Line 15	Line 15
Drop to address	5 lines	5 lines	5 lines
Length of line	40-space line	50-space line	60-space line
Margins	Pica 22-62	Pica 17-67	Pica 12-72
	Elite 31-71	Elite 26-76	Elite 21-81

Accuracy

You can never be confident that your letter is error-free unless you proofread it carefully. Even expert typists make this final check because mistakes can slip by unnoticed.

Look for typing errors and omissions as well as errors in spelling, in figures, and in English usage (see Unit 4). However, checking for typographic errors is not enough; you must read the material carefully to be sure that there are no omissions and that the message makes sense. Many errors go undetected because someone merely "eyeballed" it for typing accuracy but did not proofread it for meaning and sense. Consult your notes, dictionary, or other reference book if any word, phrase, or sentence doesn't look or sound quite right.

First, read for meaning. You may find that because of a careless typing error, the letter says something you did not intend to say—even something that may irritate or offend your reader. Mistakes in meaning often occur because the typist misreads shorthand or longhand notes, is annoyed by interruptions, or is thinking about something else. The moral, of course, is: "When typing a letter, keep your mind on what you are doing. Type ideas, not meaningless words. Be sure each sentence makes sense." If you follow this good advice, your proofreading won't flush out errors as embarrassing to you as the following were to those who wrote them.

> Please drip in at the office soon for your free copy of the pamphlet.
>
> One of my daily jobs as secretary is to open the male for this department.
>
> Our airlines offer convenient jet service from Oakland to Chicago—four frights every day.
>
> Be sure to get our expert help. It will put dollars in our pocket.

Second, read for mechanical accuracy. Proofread word by word and letter by letter. Give spelling, punctuation, and grammar a final check even though you were watchful as you typed and consulted your dictionary or reference manual.

The following frequent errors need special attention when you proofread a letter:

1. Confusion of similar words (discussed more fully in Unit 6)—*to, too, two; quit, quiet; its, it's; led, lead; hear, here; by, buy; there, their.*

2. Transposition of letters within a word—*partail* for *partial; makrs* for *marks; from* for *form; instructoin* for *instruction.*

3. Transposition and repetition of words—*it if is* for *if it is; one the or other* for *one or the other; will let let you know* for *will let you know.*

4. Omission of one or more letters of a word, especially in words with double or recurring letters—*adress* for *address; excelent* for *excellent; Febuary* for *February;*

libary for *library; convient* for *convenient; determing* for *determining.*

5. Omission of words; of phrases; of spaces between words; and of one of a pair of commas, dashes, quotation marks, or parentheses.

6. Basic English errors (review Unit 4 for details).

The right time to proofread the letter is just before you remove it from the typewriter. The right time to check the envelope address with the inside address is just before you remove the envelope from the typewriter. As you know, you can save time and worry if you make corrections while the letter is still in the machine. It is often hard to line up the typing exactly when you reinsert the paper. And making corrections on each carbon copy separately wastes time.

The right way to proofread is to scrutinize every detail of every part of the letter. Start with the date. You would be surprised how many business letters are mailed without dates and signatures because writers are careless. Did you use the correct date, not *September 31* when you meant *October 1?* And be sure to read the message with concentration.

Neatness

Fingerprints, carbon smudges, and other telltale marks on a letter indicate that its writer is careless about details. You may need to work hard to avoid these signs of carelessness that turn up unexpectedly, especially in making corrections.

The erasable feature of some plasticized bond paper causes the typewriter ink or carbon to remain on the surface of the paper instead of sinking in. Long after typing, therefore, the sheet smears when touched. Sometimes a gum eraser will remove much of the incriminating evidence of inexperience or carelessness. Keep one around for last-minute cleanups.

Through experience you can learn the art of turning out letters with a fresh, crisp appearance—but only if you really *care* how your letters look.

ASSIGNMENT: Turn to Problem 1 of the Worksheet for Unit 5 to see what can happen when proofreading for meaning is neglected. The letter in Problem 2 gives you practice in proofreading for careless errors. Problem 3 lets you apply what you have just studied.

Envelopes

The address on the envelope should match the form and content of the inside address of the letter. Follow these suggestions:

1. Type envelope addresses in blocked style—no indentions.

2. Always use single spacing, regardless of the number of lines in the address.

3. Type the city, state, and ZIP Code on the same line.

4. Type the return address on line 3 about five spaces in from the left edge.

5. On a small business envelope (No. 6¾) start the address on line 12 from the top edge and about 2 inches from the left edge.

6. On a large envelope (No. 10) begin on line 14 from the top edge and about 4 inches from the left edge.

The illustration below shows proper placement of the address on a No. 10 envelope. Note also the placement of such notations as "Confidential" and the type of mail service required.

Fold the letter correctly and insert it carefully in its matching envelope to be sure that it makes a favorable first impression. Creases from folding in the wrong places or streaks from dirty hands or desk tops can quickly turn a neat letter into an untidy one.

Folding a Letter for a Small Envelope

Bring bottom up to within ⅜ inch (10 millimeters) from top, and crease. Fold right-hand third toward left, fold left-hand third toward right, and insert into envelope.

Folding a Letter for a Large Envelope

Fold up bottom third of paper, fold top third over bottom third, and insert into envelope—last crease goes in first.

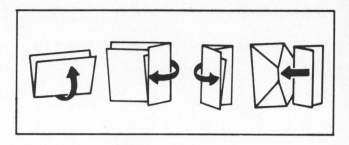

FOLDING A LETTER FOR A SMALL ENVELOPE

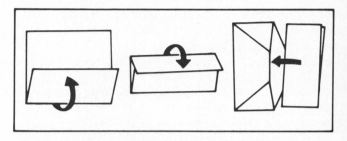

FOLDING A LETTER FOR A LARGE ENVELOPE

ASSIGNMENT: Address a large and a small business envelope, as you are instructed in Problems 4 and 5 of the Worksheet.

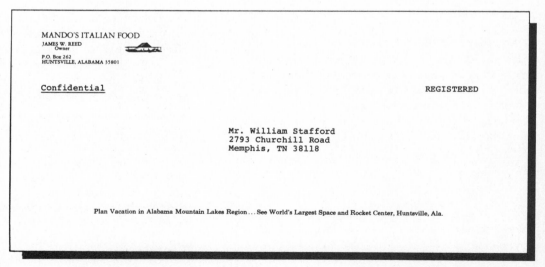

Courtesy Mando's Italian Food

CORRECTLY ADDRESSED NO. 10 ENVELOPE

The notations "Confidential" and "Registered" are each typed on the ninth line from the top edge of the envelope and about 5 spaces in from the side edge.

Principles of Good Letter Writing

You are discovering that writing better business letters is a many-sided challenge. Planning and composing effective messages requires that you put the principles and techniques in this part into practice as quickly as you can. At first you will have to use them consciously and with much thought; later (sooner than you think) you will master them and use them with ease.

When your letter makes a good first impression, you've taken the first big step toward effective communication. But the real test of a good letter—one that achieves its purpose quickly, clearly, and effectively—is the total effect it has on the reader. In this part you will learn several other steps that will help your letter make a favorable impression on the reader and accomplish its purpose.

You are not expected to master all these techniques at once, but you will quickly see that writing is a combination of things going on at the same time, not a disconnected series of "things to do in a certain order."

THE TOTAL EFFECT ON THE READER

Most people respond favorably to a letter's pleasing appearance, naturalness, courtesy, friendliness, and sincerity. Picture your reader receiving and looking over your letter. Will he or she be pleased with its appearance, be receptive to its message, and respond favorably?

If you did a good job of selecting appropriate stationery, arranging the parts of the letter, avoiding basic English errors, and giving the letter the "final touch" that made it mechanically perfect, then your letter will have that important favorable first effect on the reader.

Now follow your reader's reactions as he or she reads the letter. The total effect on the reader determines whether he or she does what you want or reacts the way you want. If your letter has done its job properly, the reader's response to each of the three questions below will be positive. You will, then, have taken three more steps toward successful communication.

Will the Reader Understand the Message?

The highest compliment a reader can pay you is to say that your letter was simple, clear, and easy to read. This reaction tells you that you have done your job well—and so has your letter.

Using simple words—words your reader will easily understand (without consulting a dictionary)—will help the reader quickly grasp the intended meaning of the whole message. Don't try to impress the reader with your knowledge by using fancy words. Be correct and natural in your use of words and construction of sentences. Your reader will understand you and be grateful to you as well.

Is the Tone of the Letter Positive?

How you say what you have to say may influence your reader just as much as *what* you have to say. Your letter will appeal to the reader if you use a natural, informal writing style, stress positive rather than negative ideas, and emphasize a "you" viewpoint throughout the letter. The friendly tone of your writing should suggest that your attitude is positive, that you are interested in the reader, and that you sincerely want to help. Naturalness, courtesy, friendliness, and sincerity are all essential to good tone in a letter.

Will the Letter Do Its Specific Job and Also Build Goodwill?

The pleasing appearance, easy readability, and friendly tone of your message attracts and impresses your reader. But the letter must do its specific job and, at the same time, increase goodwill. You can't always do all that the reader wants, but you can almost always convince the reader that you understand his or her problems and that you wanted to do something about them.

THE UNIFIED EFFECT OF THE MESSAGE

As you write, you must think not in terms of one attribute, one principle, or one attitude, but of the unified effect of the whole message. When you succeed, you will know that you understand how to make a good impression and promote goodwill through effective business letters.

You can write letters as good as the ones in this book (some of the examples were written by students!). If you keep practicing and follow the general suggestions given in Units 6, 7, 8 and 9, you *will* write successful letters. To help you further, Unit 10 will show you how to plan and prepare letters that communicate clearly and effectively.

Choosing the Right Words

Have you ever thought of writing as a matter of building? The writing process is complex, yet simple—the writer takes several steps to compose a message, but many things are actually happening at the same time. To understand how writing takes place, let's do what a writer does. A writer:

1. Chooses words.
2. Assembles them into phrases.
3. Connects the phrases to form sentences.
4. Groups the sentences into paragraphs.
5. Organizes the paragraphs into a coherent message.

To attempt to describe writing in the way the process really takes place would be difficult. So let's start with the simplest parts of language and proceed to the more complicated. We'll try to explain why some of these activities happen and how they relate to writing and the job it strives to do.

Let's start with the basic tools of writing, the words we use to communicate. Each word has one or more *denotative* meanings, or its definitions as listed in dictionaries. Usually one meaning is commonly used; the others less frequently.

In addition, words may have *connotative* meanings, or the subtle and often emotional meanings that we associate with some words. Because the emotional overtones, or connotative meanings, of words may vary from person to person, they are especially difficult to control. These connotations are often the result of the reader's intensely personal bias; and unless you enter into each reader's mind, you can't be sure how the reader will react. With groups of readers, however, you can often foresee that a particular word will evoke a negative image in those readers' minds. You can then choose another, less antagonizing word that has the same denotative meaning but that does not have a negative connotation.

The study of the meanings of words is called "semantics." There are many books on the subject that will help you understand this interesting and important aspect of our language.

Before we look at how words are used in writing, let's look at how they work in reading and listening. When a person reads or hears a word, the word goes into his or her "word bank," or memory, that part of the mind in which are stored all the words the person has ever heard or read in all their contexts. The reader or listener matches the new instance of hearing or reading a word with all the other instances stored in memory and from the context picks the meaning most likely to be the one intended by the writer or speaker.

Let's take *remote* as an example. It's not a commonly used word, nor is it exotic. It means far away, right? Such as "a remote country." But it also can mean remote in time, as in "the remote future." It can also mean having a slight relationship, as with a "remote cousin." And it is also used to mean aloof or distant, as in "a remote manner." Add *control* and you get *remote control,* meaning control (usually electronic) from a distance. This is one of the strengths of English, that we can give multiple, though necessarily related, meanings to a word, and so extend our language without making it impossibly cumbersome.

Suppose, however, that *remote* didn't fit your needs precisely or that you had just used it in the previous sentence and didn't want to repeat it. By using a dictionary or a thesaurus you could find synonyms like *distant, removed,* and *far.* And this is another strength of our language, that many words can have the same or closely related meanings. As an example, a student once counted over 220 meanings of *get*!

Crepuscule means only twilight; it has no other meanings. Between *get* and *crepuscule* lies the difference between familiar and unfamiliar words. *Crepuscule* is one of those words that one never hears and is unlikely to read. (If you knew what it meant, you are unusual.) If you think of it, you have no other uses to compare it with; so you are unable to attach a meaning to it. For *get*, you have an abundance of meanings to choose from, depending on the context in which it is used.

Here, then, is a principle to keep in mind when you are writing. Generally speaking, the more familiar a word is to your reader, the more meanings he or she will know for it and the more likely he or she will be to attach to it the meaning you intended. The more unfamiliar a word is, the fewer meanings the reader will know for it and the less likely he or she will be to give it the meaning you have in mind.

Almost all the common words you use in everyday speech are short, one- or two-syllable words. Using short words helps to keep the message readable. To communicate easily and effectively with your reader, use common, short, familiar words whenever it is possible to do so.

You can make your writing clearer and your reader's job easier by using:

1. Simple words rather than complex words.
2. Concise words rather than excess words.
3. Conversational words rather than trite words.
4. Appropriate words rather than similar words often confused.
5. Correct words rather than frequently misused words.
6. Specific words rather than general words.
7. Positive words rather than negative words.

SIMPLE WORDS RATHER THAN COMPLEX WORDS

Do you try to use high-sounding words that will impress your reader? The reader will appreciate a simple, friendly, natural tone in your writing. Your letter is a written conversation and should reflect a direct, informal writing style that communicates a message which will be easily understood by the reader. Remember that simplicity is always in good taste. The big word seldom impresses the reader.

Think twice before you *write* a word that you would not *say*. The reader's attention is shifted from the message if he or she must guess at the meaning of some of the words or reach for the dictionary in order to understand your letter. The reader is much more likely to listen comfortably and understand easily if you use words that are familiar and sound natural.

The simple word is not always a short one, however, and the high-sounding word is not always a long one. *Displeasure* and *irritation*, for instance, are used more often in conversation than *pique* is used. As a rule, though, choose the longer word *only when it expresses the meaning more clearly or more naturally than its shorter synonym.*

You can see how short, familiar words make reading easier if you contrast the following paragraph with its revision:

> Consideration of your request leads us to believe that of several alternative courses of action open at the present time the maximum effect will accrue if standard procedures are amended to permit actualization toward optimal realization of the goals of our mission.

Here's the revision:

> I agree we'll do better if we change our standard procedures.

Below is a list of high-flown, complex words and phrases and their simple, direct equivalents. Most of these formal-sounding, complicated words, often found in business letters, are perfectly good words. The point is that each has a more familiar substitute that usually does a better job of communicating.

Instead of These Complex Words...	...Use These Simpler Words
a substantial segment of the population	many people
affords an opportunity	allows
approximately	about
are fully cognizant of	know
ascertain	find out
assistance	help
consummate	complete, finish
effect the destruction of	destroy
encounter difficulty in	find it hard to
endeavor	try
gratuitous	free
hold in abeyance	delay
I wish to assure you that it has been a great pleasure to be the recipient of your gracious generosity	thank you
interpose an objection	object
interrogate	ask
it is requested that	please
numerous	many
peruse	read, study
pursuant to your request	as you asked
render services	serve
remuneration	payment
subsequently	later
sufficient	enough
take under advisement	consider, think over
terminate	end, finish
utilize	use

You can add many others to this list, for your reference. Look for complex, unfamiliar words and phrases in your writing and try to replace them with familiar words which will make the reader's job easier.

CONCISE WORDS RATHER THAN EXCESS WORDS

Every word you use that does not contribute to the effectiveness of your message wastes the reader's time and weakens interest. Strive for *conciseness* in your writing—using only as many well-chosen words as you need to convey your message. Each word in the message should help make the meaning clear or the letter friendly. By using only as many words as you need for what you want to say, you help the reader in two ways: you save the reader time in reading and understanding, and you make the letter more interesting to read.

An average of three out of ten words in the typical letter are not really needed, according to recent estimates. A reader is likely to lose all interest in a message if he or she must wade through wordiness to get to the main point. You want your reader to listen comfortably. Why use two or more words when one word will do the job well?

Let's look at this sentence from a business letter:

In reply to yours of recent date, I wish to advise you that Mr. Kenneth P. Hawthorne, about whom you inquired, was terminated from employment at Fann's on June 20, due to the fact that he frequently did not appear for work at the appointed hour.

Two-thirds of the words in the sentence can be eliminated and the message stated concisely:

Mr. Kenneth P. Hawthorne's employment at Fann's ended on June 20 because of excessive tardiness.

Notice that none of the necessary information is omitted and the message is actually clearer and easier to read.

Why not write "call you" rather than "contact you by telephone," "in that case" rather than "if that should prove to be the case," and "met" rather than "held a meeting"? In fact, why use any of the timewasters below when the timesavers express the same ideas without wasting words?

Instead of These Timewasters...	...Choose These Timesavers
arrived at the conclusion	concluded
at a later date	later
at the present time OR at this moment in time	now
costs a total of $50	costs $50
due to the fact that	because
during the course of	during
during the year of 1980	during 1980
first of all	first
five in number	five
for the purpose of providing	to provide
held a meeting	met
I want to take this opportunity to tell you that we are grateful to you	thank you
I wish to say (permit me to say, OR may I say) that we are glad	we are glad
in a manner similar to	like
in the event that	if
in the near future	soon
in this day and time	today
inasmuch as	since, because
is responsible for selecting	selects
it is the opinion of many	many believe, many think
long-lasting wear	long wear
long period of time	long time
made the announcement	announced
main problem is a matter of cost	main problem is cost
put in an appearance	appeared
self-addressed envelope	addressed envelope, return envelope
take appropriate measures	do
until such time as you can	until you can
with the exception of	except
with regard to safety precautions	for safety
in order to	to

CONVERSATIONAL WORDS RATHER THAN TRITE WORDS

Many expressions that were fashionable in business letters of years ago sound lifeless, insincere, and even boring when used in today's correspondence. If a message is filled with worn-out words, the reader probably feels that you were not thinking of nor talking to him or her when you wrote it. The letter sounds mechanical, like a record that can be played back for anyone listening, not like a personal message to the reader. Since fashions in words change, correct usage should be current usage. Don't go to out-of-date business letters to find the words to use in a letter today. Use only those words that educated business people normally use in well-planned communication.

Not only do old-fashioned expressions need to be kept out of your letters, but many modern expressions have lost their effectiveness because of overuse. For example, "contact" as a verb meaning "to get in touch with" has been worn out by overuse, as has "check" as a verb. They have become trite—meaningless.

The trite expressions in the column at the left too often appear in today's business letters. As you study them, notice how simply and naturally the suggested conversational words convey the same meanings.

Instead of These Trite Words...	...Choose These Conversational Words
acknowledge receipt of	thank you for
agreeable with your desires in the matter	as you suggested
are in receipt of	have
as per	as
at the earliest possible date	as soon as (you) can
at the present writing	now
at your earliest convenience	when you have time (are ready) as soon as you can
enclosed herewith, enclosed herein, OR enclosed please find	here is (OR here are)
give the matter our early attention	take care of this soon
in accordance with your request	as you asked
in view of the fact that	because of
kindly advise me OR kindly inform me	please write me
of recent date	of April 3
regret to inform you that	am sorry that
take the liberty of sending you	send you
the writer OR the undersigned	I, we
thanking you in advance	I shall appreciate
under date of	on
under separate cover	separately
we will thank you to	please

These are only a few examples. Unfortunately, many other trite expressions are still being used. To keep your letters alive and human, avoid using such expressions in your writing.

APPROPRIATE WORDS RATHER THAN SIMILAR WORDS OFTEN CONFUSED

By using the right word for every circumstance, you help the reader understand exactly what you mean. You also build up the reader's confidence in you and your ideas. Errors that might pass unnoticed in oral conversation are far more noticeable in the written message. If you use the "wrong" word, or one that is not "just right" for the context, you may imply a meaning that you did not intend. The reader may misinterpret your intended meaning because of your poor choice of words.

Errors often result from the confusion of *homonyms,* words that sound alike but have different meanings, such as *there, they're,* and *their; here* and *hear.* Even more confusing are words that are similar in sound but different in meaning, such as *adopt* and *adapt; affect* and *effect.* And probably most confusing are *synonyms,* words that are similar in meaning. Here it is important to choose carefully the word that says exactly what you want to say. For example, "the *balance* of your shipment" is not quite correct since *balance* usually refers to an amount of money. *Remainder* or *rest* would be more appropriate. Similarly, "you can *get* the information from him" is more appropriate than "you can *secure* the information from him."

An advertising copywriter thought he was picturing the bright attractiveness of a dress when he wrote that it was a *gaudy* print. His prospect did not buy the dress, however, because she interpreted *gaudy* as "showy" rather than "pretty."

To avoid confusing your readers, choose carefully among the following groups of words that are often confused. Use the dictionary to verify the exact meaning of any word you are in doubt about.

accept—except
ad—add
adapt—adept—
   adopt
advice—advise
affect—effect
altar—alter
among—between
amount—number
appraise—apprise
assistance—assistants
balance—remainder
beside—besides
canvas—canvass

capital—capitol
cereal—serial
cheap—inexpensive
choose—chose
cite—site—sight
coarse—course
complement—
   compliment
confidentially—
   confidently
correspondence—
   correspondents
council—counsel
eligible—illegible

eminent—imminent
farther—further
fewer—less
fiscal—physical
formally—formerly
graft—graph
hear—here
human—humane
its—it's
later—latter
leave—let
lessen—lesson
loose—lose
miner—minor
moral—morale
obtain—secure
partly—partially

party—person
passed—past
personal—personnel
practicable—practical
precede—proceed
principal—principle
respectfully—
   respectively
stationary—stationery
suit—suite
than—then
their—there—they're
to—too—two
track—tract
uninterested—
   disinterested
ware—wear

CORRECT WORDS RATHER THAN FREQUENTLY MISUSED WORDS

Some words often misused in business letters fall into two groups: redundancies and actual errors in grammar (see Unit 4) and excessive slang and other expressions in poor taste.

The list of words and phrases that are often misused supplements the common errors discussed in Unit 4. Familiarize yourself with it to help avoid misusing words in your letters.

Instead of These Frequently Misused Words...	...Choose These Correct Words
all but I	all but me
a lot of	many, much
and etc.	etc.
anywheres	anywhere
between we two	between us two
between you and I	between you and me
equally as good	equally good, just as good
if you will or not	whether you will or not
incidently (misspelling)	incidentally
inside of	inside
insight of	insight into
irregardless (no such word)	regardless
like I do	as I do
long ways	long way
might of	might have
neither...or	neither...nor
person which	person who
real pleased	really pleased
seldom or ever	seldom if ever
the reason why...is because	the reason...is that
these kind	these kinds
two pair	two pairs

You can add many other errors and their replacements to this list for your reference.

SPECIFIC WORDS RATHER THAN GENERAL WORDS

You can make your writing more *precise* by using specific words rather than general words. Specific words are those that present a clear, sharply defined picture to a reader's mind. General words are those that present a hazy, indefinite picture to the reader.

Suppose we say to you "car." What do you see in your mind? Now suppose we make it "blue car." Has the picture in your mind changed? Let's be even more specific: "baby blue sports coupé." What do you see in your mind now, and how does it differ from what you thought of when we said "car"?

As just illustrated, sometimes the more specific you want to be, the more words you must use. In terms of writing, though, being specific means finding the balance between extra words with broad, general meanings and only the words necessary to paint a precise, accurate picture in the reader's mind. Being specific in your writing is the result of practice and experience. It is often a matter of choosing one word over another, finding the word that will evoke just the right image in your reader's mind. When writing, you must constantly consider your choice of words.

POSITIVE WORDS RATHER THAN NEGATIVE WORDS

Some words carry positive meanings while others connote negative ideas. If you want your reader to feel goodwill toward you, to do what you would like him or her to do, you'll be careful to avoid negative, unfriendly words.

One type of negative words is those that are negative in almost any context, such as *complain, disappointing, inferior,* and *unfortunately.* No matter how you use them, you'll probably convey a negative meaning to your reader. Learn to substitute words like *cooperation, service,* and *sincere.*

The second type of negative words includes those that are negative because of the context they appear in. For example, *neglect, blame,* and *error* do not bring a negative response when you write, "We neglected to tell you..." or "We take full blame for the error." Yet, when used with *you* or *your,* they arouse anger: "You neglected to..." or "Your error caused..." or "You are to blame for...."

Here are some words and phrases that should be used with caution—if at all. They are likely to make the reader feel you are criticizing or accusing him or her and cause the reader to become angry with you.

apology	impossible	unfair attitude
broken	inconvenience	unfavorable reply
cannot	indifferent	unfortunately
complaint	loss	unwilling

damages	mistake	you claim
delay	problem	you neglected
difficulty	refuse	you say
disappoint	regret	your carelessness
discomfort	sorry	your failure
dissatisfied	suspicion	your inability
failure	trouble	your insinuation
guilty	unable to	your refusal

You can, of course, add many other words that deserve the label "Use at Your Own Risk."

Throughout the rest of this book, you will learn subtle ways to make the reader understand that he or she is in the wrong by carefully choosing words and positioning sentences and paragraphs in the letter.

ASSIGNMENT: Test what you have learned about word choice by rewriting the sentences in Part A of the Worksheet for Unit 6 and revising the letter in Part B.

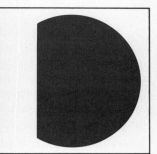

Writing Sentences and Paragraphs

Words alone do not communicate; they must be put together in the right order to do the job and according to a careful plan. Once you have planned your letter, you must choose your words and construct sentences with them, join your sentences to form paragraphs, and fit the paragraphs smoothly into a unified letter.

CONSTRUCTING SENTENCES

How well you construct your sentences plays a very important part in determining how well you communicate with your reader.

The "rules" about constructing sentences are not so very complicated. Of course, you should observe the principles of written English; otherwise, you will distract your reader. If you know these principles, you'll be able to use them to achieve the effects you want in your writing.

Generally, sentence construction in business letters is somewhat more conversational than in formal writing. Ungrammatical usage is never justified, of course. You will be wise, therefore, to choose a style that is closer to speech than to, say, a college textbook. Remember that communication takes place more efficiently when the reader is thinking about content and not about the manner in which it is expressed.

A Sentence Should Contain One Complete Thought

A sentence is a group of words that expresses a complete thought. If a group of words gives merely part of an idea, it is a sentence *fragment*. Sentence fragments, such as the examples below, split *one* thought into *two* parts.

> WEAK: To update your records and actively reflect Avant Electric's economic standing in the community. We submit the following statistics on the company.

In the above quotation from an actual letter, *To update your records and actively reflect Avant Electric's economic standing in the community* is not a complete sentence. It starts an idea that is not completed until the sentence that follows. The two statements should be joined to express one complete thought.

> STRONG: To update your records and actively reflect Avant Electric's economic standing in the community, we submit the following statistics on the company.

The next quotation, also from an actual letter, illustrates another sentence fragment.

> WEAK: It describes some of the more advanced techniques of making sound investments. Including a candid analysis of the strategies and risks involved.

Including a candid analysis of the strategies and risks involved expands the idea expressed in the first sentence but is not a complete sentence in itself.

> STRONG: It describes some of the more advanced techniques of making sound investments—including a candid analysis of the strategies and risks involved.

Sentence fragments, usually introduced by prepositions or participles, are frequently found as opening and closing ideas in business letters. They are particularly feeble in either of these spots because *the first few words and the last few words are the most emphatic of the whole message.*

> WEAK OPENINGS:
>
> Realizing that an insurance company must make fast, fair adjustments. The Sciara Insurance Agency pledges to you the best service available in the Dallas–Fort Worth area.
>
> With reference to your suggestion. I appreciate this information and will follow up within a week.

You can make these openings acceptable by substituting a comma for the first period in each of them. But you can make them much stronger by rewording the sentences as shown below.

> STRONG OPENINGS: An insurance company must make fast, fair adjustments. The Sciara Insurance Agency knows this and pledges to you the best service available in the Dallas–Fort Worth area.
>
> Your suggestion concerning our refund policy is welcome. Within a week I hope to have a solution to this problem of refunds.
>
> WEAK CLOSING: Thanking you in advance for your courtesy and cooperation in this matter.
>
> STRONG CLOSING: I shall appreciate your cooperation.

Sometimes a deliberate sentence fragment can be very effective. It can be made to express a complete thought by putting an exclamation point or a question mark after it:

> That's right—lifetime protection! Worldwide, 24 hours a day. And how?
>
> Good News! Going on *Right Now*—our special Sundown-to-Sunup 40%-off sale!

In these examples, using sentence fragments successfully tends to make the writing breezy and chatty. This informality may be useful in writing a sales letter for use in direct mail where it is necessary to establish quickly both friendliness and a feeling of trust in the reader. In general business correspondence, however, such breeziness may backfire. The reader may think you are being flippant or insincere. To a reader who is angry, worried, or fearful over something, a very breezy writing style is especially unwelcome. Your letter may convince the reader that you don't care.

Sentence fragments may be used effectively, but sparingly, in business letters. Be sure you know what you're doing when you use them and that your reader will not consider the fragment a grammatical error.

A Sentence Should Contain Only One Idea

Just as sentence fragments do not express a complete thought, sentences that contain more than one idea weaken the message. Most readers are accustomed—and rightly so—to sentences with a single thought in each sentence. Too many ideas written without a pause tend to run together in the reader's mind.

> WEAK: Thank you for your letter of May 30, and beginning with the July issue your copy of the *National Business Report* will be sent to your summer address.

Here the writer is doing two things: (1) thanking the customer for his letter and (2) telling him that his request will be taken care of. Neither idea stands out because the two are run together in one sentence. A simple change will stress both ideas.

STRONG: Thank you for your letter of May 30. Beginning with the July issue, your copy of *National Business Report* will be sent to your summer address.

The following sentence, taken from an actual memo, contains three ideas.

WEAK: Your ideas don't have to be typed, if possible though they should be written in outline form and please be prepared to discuss them when you come to the meeting.

This sentence could be confusing even if it were correctly punctuated (which it isn't). Notice how much clearer it is when split into three ideas.

STRONG: Your ideas don't have to be typed; if possible, though, they should be written in outline form. Please be prepared to discuss them at the meeting.

Try giving more emphasis to an important idea by dividing it into two parts and expressing each part in a separate sentence.

WEAK: We promise to "try harder" in the future, and please let us know of any way we can serve you better.

STRONG: We promise to "try harder" in the future. Please let us know of any way we can serve you better.

Sentence Length Should Be Moderate and Varied

For quick, clear, easy reading, all your sentences should be short and simple, right? Wrong! The length of the sentences can make the message easy to follow or hard to follow. Sentences averaging around 17 words in length are considered about right for fast reading. This means, of course, that good sentences can be longer than 17 words, and some can be shorter, for variety and emphasis. Imagine the monotony of a message in which each sentence is exactly 17 words long. It might put the reader to sleep rather than persuade him or her to respond.

Varying the length of your sentences can enliven your writing style. A short, short sentence sandwiched between two long sentences emphasizes the thought of the short sentence. A few very short sentences help to give the message "punch." But too many short sentences one after the other make the letter choppy. If you ask your reader to keep jumping from one short statement to another, you may soon lose the reader.

CHOPPY: We received your shipment of June 21. It contained sixteen #104H Klausen dresses. There were four each in Misses sizes 8, 10, 12, and 14. But we ordered four each in Junior sizes 5, 7, 9, and 11. You can see this on the copy of the order which is enclosed.

STRONG: Your June 21 shipment of sixteen #104H Klausen dresses—four each in Misses sizes 8, 10, 12, and 14—arrived today. However, the shipment should have

consisted of four each in Junior sizes 5, 7, 9, and 11, as shown on the enclosed copy of the order.

A short, choppy sentence is seldom as irritating to a reader as an extra long sentence that rambles on and on, as though the writer can't stop. One secretary said he felt almost out of breath just looking at this one-sentence letter received at his office.

WEAK: In reply to your letter of August 6, I desire to enter it upon the record that, out of our commission to be paid to us by the Callicotts for making sale of this property for them to veteran Randolph H. Lord, I agree to pay you a commission of 6 percent of the sale price, amounting to $3,000, as a service fee to you and as compensation for the work and expense of closing this loan, and I further agree that no portion of this charge shall be assessed against or paid by the veteran purchaser, and I hope that this agreement meets with your approval.

What did the writer say? Isn't the following much easier to read?

STRONG: I want to put on record the terms of the agreement you asked about in your letter of August 6.

Our commission is to be paid by the Callicotts for making sale of this property for them to veteran Randolph H. Lord. From our commission I agree to pay you a commission of 6 percent of the sale price, amounting to $3,000, as a service fee and compensation for the work and expense of closing this loan. I further agree that no portion of this charge shall be assessed against or paid by the veteran purchaser.

Please let me know if you will accept these terms.

Two careless writing habits are frequently the basic cause of too-long sentences.

The "And" Habit

The "and" habit, which leads to run-on sentences, is illustrated in this excerpt from a business letter.

WEAK: We presently employ 93,466 persons at 11 sites in the greater Denver area, and this makes us the third largest private employer in the area, and we hope you will see fit to include these figures in your brochure, and we thank you for your cooperation.

Usually you can correct this kind of error by eliminating some of the *ands* and dividing the run-on sentences into several sentences. Sometimes rephrasing the ideas makes the new sentences more varied and interesting. Don't you like this better?

STRONG: Since Mason Manufacturing employs 93,466 persons at 11 sites in the greater Denver area, we are the third largest private employer in this area. We would appreciate your including these figures in your brochure.

The "Dependent-Clause Chain" Habit

Chains of dependent clauses produce confusing sentences. Series of overlapping clauses, each hanging on to the one before, introduce new ideas and expand previous ideas so fast that the reader can barely grasp one before the next one arrives. Notice all the clauses introduced by *which* in this long sentence from a business letter.

> WEAK: Enclosed is a copy of our agreement, which is not terminable until October 1, 1982, which may be converted to a contract with no installation charge; or you can pay a short-rate termination fee of $485.59, which will relieve you from further obligation.

In breaking up long sentences of this type, be careful that each new sentence expresses a complete thought. Isn't this less confusing?

> STRONG: Enclosed is a copy of our agreement, which is not terminable until October 1, 1982. However, it may be converted to a contract with no installation charge; or you can pay a short-rate termination fee of $485.59, relieving you from further obligation.

Your Sentences Should Be Concise

Whether a sentence is long or short, it should be concise. "Concise" is not the opposite of "long"; it is the opposite of "wordy." If your sentences are concise, they contain no wasted words.

You have already studied the wisdom of avoiding needless repetition and of using concise words and phrases. You learned that when you write concisely, you express your thoughts clearly. You don't use three or four words to say something you can say just as well—or better—in one or two words.

Now go a step further. Learn to make *sentences* concise.

Eliminate Useless Words From Your Sentences

Organize your sentences to eliminate words that do not help make your meaning clear or your tone courteous. As an example, the expletive beginnings *It is, There are,* and *There were* generally add nothing to sentences except words. They also tend to lead you into stiff, artificially formal writing and passive constructions. When you have used one of these expletive beginnings, try rearranging the sentence to strengthen it and thereby achieve conciseness.

> WEAK: There are two choices open to you.
> STRONG: You have two choices.

Don't Repeat Ideas Unnecessarily

The only reason for restating an idea, once it has been said clearly and forcefully, is to gain emphasis through repetition. This way of emphasizing ideas has a danger: if you overuse it, you will bore your reader. People get restless when you tell them something they already know. They dislike even more your repeating an idea because you failed to state it clearly the first time.

> WEAK: Is the lasting beauty of your sink equal to its durability; that is, will it retain its color and brightness after long use, or will water or food acids spot or mar the surface in any way, making necessary more care and upkeep on it than on most other sinks?

Isn't the repetition in the above excerpt from a sales letter useless? Isn't the question more forceful when asked only once?

> STRONG: Will your sink retain its color and brightness after long use, or will water or food acids spot or mar the surface and make necessary more care and upkeep on it than on most other sinks?

Don't Tell Your Reader Something He or She Already Knows

If you agree that concise writing helps your letter accomplish its purpose, then you will also agree that it is wise to omit facts the reader already knows. When you tell your reader the obvious, you waste words and risk offending the reader by implying that the reader is not aware of it or has forgotten it. You also reveal yourself as forgetful or thoughtless by telling the reader what you should realize he or she already knows.

Obvious statements in business letters usually appear at the beginning. Writers who use obvious statements instead of direct beginnings simply admit that they can't solve the problem of how to begin. They do not take advantage of one of the most effective positions in the letter, the opening sentence. Too many writers begin by telling the reader that they received his or her letter, which they are answering, or quickly restate what the reader said in the letter. This is lazy writing. If you are answering the reader's letter, your answer is evidence that you received the letter. Why waste the important beginning of your letter telling the reader "In reply to your letter of February 4,..." or "In your letter of January 16 you stated that..."? The reader knows he or she wrote the letter and what it said! If the reader doesn't remember all the details, a quick glance at the file copy will refresh his or her memory. Your job is to give the reader an *answer,* not to echo the reader's letter back to him or her.

The best way to begin a business letter is usually to answer the reader's question, to get to the point. We'll discuss later a few situations when you should not begin the letter with the main point.

> WEAK: I am in receipt of your letter dated April 18. You wanted to know the current prices on our Fulton Electric fans; so I am enclosing our latest price list, which will cover all this information.
> STRONG: Here is our current price list on Fulton Electric fans.

WEAK: I am replying to your letter of November 28. With this letter you enclosed a check for $101.23, the total amount due since August.

STRONG: Thank you for your check for $101.23, which clears your account.

As with beginnings, writers often have trouble ending a letter. After answering all the reader's questions and giving explanations where needed, a writer may then fall back on trite phrases:

> Thank you again for your interest in our product. If you need further information with regard to this matter, or if we may assist you in any way, please don't hesitate to contact us.

If thanks has been given once, that's usually enough; say it twice and you will appear gushy. The best expression of gratitude is to do what the reader wanted. To offer further information or assistance may appear courteous, but it really means that you aren't sure you told the reader everything he or she should know and you hope the reader will remind you of anything you forgot to include. Isn't it safe to assume that if the reader needs more information or help, you will hear from him or her?

Deleting foggy endings, like avoiding obvious beginnings, usually improves the letter. Take this actual business letter as an example:

Dear Mrs. Romanov:

SUBJECT: GRAPHIC PRINTING PLATES

Thank you for your recent request for further information on the Graphic printing plates advertised in the June issue of *Office Products*.

Enclosed is literature which gives complete descriptive data and specifications—and we are asking our dealer in your area to get in touch with you. The dealer is:

General Printing Equipment Co.   Phone: (492) 495-3869
3961 Cumberland
Terre Haute, Indiana 58392

Attention: Mr. George S. Geller

We appreciate your interest in Graphic printing plates. This dealer is equipped to give you excellent service and will be able to answer questions about the Graphic printing plates and to show you how they will prove their value to your organization in many ways.

Meanwhile, if we can help you in any way, just call on us. We'll be glad to assist you.

Very truly yours,

Suppose you took out the first and last paragraphs of this letter. Is the letter weakened? No, not really. In fact, it would be concise and clear. A letter is concise when everything in it contributes to the job it has to do and nothing can be taken out without lessening its ability to communicate.

Avoid Passive Constructions

The passive voice is probably the worst culprit in writing that is dull and weak. Although the passive has its uses, what it does to your writing should warn you to use it sparingly.

Why does the passive voice hurt readability? Consider this example:

> Brian typed the letter.

This is a simple sentence in the active voice. The picture it should arouse in the reader's mind is of Brian typing. This is true of active-voice sentences; they emphasize the action, the "doing" that the sentences describe. Now let's put our example into the passive voice:

> The letter was typed by Brian.

Some changes have taken place. Extra words have appeared. The extra words, *was* and *by*, signal the reader that the violation of normal English word order is intentional. In the passive version, it takes six words to tell what four told in the active. The first drawback to using passive constructions is that *they require more words without adding to the meaning.*

The second drawback is more serious, and it's what makes passives so weak. In our example look how the emphasis has shifted. The mental picture is of a typed letter. No Brian, no typing, just a typed letter. *The action is gone and the person who did the acting is gone, too.* It is precisely this shift of emphasis from "someone doing" to "the thing done to" that robs passive sentences of their interest and clarity and makes them poor forms of communication.

Avoid passives by watching for them in your writing and changing them to actives. Make people the subjects of your sentences whenever possible. People doing things and saying things are interesting, not what they have done or said. Stress the "people" element in your writing; after all, a human being will read what you write.

Vary Your Sentence Structure

We have already seen that a long string of very short sentences makes for choppy writing, that a sequence of very long sentences makes reading difficult, and that sentences all the same length make a letter boring to read. Just as these faults will affect the reader's reaction, so do identically constructed sentences become monotonous and even seem to talk down to the reader. Besides varying the length of your sentences, you need also to think about varying their structure and pattern.

Monotonous writing makes for monotonous reading. A reader who becomes bored will soon stop paying attention. One way to vary your writing is to use different sentence beginnings. Since the way you begin a sentence almost always determines the pattern for the sentence as a whole, concentrating on beginnings is the logical way to control patterns.

You can also vary the structure of your sentences by utilizing simple, compound, complex, and compound-complex formations. In actual practice the ideas you are expressing and the order in which they must be stated will probably help you to vary the sentence structure.

Your Sentences Should Fit Together Naturally

Just as the words in a sentence should be arranged for smooth reading, so should the sentences in the message. Each sentence should follow the one before it and flow naturally from one thought to the next.

In writing sentences that fit together properly, you will find it often helps to (1) refer in some way to the preceding sentence, such as *this method, this plan, because this is true,* or *when it is completed;* or (2) use connectives (transitional words and phrases), such as *also, therefore, however, still, previously, accordingly, in this way, after that, during that time, for instance,* or *as a result.*

POORLY CONNECTED SENTENCES: Your proposal has a great deal of merit. There are a number of questions to be answered. Through a comprehensive market research program, we should be able to come up with an appropriate solution.

IMPROVED: Your proposal has a great deal of merit. Although many questions must still be answered, we should be able to come up with an appropriate solution through a comprehensive market research program.

POORLY CONNECTED SENTENCES: We agree with many of the suggestions in your report. We shall put some of them into effect immediately. We shall delay action on the remainder and get reports from other sales representatives.

IMPROVED: We agree with many of the suggestions in your report. We shall, therefore, put those points into effect immediately. Later on, after we have studied reports from other sales representatives, we shall decide what to do about your other suggestions.

POORLY CONNECTED SENTENCES: You were right when you suggested that your April statement was not correct. A payment you made on February 28 had not been credited to your account.

IMPROVED: You were right when you suggested that your April statement was not correct. The error occurred because a payment you made on February 28 had not been credited to your account.

Your Sentences Should Be Punctuated Correctly

Let good usage and common sense be your guides to correct punctuation. If you do not follow accepted rules in punctuating, will your reader know what your

punctuation marks mean? Maybe not. **Review the punctuation rules in the Reference Section. To check on punctuation errors that often appear in business letters,** review the discussion of them on pages 22 to 25.

Your Sentences Should Be Error-Free

Basic English errors in your sentences may make your reader think you are ignorant or careless—or both. To avoid such errors, review the rules and examples on pages 129 to 134 of the Reference Section and in Unit 4 until you are confident that you can apply the rules correctly. Remember that no letter is completely satisfactory unless it is mechanically acceptable. Write and edit each sentence until it is correct.

ASSIGNMENT: Revise the poor sentences in Section A of the Worksheet.

DEVELOPING PARAGRAPHS

After choosing the words and combining them into sentences, the next step in "building" a letter is grouping the sentences into paragraphs. Paragraphs deserve the same care you give to words and sentences. Here are some suggestions for paragraphing business letters.

A paragraph deals with one idea—with one set of thoughts related to a particular topic. When you introduce a new topic, start a new paragraph. Beginning a new paragraph is how you let the reader know that new ideas are coming up.

Business letters usually deal with one major subject or have one major purpose. This major subject is made up of several items or parts, and each of these items is developed into a paragraph. Writing a business letter, then, is a matter of identifying the major subject or purpose and deciding on the items that make it up. How to organize the items, the paragraphs, in the best order is the next job.

Even when a letter deals with more than one major subject, as sometimes happens, its organization should not be too difficult. You begin by identifying each of the major subjects, then the items or parts within each subject, and finally you put everything into logical order—the order most likely to achieve your purpose.

The Paragraphs Should Be Reasonably Short

Short paragraphs can, as a rule, be read faster than long paragraphs. Also, most readers like the breaks that "white space" gives. A paragraph as short as one typewritten line—or even one short line—may be effective. If any paragraph runs over nine lines, you should usually consider breaking it into two or three short paragraphs. Think of "reasonably short paragraphs" in a business letter as varying from one to seven lines, with an average length of four or five typewritten lines.

The First and Last Paragraphs Should Be Shorter Than Average

Usually, brief opening and closing paragraphs give the letter a brisk, businesslike appearance and make it easier and more interesting to read. Since a reader hesitates to wade into a long, solid mass of words, a short opening paragraph is especially important. A two-, three-, or four-line paragraph invites the reader to start reading. And you can often stress the one idea that you want to leave with the reader in a short closing paragraph like the following:

> To get your copy of our free brochure, just fill in the enclosed prepaid card and return it.

> Call 482-3958 and ask for Tom or Janice.

Each Paragraph Should Contain One Part of the Major Subject

A paragraph containing unrelated ideas confuses the reader. By starting a new paragraph, you prepare the reader for the shift from one phase of the subject to another.

Paragraphs Should Be Related to Each Other and to the Whole Message

You want every letter you write to be developed logically and to have a pleasing appearance. You also need to avoid choppiness and to emphasize the important ideas. To reach these goals, you can do these three things:

1. Break a short letter into two paragraphs, even when the letter is only two or three sentences. A one-paragraph letter rarely looks attractive, and it may give your reader the initial impression that you didn't care enough to write more than a few lines.

2. Vary the lengths of paragraphs in a long letter. Too many short paragraphs—just like too many short sentences—give a choppy effect. At first glance, the reader may feel that the page is crammed with ideas.

3. Use very short paragraphs to emphasize important ideas. One-sentence and two-sentence paragraphs tend to stand out in a letter, especially if longer paragraphs precede and follow. They attract the reader's attention and signal "This is important."

Remember, however, that like all artificial devices in writing, overusing these suggestions will make them less effective.

Your Paragraphs Should Fit Together Smoothly

You have learned the importance of smooth movement from one sentence to the next. For ease in understanding a message, the paragraphs in the letter must also fit together so that the reader is led naturally from the opening paragraph to the closing paragraph without having to reread. Sometimes you can show the relationship of paragraphs more clearly by numbering them or by using transitional words, phrases, or sentences.

Now let's first consider a business letter that is poorly paragraphed and then decide how we can improve it according to the five suggestions above.

INEFFECTIVE PARAGRAPHING: Six years ago, when the Gems brand first appeared in our Annual Brand Preference Survey, it was at the bottom of the list—in 13th position, to be exact. It didn't stay at the bottom for long.

Every year since, Gems' brand preference rating has risen. And in this year's survey, it *zoomed!* Now Gems is Number 2 in brand preference.

It has passed Fisher and Neilson—and it's closing in fast on Number 1 Tandy! At its present growth rate, Gems should be Number 1 by next year.

From 0.47 percent brand preference six years ago to 16.9 percent today is a growth history unmatched by any competitor in the industry! And during this period Gems has been a major advertiser in *The American Dream.* While we won't take all the credit for Gems' accelerated brand preference, we, too, have helped!

MORE EFFECTIVE PARAGRAPHING: Six years ago, when the Gems brand first appeared in our Annual Brand Preference Survey, it was at the bottom of the list—in 13th position, to be exact.

It didn't stay at the bottom for long. Every year since, Gems' brand preference rating has risen.

And in this year's survey, it *zoomed!*

Now Gems is Number 2 in brand preference. It has passed Fisher and Neilson—and it's closing in fast on Number 1 Tandy!

At its present growth rate, Gems should be Number 1 by next year. From 0.47 percent brand preference six years ago to 16.9 percent today is a growth history unmatched by any competitor in the industry!

And during this period Gems has been a major advertiser in *The American Dream.* While we won't take all the credit for Gems' accelerated brand preference, we, too, have helped!

ASSIGNMENT: Make the letter in Section B of the Worksheet "stick together" by applying the suggestions for effective paragraphing you have just studied.

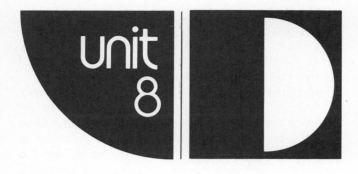

Projecting a Positive Tone

The words you use and the way you put the words together into sentences, sentences into paragraphs, and paragraphs into a letter play a large part in the impact the letter has on a reader, as you learned in Units 6 and 7. The tone of a letter may influence the reader as much as the words themselves. The tone is conveyed by the words, sentences, and paragraphs and by the *spirit* behind them. All these together form the impression that the message makes on the reader—the reader "sees" not only the words and sentences but also between the lines of the letter. The spirit in which you write must be warm and friendly. It should also be sincere, for most people quickly discover the hollowness of fine words that lack sincerity.

The "you" attitude gives a business letter a desirable tone and shows sincere interest in the reader.

PROJECT A "YOU" ATTITUDE

Your attitude is influenced by your frame of mind at the time you are writing. If you are worried, frustrated, or angry, your attitude may color the tone of the letters you write. Everyday matters—personal or business—may affect your attitude and can actually determine what you write and the way you write it. You would be wise, however, to put these aside and concentrate on representing the company you work for and satisfying the reader.

The attitude projected by the tone of your letter, then, should be one that shows the reader that you care, that you are looking at things fairly, and that you are genuinely interested in communicating with the reader.

Avoid writing from a selfish point of view. If the tone of the letter shows a "me" attitude—that is, if the letter is slanted toward the writer and his or her company—the reader sees that the message is one-sided. Instead, make the "you" attitude, or emphasis on the *reader,* evident throughout your letter.

One way to show the "you" attitude is to use *you* and *your* often in your writing. But remember that writing *you* and *your* does not always give the letter a "you" attitude. For example, which sentence has the better tone: "*Your* error caused the delay, and *you* alone will be responsible for the extra charges on *your* bill" or "*We* are sorry about the delay and will have *our* shipping department look into it; *we* will, of course, accept responsibility if *we* are at fault in any way"?

It is not a good idea, however, to overuse "we" words and project a "we" attitude, as you can see in the following excerpt.

> We have been selling fine furs for more than half a century. We ship furs to thousands of customers all around the world. We keep our prices low so that we can sell more furs. We are proud of our record of at least a 10 percent increase in sales volume every year since Tuppers' House of Furs was founded in 1915.

The ideas are good, but they are expressed so selfishly that the reader "couldn't care less." Notice the greatly improved tone when the same ideas are expressed with "you" words and a "you" attitude and the writer talks directly to the listener.

> When you walk into Tuppers' for the first time, you will find yourself surrounded by the most beautiful furs imaginable, at equally pleasing prices! In our showroom you will be wrapped in the warm luxury that has kept customers coming back to Tuppers' since 1915. You can depend on our experience to help select the right fur for you.

Your letters will have a "you" point of view if you take this advice from a correspondence supervisor: "The letterhead takes almost one-fifth of the page, and the closing and signature lines take another one-fifth. Let's give the reader the other three-fifths!"

SHOW SINCERE INTEREST IN THE READER

If you are genuinely interested in the person to whom you address a "written conversation," write to show your respect for that person's intelligence, judgment, opinions, and preferences. Avoid making statements that are distasteful to the reader, statements that will have the opposite effect from the one you intended.

Avoid a Formal Tone in Your Writing

Your letters can show warmth and friendliness if you write with an informal, conversational style. Remember that formal English seems stiff and unnatural to the reader. As you learned in Units 6 and 7, a simple, personal style is much more appealing.

Stiff, formal writing reads like this:

In accordance with your request of recent date, in which you expressed concern about the damaged merchandise you received on May 18, I have reviewed your case and have reached the decision that full restitution should be made to you.

In view of the circumstances, I am sending to you today the replacement shipment of merchandise, accompanied by an invoice. If you will please send a remittance for the total amount due at your earliest convenience, your cooperation in this matter will be appreciated.

Please accept our most sincere apologies for delivering damaged merchandise to you, and we deeply regret the delay and inconvenience which you have suffered.

If this message were written naturally, it might read like this:

> The new shipment of Delmak dishes should reach you within five days, Mrs. Hosinski. So that you will be able to display them in your shop as soon as possible, our driver will deliver them and will pick up the damaged dishes.
>
> We are sorry for the slight delay, but the dishes should be on your shelves and ready for your customers by the end of the week.

Do you see how much more friendly a message is when written naturally?

Don't Talk Down to Your Reader

A person new to letter writing often talks down, or "preaches," to the reader. A condescending tone communicates lack of respect and will surely arouse resentment. You will get better results if you share ideas or make suggestions instead of writing to the reader as a subordinate and trying to force him or her to accept your views. Like most of us, your reader would rather be treated as an *equal* and would appreciate being *asked* rather than *told*.

Would this letter persuade *you* to go to Levy's Back-to-School Sale?

> Now is the time when all smart shoppers are taking advantage of the special money-saving buys at Levy's, while our Back-to-School Sale is in progress.
>
> School will be starting soon, and crowds of shoppers are trying to buy their children's clothes.
>
> Why not come in now while we offer the lowest prices of the year and a pleasant shopping atmosphere.

When a reader is told that everyone else is doing something, the implication is that the reader is "out of step" if he or she is not doing it too. In this letter, the writer is telling the reader that "all smart shoppers" are coming to Levy's. Does this mean that the reader is lacking in intelligence if he or she does not come to Levy's? Better be careful! The reader already knows that "school will be starting soon"; and writing that "crowds of shoppers" are in the store may convince the

reader to go elsewhere! Wouldn't it be better to stimulate the reader's interest by giving examples of specific sale items and then letting him or her decide that "now is the time" to shop at Levy's for school clothes?

Keep in mind that the reader, like everyone else, prefers to think and act independently and is more likely to respond favorably if you appeal to the reader through sound reasoning. You will guard against talking down to your reader if you put yourself in the reader's place and imagine *your* response to the letter you have written.

Don't Exaggerate

Exaggeration in the form of bragging, gushiness, flattery, overhumility, and unlikely promises makes a letter sound insincere.

Bragging

When describing your products and services, avoid bragging—be prepared to back up everything you say. Overstatements and superlatives such as "the best," "outstandingly superior," and "incomparable" seldom sound convincing to the reader unless you give evidence to back up your claims.

The unreasonable claims made in this boastful message make it sound absurdly insincere.

> In your wildest dreams you have never pictured bargains in used cars like those on our lot today. They are truly the ideal buys of the century! Competitors envy—but never approach—the magnificent choices and prices and the unbelievable service we offer. They are aghast at the fabulous way our cars move. Visit us today to find your dream car of matchless beauty and performance fit for a king at a price a peasant could afford!

Make your letter believable by telling the reader *specifically* what your product or service can do for him or her. If you have a reasonably good product or service, you won't have any trouble finding specific points to make about it. If your product or service has no reasonably good features, there won't be much you can say—and you won't have the problem of finding something to say about it for very long.

Gushiness

Gushy language in business letters indicates that the writer is insecure about the product or service and is trying to overcompensate by using flowery words and too many strong adjectives and adverbs.

Excessive politeness makes the following letter confirming a repeat reservation sound insincere and inappropriate. The overlong paragraph and the repetition of the reader's name within it are also unbusiness-like.

> Yes, indeed, Mrs. Appleton, we shall be more than happy to reserve a suite for you and your daughter at the

Mountain View Resort for the first two weeks in June. You certainly are remembered from last summer. How could we forget two such extremely vivacious, glamorous—and altogether charming—ladies! It will be marvelous to have you and your daughter with us again, Mrs. Appleton. We appreciate to the utmost your desire to return for another delightful visit and are even now waiting—eager to welcome you on June 1, Mrs. Appleton.

The gushy language which makes this letter sound insincere can be eliminated, and the message can become a simple but personalized confirmation.

> We appreciate your desire to return to the Mountain View Resort and are happy to confirm your reservation for June 1–14.
>
> Your daughter Carrie will be glad to know that, since your last visit, riding stables have been added to our recreational facilities. Also, a larger swimming pool has been built, for your vacation pleasure.
>
> A brochure of Mountain View Resort's June activities available to our guests is enclosed. Your suite will be ready on June 1, Mrs. Appleton.

Flattery

Flattery can be more damaging than gushiness. There is nothing wrong with giving a compliment that has been earned, but subordinate it to avoid embarrassing the reader with outright flattery.

Does this opening paragraph of a request sound sincere?

> Since you are an authority on life insurance, I am sure you can help me. Twenty years' experience as a successful insurance agent should qualify you to answer all of my questions.

The writer flatters the reader and then implies that the reader may not deserve the compliments if he or she cannot answer all of the writer's questions!

Overhumility

Overhumility merely shows the reader what little self-respect the writer has. If you apologize to the point of degrading yourself and your company, you are destroying the reader's faith. What effect would this message have on a reader?

> Please accept our deepest apologies for the thoughtless error we made in sending you a second bill for your March 28 order when you had sent us your check two weeks earlier.
>
> Our accounting department is extremely embarrassed and sorry, as are all of us here at J. T. Miller and Sons, Inc. We need your business, and we hope you will forgive us this time. From now on we are dedicated to serving you better, and you can be sure that we will check all records before billing you again in the future.

There's nothing wrong with saying you're sorry, but don't beat that subject to death. You have more important things to say to a reader, and excessive apologies aren't among them if you have taken steps to remedy what went wrong.

Unlikely Promises

If you make promises like "We will take care of each of your orders the minute it comes into our office" or "Just a telephone call and our technician will be right there," your reader may take a skeptical attitude toward *everything* you say in your letter. And as with other forms of exaggeration, you must guard against making rash promises you may be legally held to.

You know that no legitimate lending company can promise instant solutions to everyone's money problems. Don't try to entice the reader with promises that do not sound plausible, as this writer did.

> Whether your unpaid bills are many or not so many, Famous Finance Company will SOLVE ALL YOUR MONEY PROBLEMS in the batting of an eye! A moment's chat in one of our friendly offices...a confidential personal payment plan...a Famous Finance check...and you can jauntily bid all your financial worries goodbye!

Don't Show Doubt, Irritation, or Indifference

Negativism and doubt destroy the sincere tone you want your letters to have. Be careful in your writing not to imply doubt about your reader. Referring to "your claim" or saying "We are surprised" about something the reader said or did implies that you do not believe the reader. Do you detect the tone of disbelief in the following example?

> We have not overlooked the $35 payment on your account that is two months past due. We received your explanation of your failure to pay on time a month ago, and we are still waiting for you to pay.

Revealing that you are irritated does not help you accomplish your purpose. It merely arouses the reader's indignation at your lack of respect. Notice how this message irritates and belittles the reader:

> We have investigated your complaint about your Ever-Glow Mod Light and found that you neglected to charge the battery. We charged it for you and trust that in the future you will take care to check the battery before making unfounded claims about defective merchandise.

A letter such as this would surely make the reader vow never to buy from that company again.

One reason retail stores lose customers is indifference. Whether the store's employees actually display an attitude of indifference or whether the customer imagines it, if that's the way the customer feels, then the customer will take his or her business elsewhere. A major concern of retailers today is to convince their customers that they really care about them.

Do you think that Burns, Hart & Co.'s customer relations could be improved by revising this cold and indifferent form letter which was sent to a customer who complained about a dress she bought?

> While Burns, Hart & Co. attempts to assure every customer that he will get the highest quality merchandise available at the price, our enormous volume makes it impossible for us to achieve this goal 100 percent of the time.
>
> If you will bring your garment in, we will try to have someone look at it to ascertain whether we are responsible. Should Burns, Hart & Co. accept responsibility, satisfactory arrangements will be made with you.

If that "he" in the first paragraph leads you to think this is a "fill-in" form letter, you're right. The errors in the tone of this letter are obvious, from the poor excuse that the store's "enormous volume" makes the reader unimportant to the ending which leaves the reader asking "satisfactory to whom?"

Avoid the Temptation to Criticize, Argue, or Be Sarcastic

When you talk with someone face to face, you usually do your best to keep the conversation pleasant. You try to put the other person at ease, and you avoid sounding critical or saying anything he or she might resent.

When you are tempted to criticize, argue, or make a sarcastic remark, remember that in a written message you can't soften the tone by smiling or listening to the reader's side, as you can face to face. The reader can only read the words you have written, harsh as they may be, and can't talk back.

Would you agree that the man who wrote this letter gave in to the temptation to be sarcastic and critical?

> I received my order today, after waiting over two months for it. Needless to say, I had to go elsewhere to buy the sprayer-compressor because you were unbelievably slow in sending it. After examining the sprayer-compressor, I found that it was not the high quality which I demand anyhow. So I'm sending it back, and you can keep it for someone who is not in a hurry to use it.

Sarcasm is more likely to wound the user than anyone else. Even when the temptation to "needle" a reader with sarcasm is great, giving in to the temptation can hurt. There is no way to take the sting out of a sarcastic remark that is written, as there is in speech.

How would you feel if you, a supervisor, received this memo from your boss?

> Congratulations to you and your staff, Donald, on the new XL Copier III brochure. You people must really have put in some overtime to get it out to our sales representatives only 8 months after they started selling the product.

Remember that an *effective* letter will persuade or convince rather than criticize, argue, or be sarcastic. You will read more about the persuasive approach in Unit 10.

Never Show Anger in Your Writing

Showing anger in a letter provokes the reader's hostility and makes it impossible to transact business. Even though your anger may be justified, *never* show it in a letter. Remember that it pays to be courteous, not to "burn your bridges behind you."

The best advice is to wait until your anger has passed and you can see the situation clearly and calmly. Then sit down and approach the reader logically with a good, psychologically sound letter that will make him or her see your point. "Keeping your cool" when writing is important to effective communication.

How would you describe the mood of the writer of this letter, which was addressed to the president of a large company?

> Did you really think you could get away with taking my cash register back to "fix it" and not refunding my money? This piece of junk has never worked right, and I don't want it "fixed," or a new one—I want my money back so I can buy one that works. Is this plain enough for your dense employees?

How is the company going to *feel* about this customer in the future?

FOCUS ON POSITIVE IDEAS

The reader is more interested in what you *can* do than in what you *can't.* True—you can't always answer "yes" to a request, but you can say "no" with a friendly tone if you show consideration for the reader by stressing the positive and playing down the negative. By doing this, you will make your letters sound as friendly and helpful as possible and encourage the reader.

Why write: "We are sorry that we can't deliver your furniture by December 1"? The customer would rather hear: "We will deliver your furniture just as soon as it arrives from our Chicago warehouse. We expect it to arrive during the week of December 7."

While the tone of the entire letter should be positive, the *beginning* of a letter sets the mood. It is *very* important, then, that the beginning contain something positive and pleasant to the reader. In a "bad news" letter, however, it should *not* lead the reader to believe that you are going to say "yes" in the next paragraph. Try to stay optimistic while you write the bad news, using as few negative words as possible. How many positive ideas can you find in the letter that follows?

It is my unpleasant duty to inform you that your application for a research grant was not approved. Only five grants were awarded. Unfortunately, the selection committee placed your application sixth on the list, which means it is not eligible for reconsideration until next semester's grants are awarded.

What a depressing letter! But what if it were rewritten to stress the good news that is almost hidden among the many negatives?

Your application for a research grant placed sixth on a list of 200. Since only five grants were available this time, Miss Griesbeck, the Selection Committee invites you to renew your application when next semester's grants are considered.

The difference in these two letters is a matter of attitude and tone. Each tells the reader that she was not awarded a grant this semester; but the second letter softens the blow by telling her that her application was close to the top and may be renewed for consideration next semester.

A letter may sound negative or unpleasant if the tone is not one of pleasant conversation. If it contains negative words, the overall effect on the reader is negative, as you read in Unit 6.

Notice the negative implications in this letter:

We were sorry to receive your letter stating that there is something wrong with your Pauley broiler-oven. It is too bad that this merchandise was found to be unsatisfactory.

Just ship it back to us, and we will send you another one just like it.

Let's take the message apart and see if we can find out what gives it such poor tone.

"We were sorry to receive your letter..." Should you ever tell anyone that you are sorry to receive his or her letter? Is the writer sorry to receive the letter or sorry that the merchandise wasn't just right?

"...there is something wrong..." This negative clause implies that the reader may be at fault.

"It is too bad..." The writer may have felt sincere regret. But does the writer regret that the reader is not pleased or that the company has to make an adjustment?

"...merchandise was found to be unsatisfactory." Isn't the writer giving the customer a negative suggestion that the company's merchandise is unsatisfactory?

"Just ship it back..." Isn't this a rather cold way to take care of a customer?

And do you think the reader wants "another one just like it"? Or does she want one that works properly?

Here's the way the letter might have been written if the writer had been thinking of the listener.

Thank you for writing us about the Pauley broiler-oven we sent you recently. We are sorry that it is not working properly. If you will please ship it back to us, we will send a replacement immediately.

I'm sure your new Pauley broiler-oven will give you many years of service.

These two letters contain the same facts—but do you *feel* the difference in tone?

Our language helps us to think and write positively; all we have to do is choose words to which people react favorably. Good letter tone depends on positive statements, a "you" attitude, and sincere interest in the reader.

ASSIGNMENT: Put to work the suggestions you have studied in this unit by rewriting and improving the tone of the letters in the Worksheet.

Building and Keeping Customer Goodwill

Every business is concerned not only with selling products or services but also with selling itself. Goodwill is the favorable attitude customers have toward a business. Genuine interest in the customer, fairness, courtesy, and friendliness should be projected by all employees of the organization. These qualities all help to build goodwill.

One of the ways you can build and maintain goodwill is to write good business letters. Every letter you write should accomplish its specific purpose and, at the same time, try to increase the reader's positive feeling toward your company. Your letters should create an impression of a friendly company that is interested in the people it serves.

Letters influence what people think about the company. And what people think often determines where they buy. Consider each letter you write as an opportunity to influence a person's attitude toward your company—possibly even an opportunity to make a sale. Even though you don't try to sell goods or services in every letter, you do try to sell ideas and the personality of the company.

Of course, no business or individual would intentionally destroy goodwill. But many letter writers do drive away old or potential new customers by conveying an attitude of indifference or by failing to make a conscious effort to build and keep customer goodwill.

PROMOTE GOODWILL THROUGH A SERVICE ATTITUDE

If you care about building goodwill, you will think of many ways to project a service attitude in your business correspondence. A service attitude is made up of sincere interest in the customer's welfare and the willingness to do a little more, to give a little extra. A service attitude, well expressed, will pay dividends both for your company and for you. The rewards will often be monetary; both your firm and you may profit. In addition, of course, you will also have the personal satisfaction of doing a job well.

For instance, you can anticipate a question the customer did not ask—but might want to ask later—and give him or her the information now. You can include information that you know will be of particular interest to the reader, such as an article on a subject the reader is concerned with or a brochure describing your product. And you can make it easy for the customer to do what your letter asks by enclosing an addressed, postage-paid reply card or envelope. Thoughtful gestures like these build *and* keep goodwill. People will notice and appreciate your thoughtfulness.

Let each of your letters remind the reader of your genuine desire to serve. Be sure to emphasize this desire rather than the profit motive and any selfish interests.

In letters that contain good news, building goodwill is fairly easy. But when company policy or other circumstances do not allow you to give customers the replies they would like to have, building goodwill is not easy at all. For instance, you may need to write that you can't answer "yes" to a customer's request, or that the customer has made an error, or that his or her criticism of the company's products or service is unjustified. Such "problem" letters call for skill and tact—and imagination.

Let's look at a few ways to build goodwill even in these problem letters.

Begin With a "Goodwill Idea"

Open the letter with something the reader will be pleased to hear, even though the letter may contain bad news. This is a good way to get in step with the customer at the beginning rather than starting with an unpleasant idea and setting up a barrier between you and the reader. Then you have the difficult task of persuading the reader to stop thinking about his or her disappointment long enough to listen to your side of the story. If, instead, you start with an idea the reader likes and agrees with, you have a chance to gain the reader's attention while you gradually introduce your point of view.

In Unit 10 we will discuss in detail how to get letters off to a good start.

Consider the Customer's Side

You can build and maintain goodwill by keeping the customer's point of view clearly in mind at all times. But how can you build goodwill when you must say "no" or "you are wrong—this is how it really is"?

The first step is to find out where the customer stands. In other words, try to assume the other person's attitude and to look at things the way he or she looks at them. You wouldn't, for example, try to sell Mr. Cohen a suit by telling him how long it would wear or that it is on sale if you knew he was a wealthy, fashion-conscious man interested only in how well he would look in it. If you wish to sell suits to men like Mr. Cohen, you must try to find out *how* they feel about suit colors, fabrics, and styles and *why* they feel as they do. Then you will know that you should stress style and quality as the major selling points.

Then, try to think how you would react if you were in the customer's place. Try to discover the benefits to the customer in a situation where few or none may be apparent. You may be able to use gentle persuasion by reminding the customer of likely benefits and the advantages of going along with you. Your letter should make it easy for the customer to agree with you. Above all, try to express the company's point of view in such a way that the customer accepts it and is still friendly toward the company.

Sell Your Company's Viewpoint

In writing business letters dealing with problem situations, keep in mind that you do *not* build goodwill by losing your temper or showing annoyance, as the following excerpts reveal.

> You certainly are not entitled to the 2 percent discount you took, as you could clearly have seen if you had read the terms of our invoice.

> You are mistaken in thinking that we would consider stocking petite sizes in our Ladies' Wear Department simply because it would be convenient for you.

To sell the company's point of view: (1) explain the reasons behind the policy, (2) point out that this policy is fair to all customers, including the reader, and (3) show the customer how this policy may benefit him or her in the long run. By doing these things, you can handle the same situations diplomatically.

Dear Mr. Vergas:

Thank you for your check for $1372.84 in payment of our invoice 8970K in the amount of $1400.86.

We notice that you have deducted from the invoice the 2 percent discount offered on payments made within ten days of the date of purchase. Your check is dated September 17, however, and our invoice August 20. We assume that this was an oversight—that you intended to send your check within ten days.

Naturally we wish we could allow a discount on payments made within thirty days. Payments made within ten days represent a savings to us, and we are glad to pass these savings on to our customers by giving them lower prices. But, as you can understand, payments made at a later date do not give us these savings to share with our customers.

May we have your check for $28.02?

Sincerely yours,

Dear Mrs. Coletta:

Your suggestion that we stock petite sizes in our Ladies' Wear Department is welcome—particularly since it comes from one of our good customers.

You may be interested to know that a selection of petite styles was recently featured at our branch store in Greensboro. But these did not sell so well as had been expected, and the line was discontinued. As a result, The Toggery is somewhat reluctant to stock petite sizes here in Raleigh just now. We shall keep your suggestion in mind, however.

We understand that Susie's, in the Beale Street Mall, carries a selection of petite styles. You may be able to find what you need there. In the meantime, we look forward to helping you with your other clothing needs.

Sincerely yours,

Shortsighted businessmen and businesswomen often act as if there were no competition—an unrealistic attitude, to say the least. Recommending another company as a source of supply for something you don't carry is evidence of a service attitude. Not only is it helpful, but it tends to make you look big in the customer's eyes—it's the little extra that you didn't really have to give. Nor does it cost you sales, as some people fear ("if the customer buys from my competitor what I don't have and likes my competitor, I may lose the customer's business to my competitor"). Remember that you are the "favored vendor." The customer came to you *first* and wanted to buy from you. You'll still have that in your favor after sending the customer elsewhere for something you don't have. If you are afraid the customer will like your competitor's service better than yours, maybe you should take a close look at your own business!

Now read the following collection letter from Ozark Fisheries to see how skillfully a customer can be persuaded to accept the company's point of view.

Dear Mr. Mino:

"How long does it take to grow a goldfish to marketable size?" is a question asked by most customers visiting us.

The answer is—

Sizes ranging from 2 to 4 inches long require five or six months; 4 to 7 inches, up to eighteen months; and the larger ones, as long as three years.

During all this time a lot of work is required to see that they get

proper care—especially plenty of feed—so that they will grow normally and be strong enough to withstand the long trips in the shipping cans and display to the best advantage in your aquarium.

Many customers remark: "I can't understand, with all the work and time required, how you can grow a 2- to 2½-inch fantail and sell it for 15 cents and make any money out of it."

The truth is—we don't make much. The margin of profit is slim. We must grow them in large quantities and sell them that way, too.

And you know five months is a long time to be turning out one little 15-cent item—so we know you won't mind when we say in a friendly fashion: "Have you overlooked your last invoice which is now 15 days past due?" The amount is $36.53.

Sincerely,

OZARK FISHERIES, INC.

Jay Hughes

Notice that Mr. Hughes doesn't *demand* payment; he *invites* the customer to pay. He gets the reader's interest at the start by asking and answering a question that many customers ask. Through sharing ideas, he leads the customer gently to the company's side of the fence. When the reader gets to the last paragraph of the message, he is ready to answer the question, "Have you overlooked your last invoice, which is now 15 days past due?"

These are only a few examples of the "problem" letters that must be written *every* day in business. Each letter presents an opportunity to build goodwill or to tear it down. Before you begin to write such a letter, think the situation through carefully to decide exactly how you can best do the job and still keep the reader as a friend.

USE LETTERS AS GOODWILL MESSENGERS

You can build goodwill only if you *care* how your letters sound. Try to visualize each letter as your company's ambassador, as a salesperson meeting a customer. Ask yourself the same questions about the "letter salesperson" that you might ask about a real salesperson to determine whether he or she is doing a good job.

1. Is the salesperson well-groomed and personable? You may review Units 1 through 5 to be sure your "letter salesperson" looks good for its visit with the customer.

2. Does the salesperson use correct English and speak clearly? You may review Units 4, 6, and 7 to be sure your "letter salesperson" talks well during the visit with the customer.

3. Is the salesperson friendly but persuasive? You may review Unit 8 to be sure your "letter salesperson" smiles and holds the customer's attention and interest throughout the visit.

4. Does the salesperson give the customer satisfaction? Even if the customer cannot be given exactly what he or she asks for, the good salesperson tries to keep the customer's friendship.

5. Does the salesperson answer all the customer's questions fully, giving all the facts needed to act or to make a decision?

6. Does the salesperson show interest in the customer's point of view and a genuine desire to be helpful?

You can supply positive answers to the last three questions about your "letter salesperson" if you follow the suggestions in this unit.

Answer All the Customer's Questions

A salesperson may be both personable and friendly but still not be successful. The salesperson leaves the customer dissatisfied if all of the customer's questions about the company's products and services are not answered. In the same way, an incomplete letter leaves the customer dissatisfied and weakens the company's chances of building goodwill. It may even lose a customer.

The friendliest and most tactful letter you can write does not build goodwill if it fails to satisfy the customer. When you do not know the answers to all the questions asked, you should supply the answers you know and tell the reader what you are doing about the others. Always check your reply with the inquiry to be sure you have not overlooked any of the customer's questions—actual or implied.

Suppose you are replying to a customer about a reconditioned bicycle she is thinking of ordering for her young son. In her letter, she asks about the cost of a 3-speed model, the guarantee, the condition of the tires, and the sizes in which the bicycle is available. In your reply, you stress the low price of $39.95, the one-year guarantee, and the fact that the tires are new and the paint job is fresh. You urge her to send her order promptly because you have only eight 3-speed bikes left in stock.

Your letter is friendly, courteous, and convincing. But it is not complete. What did you overlook? You did not answer the question about sizes. The customer is naturally annoyed. She hesitates to order a bicycle with a 20-inch wheel because she is afraid that the eight bargain bicycles left may not include this size. The customer wants the bicycle in time for her son's birthday, which is only two weeks away. She may decide to write again for the information. Or she may try another supplier.

Failure to answer a customer's questions makes the customer suspicious. Why didn't you answer the question? What are you trying to hide? Is there some drawback to your product or service you don't want the customer to find out about? If so, what other dishonest thing may you try to do?

The customer assumes that you are out to do the best you can for yourself or your company. Suspicion leads directly to distrust—perhaps not logically, but that's human nature. And distrust is unlikely to lead to sales.

Admitting you don't have an answer to a customer's question is not wrong. If this is the case, promise to get the answer and then follow through. If there is no answer, say so and explain why. Either course is preferable to ignoring what you can't answer positively or what you don't have an answer to.

Don't Make the Reader Guess

Often a reply to an inquiry—like the letter about the bicycle—is incomplete because the writer has overlooked a question asked in the inquiry, as you have just seen. You can answer all the customer's questions, however, and still not tell the customer everything he or she needs to know. You may leave out an important detail just because you assume that the customer knows more than he or she does know about the subject on which you are writing.

Have you ever watched a TV game show in which the audience was given the answers to the questions but the players were not? How simple the answers seemed when you knew them! But it was a different story for the players—they had to guess! And often they missed.

When you are writing a letter, the "answers" seem simple to you. But often the reader has to guess because you assumed too much.

For example, in response to an inquiry, a writer may fail to answer a question because the question should be directed to someone in another department. Perhaps after answering the letter, the writer will turn the letter over to the appropriate person who will then supply the missing answer. But does the reader know this? Even though the writer cannot handle part of the letter, for the customer's sake he or she should not ignore that part of the letter.

The writer cannot assume that the reader will know that the question will be answered by someone else. The reader will probably assume that the writer did not read the letter carefully enough to see the question or did not want to give a negative answer.

The writer could avoid making the reader guess simply by adding a short paragraph, such as this:

I am referring your question about subscribing to *Electronics* to Mr. Jenkins, Circulation Manager. You will hear from him in a few days.

RESELL THE PRODUCT AND YOUR COMPANY

A major purpose of each letter you write should be to promote goodwill and resell the product and the business. "Reselling" means doing a second time the selling job that led to the purchase. The writer attempts to confirm the reader's faith in the writer's products, services, and company. The purpose of reselling is to assure the customer that he or she made a wise choice in buying the product (even though it may not yet be delivered) and to keep the customer from complaining or returning the goods.

Reselling your company involves pointing out the services you render and the guarantees, policies, and procedures that will benefit your readers. Reselling is appropriate in letters to new customers, but it should also be included whenever you can tell your customers about a new service or benefit that your company provides.

The woman who received the following letter probably felt that she had made a wise choice in subscribing to *The Executive's Guide to Communication and Motivation*, a monthly magazine of tips and case studies.

> Your first issue of *The Executive's Guide to Communication and Motivation* will arrive in a few days, Ms. O'Neill. The feature article should be particularly interesting to you because it discusses ways you can increase productivity and profits by improving interpersonal skills among your employees.
>
> In the coming months, *The Executive's Guide to Communication and Motivation* will cover methods you can use to your advantage when communicating with either superiors or subordinates. For example, you will learn an ingenious technique that helps get ideas approved and a unique approach that is usually successful when you want to persuade anyone who is hostile toward your plans.
>
> We know that you will enjoy reading every issue of *The Executive's Guide to Communication and Motivation*, Ms. O'Neill, and that it will be as helpful to you as it has been to other executives in the past ten years.

As you can see, the purpose of this letter is to promote goodwill and resell the product. Unit 14 will give you more "goodwill ideas" as you study special goodwill letters.

ASSIGNMENT: How successfully will you build goodwill for your company? To find out, complete the Worksheet for Unit 9.

unit 10

Planning and Preparing Letters

As you have discovered, writing effective business letters is a complex process. But having considered everything we have discussed so far, you are now ready to take another important step—planning the letter—and the most important step—actually writing it.

PLANNING THE LETTER

When a letter is written without planning, the writer may forget the important details so necessary if the letter is to do its job well. Then a second letter is usually required to complete the job.

The kind of plan you make depends on you and on the letter you are writing. But you should always start by considering the person who writes the letter, the person the letter is written to, and the background and purpose of the letter. Then decide on the best approach and what you will say.

The Person Who Writes the Letter

Naturally *you* are the person who writes the letter. When you are writing for a business rather than for yourself personally, you should learn all you can about the business you represent and make sure that your letter sincerely reflects company attitudes and policies.

Remember that your personal views are secondary when you are paid to speak for the company. Occasionally you may feel that the company's policy is unfair; you may even suggest to your supervisors that it be changed. But until it is, you are bound by it. Never let a customer know that you disagree with company policy. Nor should your letter seem to blame another person or department for an error or an unpopular decision. In writing company correspondence, you speak for the company as a whole—not for yourself or for your department.

The company, the group, speaks through you, the writer. It is your job to put what the company has to say in terms that your reader can accept, to bring both sides to the same point of view. The good letter writer tries to represent both the company and the reader.

The Person the Letter Is Written To

The most important factor to consider when you are planning a business letter is the person who will read it. The letter is successful only if the reader reads it, understands it, and reacts favorably to it.

Adapting to the reader means writing with the reader in mind, writing to fit the reader's capabilities, frame of mind, and so on. The more you know about how your reader thinks and feels, the better chance you have of getting the message across. If you know something about the reader's education, for example, you can adapt your vocabulary accordingly. If you know something about the reader's position and ambitions, you can choose a suitably challenging appeal.

To interest and influence the reader, you must be able to look at both your side and the reader's side of things at the same time. By doing so you can learn what kind of help the reader expects to find in your letter. It takes practice, but you *can* do it. With the ability to see things from the other person's side as well as your own, you will soon be successful at persuasion.

If you have a letter to answer, you can learn much about your reader from the message he or she wrote. Sometimes previous correspondence, reports of sales representatives, and other records in the files will tell you more. If you have no letter to answer and no file records on which to draw, your general resourcefulness and knowledge of human nature can help you plan an appropriate letter.

Consciously practice adapting to the reader as you write letters for the rest of this course, and you'll soon master it. Just remember to think through the situation, imagine your reader as best you can, and then write directly to him or her.

The Background and Purpose of the Letter

A business letter grows out of a *need to communicate.* For example, the credit manager of a store may write to customers whose bills are overdue and ask them to pay. Some customers may respond with letters enclosing checks; others, with letters explaining that they can't pay until later.

To plan a letter efficiently, you must understand *why the letter is needed and how it can satisfy the need.* The credit manager should know the amount each customer owes, what it is owed for, how long it has been owed, and any special circumstances concerning the debtor or the bill. The credit manager must also know the store's policy concerning overdue accounts.

If you are answering a letter, use the background information contained in the letter itself. Always read the letter carefully to be sure you have learned all you can from it. If you need additional facts or if you have no letter to answer, check the files for previous correspondence and pertinent company records. And, of course, use common sense, as well as your general business knowledge and your specialized knowledge of the company, to decide what background facts are important and how they can best be used to make the letter successful.

As you think through the reasons for the letter and the background facts, you will find that the *purpose* of the letter becomes apparent. The purpose of a credit manager's writing a collection letter might be "to collect $75 from Louise Gavin without losing her as a customer." And the purpose of Louise Gavin's reply might be "to pay $25 on my account and promise the store the $50 balance in 30 days."

The Best Approach

As you continue to plan, your next job is to decide on the idea that will get the letter off to the right start. All the facts you have been thinking through will help you select an opening which will make a pleasant contact with your reader and which is appropriate to the situation and the purpose behind the letter. You will also be able to decide the most effective order in which to present the ideas in the letter.

Business letters can be grouped roughly into three categories:

1. Routine and "Yes" letters.
2. "No" letters.
3. Persuasive and sales letters.

By far the largest part of business correspondence is the routine correspondence that requests or transmits information necessary to the daily conduct of business activities. If no problem is foreseen in getting information requested or if the information supplied is routine and not displeasing to the reader, simple letters are written or form letters are used.

These letters can be written in a straightforward manner, using the same approach best for "Yes" letters that tell the reader what he or she wants to hear or something that will please him or her. This kind of letter can get directly to the point; therefore, the way its parts are usually arranged is called the *direct approach.*

The problem letters in business are those that give the reader bad news or refuse something the reader has asked. These "No" letters have to be carefully prepared to avoid causing anger or loss of goodwill. For this type of situation, an *indirect approach* is called for.

The third group of business letters includes letters in which the reader must be persuaded to do what you want him or her to, to be "sold" on an idea—for example, sales letters that attempt to obtain an order for a product or a service, or sales promotion letters that try to set up a sale in the future without pressing directly for an order. Letters of this type use the *persuasive approach.*

Let's look at these three approaches so that you can see how they work and learn to choose the right one for the situations you handle. As we discuss common business situations in later units and apply these three approaches to them, we will see how they can be varied to meet a wide range of writing problems.

The Direct Approach

When you can tell your reader "Yes" or transmit some good news, you have the easiest and most pleasant of writing tasks.

In these situations there is only one rule: *Start with the good news.* This will put the reader in a friendly, receptive frame of mind for anything else you may want to say.

If you have other things to say after the "yes" opening, go on to the next most pleasant point for the reader, then to the third most pleasant, and so on until the end of the letter. The last paragraph of the letter, the ending, should refer to the good news in the opening, leaving the reader in a friendly frame of mind.

With a few exceptions, routine requests for information follow the direct approach, since such requests are a normal part of business. Examples are requests for credit information, requests for information on personnel, and requests for information about products and services. If there is no reason for the reader not to supply the information or if it is to the reader's advantage to do so, the direct approach should be used. Begin by giving the information the reader requested. If the information is obviously bad news for the reader or if it reflects badly on another company or person, however, you may want to consider using the indirect approach instead.

In summary, then, whenever you can say "Yes" to your reader or otherwise tell the reader something he or she wants to hear or will be pleased to hear, start your letter with that information. Here's an example.

The background: As credit manager for the Lennox Wholesale Company, write a letter approving credit for Mr. Charles Bradshaw. His credit card is enclosed.

The customer's request: Mr. Bradshaw asked for credit by filling out one of your forms and supplying references, which you have checked.

Your company's policy: Mr. Bradshaw's credit limit is $500. He will be billed on the tenth of each month for purchases made the preceding month. Payment is due by the 28th.

The letter's job: Welcome the customer, explain the credit terms, talk of company service, and look forward to the customer's orders.

The approach: Since Lennox is doing as Mr. Bradshaw asked, you select the direct approach.

Dear Mr. Bradshaw:

Lennox welcomes you as a credit customer. All you have to do to charge your purchases at our store is to present the enclosed charge card and sign the sales slip. The people whose names you gave as references paid you compliments that you should be proud of.

You may charge purchases up to $500 a month. On the tenth of each month, you will receive a statement of your purchases made through the end of the preceding month. Your payment is due on or before the 28th.

When you order from our catalog, please include your account number (113-737-40) on the order form so that the clerk can process your order quickly. The merchandise you request will be shipped within 24 hours after we receive your order.

The Indirect Approach

Having to give the reader bad news or to say "No" to a reader poses a problem in letter writing. If you blurt out the bad news in the first sentences of your letter, the reader will quickly become disappointed, angry, or both. Such feelings will color the reader's interpretation of everything else you say. If you start with the refusal, the reader isn't likely to accept your explanations, if he or she reads them at all! Why put the reader in a bad frame of mind at the start and destroy the effectiveness of the rest of the letter?

Instead, use the indirect approach. This often means simply using a "buffer paragraph." You try to place a "buffer" between the reader and the bad news, so as to avoid putting the bad news in the emphatic first-paragraph position.

The buffer paragraph is based on sound, practical psychology. People would rather hear good news than bad news. So if you have some bad news for them, tell them some good news first to help break the bad news as gently as possible.

The buffer-paragraph technique has two more advantages: (1) it can always be used in arranging the parts of a bad-news or "No" letter, since it is flexible enough to meet all such situations; and (2) anyone can use it effectively with a little practice.

Begin with something in the situation that you and the reader can agree on. It may only be that you agree the reader was right to come to you with his or her problem. If there are no facts you can agree on, pay the reader a compliment (don't flatter the reader!) or say *something* friendly. You must not appear to be saying "Yes," however, because the reader will not forgive you for misleading him or her when later on in the letter you say "No." And your buffer paragraph must be on the subject of the letter; it should not be a time-waster.

After the buffer paragraph, you give the reasons for refusing or for giving the reader bad news. Begin with your best reason for refusal, go on to the next best, and so on. After you have given the explanation, use a middle paragraph for the actual refusal. What is important is that the reader does get the message clearly, even though it may be subtly implied, and that he or she is in the most receptive frame of mind for it that you could manage under the circumstances.

By the end of the letter, you are over the rough parts. You can then offer a counterproposal to what the reader asked or resell your point of view. This type of letter usually ends on a hopeful note.

Later we will show you other indirect approaches for letters, but the buffer paragraph usually works best. Here's the technique in action.

The background: As advertising manager for a farm implement manufacturer, answer a letter from one of your dealers, an independent store owner with an exclusive franchise to sell your products in his area.

The dealer's request: You purchase an advertisement for him in his city's classified telephone directory. He also wants you to purchase advertisements in the two suburban editions of the telephone directory.

Your company's policy: You purchase advertising only in classified telephone directories serving areas in which your dealers are located. Since this dealer is not located in the suburbs, but inside the city limits, you will continue to place advertising only in the city directory.

The letter's job: To refuse the dealer's request for company-paid advertising in the two suburban directories. To explain the company policy on telephone-directory advertising and the reasons behind it: over 800 dealers; if you buy something for one, you must do it for all; the costs would be out of sight; requests would come in for the company to purchase advertising in directories for neighboring counties and towns; and so on.

The approach: Since you will have to say "No" to the dealer, an indirect approach is called for, the buffer paragraph opening.

Dear Mr. Weidner:

We agree that advertising in Yellow Pages directories is important in calling the attention of prospective buyers to the availability of our products. We also agree that the more of it we do, the better.

Last year we considered the possibility of altering our policy on telephone-directory advertising. For each of our 806 dealers we found out the cost of placing advertising for each dealer in all the telephone directories within 125 miles of his or her location. It came to a staggering $965,000 a year! Even for just those directories in areas actually served by our dealers, the cost was over $650,000.

Since we would, of course, have to apply the same policy to each dealer, we regretfully set aside the question of increasing our telephone-directory advertising.

Any increase in one area of our advertising budget would have to be at the expense of other areas, and we know how reluctant you would have been to see us cut out sponsorship of the State Fair plowing contest, advertising in your state's farm magazines, or our successful outdoor advertising.

Such activities, as well as telephone-directory advertising, are

all part of the master marketing plan for Premier Farm Implements, and mid-year changes tend to have a "ripple effect" on the plan far beyond the actual changes themselves. Because the various telephone directories around the country are published at different times during the year (according to no discernible pattern), the "ripple effect" would be magnified.

In spite of the recent downtrend in farm implement sales, Premier dealers have increased their share of the market, an achievement we are all proud of. We intend to continue to make the best farm implements we know how and to aggressively support you in your successful selling efforts.

Sincerely,

The Persuasive Approach

Getting the reader to do what you want, to accept what you say, or to agree with you means using the persuasive approach. In one sense, all persuasive letters are sales letters.

In direct mail, especially the kind sent to a person's home, some device is often used to get the prospect to open the envelope and read the message. "Free Gift Inside!" or "Urgent—Open Immediately!" or a similar message may be printed on the envelope. Inside are a letter (printed in color), a brochure, a coupon, plus other items to make up an impressive package. Yes, much of it is "junk mail," but people have become so used to it in their mailboxes that even companies with products or services of real value sometimes feel they have to "shout" for attention.

Sales letters to a business person may use all the devices of direct mail but usually get to the point without resorting to gimmicks. We will focus on sales letters as they are used in business.

If you want to write effective sales letters, you should take this advice from an advertising copywriter: "Don't use formulas. Rely on your knowledge of *why* people buy things." Successful copywriters are those who are able to make readers imagine themselves using the product or service. When you can get your reader to imagine himself or herself successfully using your product or service, you can close the sale.

Essentially, a good sales letter will be structured something like this. First will come the opening paragraph in which some benefit or reward is promised or implied for the reader. Done properly, this sets the tone of the letter, prepares the reader for what follows, and arouses the reader's interest so that he or she will read on. Immediately after come descriptions of how the product or service would benefit the reader. In the description the "you" attitude would be used to help the reader imagine himself or herself using the product or service. After this can come physical details of the product or service, such as dimensions and materials, and specifics about the guarantee, service, and so on. These details won't make the sale but will help clinch it. Finally, ask for the reader's response—or for the order, if appropriate. Naturally, the request should make it as easy as possible for the reader to respond.

This is as much of a "formula" for a sales letter as you will find useful. No two products or services are alike, nor are any two groups of prospects. Each has to be treated individually if you are to be successful in getting the response you want. See the letter below.

What You Will Say

So far you have been *thinking* about your plans for writing the letter. Often when you just think, your ideas are not very clear. Now that you are ready to plan the content and organization of the message, you can make your ideas more concrete by writing them down.

Besides clarifying your thoughts, a written plan helps to assure that you won't forget any important details and makes the actual writing of the letter faster and easier. A written plan is especially helpful when you are first learning to write business letters. After you have had more practice, you may find that you need to write out your plans for only the most complicated and the most important messages you prepare.

Keep your written plan as brief and simple as you can. Don't put into it everything you will say in your letter. Just jot down a few words that will suggest the points you are thinking through and the things you want to say. Write the plan in the margin of the letter you are answering or on scratch paper. To save time, write in shorthand or abbreviated longhand—just be sure that what you jot down will be readable later.

Many beginning letter writers have found it helpful

**ANCHOR
LIFE INSURANCE
COMPANY**

December 10, 19--

Mr. Jason E. Talbert
1632 Woodbridge Road
Warren, MI 48091

Dear Jason:

I have been reviewing your Anchor Life policy No. 275330 and find that you have $1,431.63 in accumulated dividends at interest. As you know, the interest earned on the dividends is reportable as income each year.

Here is a suggestion that will be of benefit and interest to you: Take your present dividends and buy $2,367.62 in additional paid-up insurance and arrange for future dividends to also buy paid-up insurance.

This would be a wise move, in my opinion, because:

1. You will no longer have interest to report as income.

.2. The paid-up insurance will increase the death benefit to your wife.

3. The cash value of the additional paid-up insurance is guaranteed never to be less than the dividends declared.

4. The purchase is made at net--there is no charge to purchase these dividends. As you can see, at present each $1 in dividends will buy about $1.65 of additional paid-up insurance.

If you would like to take advantage of this arrangement, please sign the enclosed form and return it to me.

Cordially,

L. C. Parkinson

L. C. Parkinson, C.L.U.

dc
Enc.

328 BENNINGTON DRIVE, LANSING, MICHIGAN 48917   TEL. (517) 542-6000

This sales letter will be effective because it opens with a specific benefit to the reader, prepares the reader for what follows, and arouses the reader's interest.

Procedure	Example
Step 1. Write down the main purpose of the letter in as few words as possible.	To provide cost estimates for printing
Step 2. List all secondary purposes concisely.	To convince the reader that we are dependable To confirm exact printing specifications
Step 3. Jot down all points to be covered in developing both primary and secondary purposes. Try to think of every detail you might need to include in the letter. Put these items down *as you think of them,* whether they are important or not. This process (called *brainstorming*) will stimulate both good and bad ideas that can be sorted out later.	*Itemize paper, printing, collating, and shipping costs for 750, 1,000, and 1,250 copies* *Abbot to supply binders* *Thank her for estimate request* *Representative will call* *Confirm specifications in her July 14 letter* *Delivery within ten days* *Refer to her July 14 letter*
Step 4. Cross out any of the listed items that can be omitted without sacrificing friendliness or completeness. Watch particularly for the repetition of ideas that brainstorming often produces.	Draw a line through "Refer to her July 14 letter"—you already listed "Confirm specifications in her July 14 letter." Then, when you have arranged the items in proper sequence, you will have:
Step 5. Check your plan for sequence and then number the items. Select an item from your list that would make a pleasant contact with the reader, either telling the reader what he or she wants to hear or putting the reader in a favorable mood to listen to something you want to say. *Number this item 1.* Arrange the other items on your list in the best order for emphasis and follow-through. Remember to keep the reader interested. Be sure the last item leaves the reader with a good impression of your company and suggests any further action to be taken. *Number these items 2, 3, 4, and so on,* according to their places in the letter. You now have a complete outline from which you can quickly write the letter.	*Thank her for estimate request* *Confirm specifications in her July 14 letter* *Abbot to supply binders* *Itemize paper, printing, collating, and shipping costs for 750, 1,000, and 1,250 copies* *Delivery within ten days* *Representative will call*

to use the planning procedures outlined in the left column of the Letter Planning Chart above. Probably you will be wise to follow these steps exactly in planning your first letters. Later, as you gain experience, you may eliminate some of the steps and in other ways adapt the procedures to your own work habits.

The right column of the chart lists example steps for planning a specific letter—one that might be written by the manager of a printing company to acknowledge receipt of an estimate request. The writer of the estimate request letter asked for estimates for printing a new company manual, *Quality Control Procedures.* She asked for an itemized cost estimate for the paper, printing, collating, and shipping of the 320-page, 8½- by 11-inch manual in quantities of 750, 1,000, and 1,250 copies. Her company, Abbot, will supply its own loose-leaf binders. The chart shows how a response to this estimate request letter might be outlined.

WRITING THE LETTER

After studying all the facts related to the letter, you outlined what you should say and decided on the best order for saying it. Now, as you develop the outline into a letter, keep in mind two of the factors that influenced your planning: (1) the person to whom you are writing the letter and (2) your reason for writing the letter.

You know that if a letter is to make a good impression, its form and construction must be correct and appropriate, its style clear and natural. You remember also that you should build goodwill in every letter you write. You can do this (1) by emphasizing the things the reader wants to hear, (2) by avoiding or subordinating negatives and other ideas unpleasant to the reader, and (3) by using friendly words and reflecting a sincere desire to serve.

Revised Rough Draft

<del>We want to</del> thank you for asking us to estimate the cost of printin(g) your new company manAul, *Quality Control Proce(e)dures.* We are delighted to be of service <del>to you</del> In your July 14(th) letter, you specified that the new manual will be 320 pages long, *and* <del>It</del> will be printed on 8½ by 11-inch, 20= pound white paper, <del>and</del> all pages will be three-hole= punched, collated, *and* inserted into your Abbott loose= leaf binders, which you will <del>be</del> provid(ceo) As you <del>have</del> requested, based on these specifications we have itemize(d) the costs of paper, print(h)ing, colla- ting, and <del>the cost of</del> shipping for quan(ti)ties of 750, 1,000, and <del>and</del> 1,250 copies: <del>of the manual.</del>

	750 Copies	1,000 Copies	1,250 Copies
Paper	$336.75	$449.00	$561.25
Prin(t)ing	123.75	151.00	176.25
Collating	29.25	39.00	48.75
Shipping	23.25	31.00	38.75
TOTAL:	$513.00	$670.00	$825.00

Whichever quantity you select(s), Mr. Weems, We will be able to deliver the complete order to your of- fice within ten days <del>within ten days</del> of receipt of your typed pages and your Abbot(')s looseleaf binders.

Explanation of Changes

Roundabout wording (should be more direct)

Misspellings; Underline book titles

Delete unnecessary words; Correct number style

Add hyphens

New sentence for easier reading; Add hyphen

Comma to set off restrictive clause
New paragraph for easier reading

Misspellings

Misspelling

Comma in series of three or more items

Misspelling

Sentence fragment
Subject and verb must agree
(you select)

Repetition

Misspelling (add hyphen)

Of course, our represent^at^ive, Tom Blaney, will be

happy to discuss these estimates with#you when he

visit^s^ you ~~at your office during the~~ next week.

Add space

Subject and verb must agree
  (he visits)
Unnecessary words

1189 PLAZA WAY, ATLANTA, GEORGIA 30303, TEL. 404-568-2000

January 8, 19--

Mrs. Henrietta Weems
Manager, Purchasing Department
Abbot Chemical Corporation
90 E. Hooper St.
Atlanta, Georgia 30340

Dear Mrs. Weems:

Thank you for asking us to estimate the cost of printing your new company
manual, Quality Control Procedures. We are delighted to be of service.

In your July 14 letter, you specified that the new manual will be 320 pages
long and will be printed on 8½- by 11-inch, 20-pound white paper. All
pages will be three-hole-punched, collated, and inserted into your Abbot
loose-leaf binders, which you will provide.

As you requested, based on these specifications we have itemized the costs
of paper, printing, collating, and shipping for quantities of 750, 1,000,
and 1,250 copies:

	750 Copies	1,000 Copies	1,250 Copies
Paper	$336.75	$449.00	$561.25
Printing	123.75	151.00	176.25
Collating	29.25	39.00	48.75
Shipping	23.25	31.00	38.75
TOTAL:	$513.00	$670.00	$825.00

Whichever quantity you select, Mrs. Weems, we will be able to deliver the
complete order to your office within ten days of receipt of your typed
pages and your Abbot loose-leaf binders. Of course, our representative,
Tom Blaney, will be happy to discuss these estimates with you when he visits
you next week.

Sincerely,

Martin P. Loomis

Martin P. Loomis
Manager

A rough draft must be carefully edited before it is retyped, and the retyped
letter should be proofread while it is still in the typewriter.

Prepare a Rough Draft

Because there are so many things to keep in mind while writing the letter, you will probably do a better job faster if you prepare a rough draft. In composing the first draft, concentrate on content alone. Afterward you can revise the draft—with particular attention to correct mechanics, style, and tone—before you type the letter in good form for mailing.

Later, when you have had practice in business letter writing, you should find that correct and effective expression of your ideas becomes a habit. Then you can dictate or type many of your letters directly from an outline.

In actual business practice, most letters are dictated directly without a detailed written outline. But for long, complex letters, and for "problem" letters, most people do jot down an outline and make a rough draft.

Write Naturally

Write the message in your own words. Remember, there is no special vocabulary for business. The words you use in everyday conversation are the words that will sound natural and friendly to the reader. Try to imagine that the reader is across the desk from you or at the other end of the telephone. Perhaps then you can write what you want to say as naturally as you would say it.

Write as Quickly as You Can

Develop your rough draft directly from the outline you prepare when planning the letter. Write the first draft as quickly as you can. Use abbreviations and any other helpful shortcuts you know. Don't waste time checking spelling of words or points of grammar or referring to principles in your text—yet. While looking up a point, you might forget what you started to say. Or you might write a letter that sounded jerky because it was composed of disconnected sentences or paragraphs instead of being written as one complete message. You can probably finish the letter-writing job faster if you write the first draft without stopping and then do all the correcting as you edit.

Leave plenty of space in the margins and between the lines of your first draft for revisions. If you are composing on the typewriter, use double spacing. If you are writing in longhand on lined paper, write on every other line.

Edit for Appropriateness

It is now time to give the message an overall check for content, style, and tone. Ask yourself, does the message contain everything it should and nothing else? Is its arrangement effective? Is its meaning so clear throughout that it cannot be misread or misunderstood? Does it sound natural and sincere? Will it keep the reader's friendship and interest? If the answer to any of

these questions is "no," then you may need to rewrite one or two paragraphs or the whole letter.

When you can answer "yes" to these questions, you are ready to give the copy a word-by-word check to be sure the message is appropriate and correct in every detail. Review the principles of good letter writing and the rules for correct usage in the text and in the Reference Section, and consult a dictionary or a handbook for any other help you need.

To correct the rough draft, simply draw a line through any inappropriate letter, word, or phrase. Then write the revision directly above or in the margin near it. Usually it is easier to make the changes in longhand, even when your rough draft is typed.

In making corrections on the draft, watch for:

• *Words* misspelled, words incorrectly used, and words that can be eliminated.
• *Sentences* that are incomplete, choppy, too long, confused, wordy, or awkward.
• *Paragraphs* that are choppy, too long, or poorly organized or connected.
• *Punctuation* marks that should be inserted or omitted to make the letter clear and easy to read.
• *Capitalization;* writing of *numbers;* and use of *apostrophes, hyphens,* and the like.

For an example showing the revision marks to use in editing a rough draft, see pages 58-59.

Type the Letter

After the message has been carefully edited, it becomes the body of the letter, which you now type in good form before mailing or handing in to your instructor.

See the letter on page 59, which shows how the rough draft appears when it has been retyped.

In preparing the finished letter, follow these steps:

1. Select the appropriate stationery, letter style, and side margins for the letter. If you need help, you can find answers to your questions in Units 1, 3, and 5.

2. Type the heading, inside address, salutation, body—the edited message—complimentary closing, signature, and any special notations. As you type, you may review Unit 2 for help with the parts of the letter and Unit 5 for help with techniques of typing and arrangement, including erasing and word divisions.

3. Proofread and correct the letter word by word, sentence by sentence, and as a whole *before you take it from the typewriter.* For specific suggestions about your responsibility in proofreading your own letters, see Unit 5 (page 29).

ASSIGNMENT: The Worksheet for this unit will help you to develop your skill in planning, organizing, and preparing written messages.

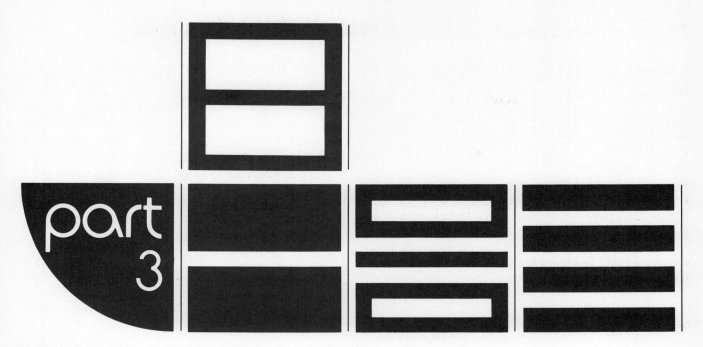

Writing Effective Business Letters

Now it is time to apply the techniques and principles you have learned to writing various types of business letters. Many of the examples you will read in this part are real-life business letters—some good and some bad. Analyze each to determine what makes it good or bad and why. You will then begin to try writing simple letters first, then more complex ones. Remember to look at each example—and your own writing, too—from the reader's viewpoint. Before you begin to study and write these letters, you should have a checklist of the ideal contents of a business letter. The "Checklist for an Effective Business Letter" on page 62 will help you analyze the letters that you are about to read and the ones you will compose.

As you write the letters for Worksheets 11-20, remember that:

1. Every letter is a unique blend of writer, reader, circumstances, and purpose.

2. A good letter reflects a writer who is sincere and interested in the welfare of the reader.

3. The circumstances surrounding a particular letter must be considered.

4. To be successful, the letter must achieve its purpose.

As you come to understand the principles of effective letter writing and develop your skill in writing through practicing these principles, you will find yourself writing more quickly and more confidently. Your first letters may not be sparkling, but they will do their job efficiently and build goodwill...which is really what modern business correspondence is all about.

CHECKLIST FOR AN EFFECTIVE BUSINESS LETTER

A Good Letter Is Unmistakably Clear

Unless a letter is easily read and its meaning immediately clear, it is a barrier rather than an aid to communication. As you analyze good and bad letters, begin by asking yourself:

1. Is this letter easy to read?

2. Is its message clearly written so that it cannot be misunderstood?

A Good Letter Does Its Specific Job Well

A business letter is written to accomplish a definite purpose. Usually it plays a specific part in a business transaction. The letter should do what it set out to do; it should help push the transaction to a successful outcome. A letter which, for example, is well written, friendly, and builds goodwill but fails to answer the customer's request does not fulfill its purpose or satisfy the customer.

Continue to build your concept of a good letter by asking yourself:

1. Of what business transaction is this letter a part?

2. What is the letter's specific job in carrying out the transaction?

3. Does the letter accomplish its task?

4. Does the letter tell the reader clearly what he or she is expected to do and how to do it?

A Good Letter Has a Pleasing Personality

Just as your own personality is made up of many distinctive traits, so is the personality of each letter you write. In determining what traits in a letter will please the reader, ask yourself:

1. *Is its appearance attractive?* A letter, like a person, should make a good first impression.

2. *Is its expression correct, concise, and natural?* A letter, like a person, is judged by "the way it talks."

3. *Is its tone friendly?* A letter, like a person, attracts friends by being friendly. And letters CAN SMILE.

4. *Does it reflect a sincere and helpful attitude?* A letter, like a person, influences others if it convinces them that the writer's thoughtfulness and desire to serve are more than merely pleasant words and polite manners.

5. *Does it stress a "you" viewpoint?* A letter, like a person, pleases if it focuses on the reader and emphasizes that the reader's interests are important to the writer and the writer's company.

6. *Are negative elements positioned carefully and explained or minimized?* A letter, like a person, should emphasize the positive aspects.

A Good Letter Is Interesting to the Reader

A business letter need not be clever and entertaining, but it should attract and hold the reader's attention so that he or she reads the message through and then acts on it—or at least reacts to it. To determine whether a letter is interesting, ask yourself:

1. Does the opening sentence say something of interest to the reader? Will it capture the reader's attention?

2. Do the friendly tone and "you" viewpoint make the reader want to go on reading?

3. Do the clear, natural style of writing and the logical development of ideas make the letter easy to read and understand?

4. Does the letter continue to keep the reader involved?

5. Does the ending drive the point "home"?

6. Does the letter's sincere and helpful attitude make the reader feel that the writer actually *wanted* to write the letter and is genuinely interested? Or does it sound as though its writer is tired and bored?

Writing Inquiries and Requests

When people want to know more about a product or service, they write "inquiry" letters—letters that request or ask for information. Such letters can be grouped into four types.

1. Requests for simple confirmation of reservations and appointments.

2. Requests for information about products or services in order to purchase them. These are sometimes called *buying inquiries,* and they use the direct approach.

3. Requests for information without any intention to buy or sell. Such requests (called *general requests*) ask for details and facts the reader can give with little time and effort and at practically no expense.

4. Requests for cooperation, gifts, or favors without any intention to buy or sell. Since you are asking the reader to spend time or money, or to go to some trouble to help you—without benefit to the reader—you need to first interest the reader in your cause to get his or her cooperation. These letters are called *persuasive requests,* for they attempt to persuade the reader to do something.

Let's look at each of these types of inquiries and requests, from the simple to the persuasive. Notice the change in approach as the benefit is to be received by the reader or the writer.

WRITING LETTERS ABOUT RESERVATIONS AND APPOINTMENTS

Business people often write letters asking for or making changes in reservations and appointments. These letters are short and businesslike to save time for the writers as well as their secretaries and readers. In such a letter, the writer is careful to include exact dates and other facts needed to prevent misunderstandings.

Follow these suggestions when you write a letter about a reservation or an appointment.

1. *Make sure the facts are accurate.* Think of the confusion, inconvenience, loss of goodwill, and possibly even loss of business that might be caused by one error in the date—such as August 12 instead of August 21. Guard against such errors by mentioning also the day of the week.

2. *Give all necessary details concisely, but use judgment in selecting details to be included or omitted.* You should, for instance, stress the time, date, place, and purpose of proposed meetings rather than draw the reader's attention to incidental, unimportant remarks.

3. *Consider the other person's convenience.* If you must change the time and/or date of an appointment or reservation, do it just as soon as you can, and give a satisfactory reason. The other person deserves better than a last-minute excuse. It is wise to try to suit the other person's convenience if you must set up a second appointment.

4. *Keep the tone courteous and friendly.* A condescending or demanding tone can easily creep into these letters and leave a bad impression of the writer.

5. *Close by expressing appreciation, indicating possible action, or looking forward to the next meeting.*

Practice until you can write these simple letters quickly and effectively.

A letter asking for a hotel reservation should be both concise and specific, as the following letter is.

Please reserve a moderately priced single room (downstairs, outside) for me for the week of August 11 through 17. Will you have the room ready before one o'clock on Monday afternoon?

Please confirm my reservation immediately, since I plan to be out of the office after August 1.

The following letter asks for a change in the date of an appointment, states the reason for the change, and then gives the reader the opportunity to set the time for the next conference.

Will it be convenient for me to demonstrate our new Speedy-Print copier to you next Friday instead of next Wednesday? Can we reschedule our meeting for July 28 at 3 p.m.?

We are exhibiting at the annual Blue Ribbon Machines Show in Chicago on July 24-26, and I have been assigned to work that exhibit.

If Friday, July 28, is not convenient for you, would you suggest a later date?

WRITING REQUESTS FOR INFORMATION

Follow these suggestions when you write a simple request for information.

1. *Begin with your questions.* You help the reader to understand and answer your inquiry quickly when you get to the point immediately and tell the reader exactly what you need to know.

2. *Word each question carefully.* Make sure that each question asks for specific information and that each is unambiguous.

Use questions rather than statements. Notice that the question below is shorter than the statement. In addition, the question mark immediately suggests to the reader that an answer is expected.

> POOR: I would like to know the colors in which Brady sculptured shag carpet is available.
>
> BETTER: In what colors is Brady sculptured shag carpet available?

Make the question specific—not general. A general question usually brings a general answer, which often repeats what you already know instead of giving you the details you want.

> POOR: What can you tell me about the value of your Jr. bean bag?
>
> BETTER: How does your Jr. bean bag compare with the Giant bean bag in size, price, quality, and durability?

Be careful of the question that can be answered with a "yes" or "no" and still not tell you what you really want to know. A "yes" answer would be satisfactory for a question such as "Can you deliver it within ten days?" But what about a "yes" answer to: "Is it available in any other styles?"

> POOR: Is the guarantee on your Crafty table saw a good one?
>
> BETTER: What does the guarantee on your Crafty table saw cover, and what is the life of the guarantee?

3. *Briefly explain why you are asking.* Include all facts—such as the use you plan to make of the information requested—that will help the reader answer you.

4. *Omit details not helpful to the reader.* The person to whom you write usually has many letters to answer—and no time to read your life story. Incidental comments clutter up a letter and make it harder for the reader to determine the exact information you want.

5. *Stop when you are finished.* Say what needs to be said, and end the letter courteously. Too many beginning writers tend to repeat in the closing sentences things they have already said, just because they do not know how to stop.

If you are going to ask several questions in one letter, you can help the reader by putting each question in a separate paragraph. A letter that groups several questions in a single paragraph is hard to answer. The reader must make a special effort to identify each question and may easily overlook one.

You can make your questions stand out by numbering them, as in the inquiry below. You may include

explanations at the beginning, at the end, or in the paragraph with the question (see question 3), whichever is most appropriate.

Please send me answers to the following questions about the Permaweave Draperies advertised on page 43 of the May HOME DECORATOR.

1. Will these draperies retain their colors and sheen if washed?

2. What method (or methods) do you recommend as satisfactory for cleaning them?

3. Will the colors fade under continued exposure to sun? I would like to have dark green draperies in one room, but I hesitate because dark green tends to streak if it gets too much sun.

I shall appreciate receiving this information before I select draperies for my new home early next month.

As you begin to *answer* inquiries in Unit 12, you will see the importance of *writing* inquiries that follow the suggestions above.

Sometimes a writer requests general information with no intention of buying products or services. For instance, you might write your local chamber of commerce requesting figures on wholesale and retail sales in your city over the past ten years. If such information is easily accessible to the reader, you can assume he or she will be willing to send it. Make this request letter as direct and concise as a buying inquiry. Begin by requesting the information, then explain briefly why you need it and what use you will put it to, and end by expressing appreciation.

WRITING PERSUASIVE REQUESTS

If you read the persuasive letter on page 65 sent to all the residents of Brookdale, you will see how effectively it captures the interest and secures the cooperation of the reader with its approach and its use of the "you" attitude. When you write a persuasive request, follow these suggestions:

1. *Begin with something that will interest the reader.* If you review the discussion under "The Best Approach," Unit 10, pages 53 to 57, you will find that you already know a great deal about the opening paragraphs of persuasive letters.

The approach for these letters is entirely different from the approach for direct inquiries. When you ask someone about a product or service he or she is trying to sell, the reader sees the inquiry as an opportunity to sell and becomes interested. But when you ask for a gift or favor, you must point out the advantage to and stimulate the interest of the reader. If the request is made bluntly or selfishly, the reaction is likely to be "why bother?" Since you want a favorable response, avoid starting with the request. Get the reader interested in your story before asking for an answer.

Successful persuasive approaches often stress the following themes:

Altruistic appeal with emphasis on benefits to others, as illustrated in this opening paragraph of a letter from the Easter Seal Society:

> Nobody works harder than crippled children to overcome their handicap. But they need help...your help and ours.

Reader-benefit appeal, as illustrated in the following excerpt from a sales manager's plea to salespersons to improve their personal appearance:

> How often do you take time for a second look at your appearance? Your customers do every day.
>
> Your appearance is a preview of the way you might handle your customer's affairs. When you take pride in yourself, your customer feels that you also take pride in what you do for him or her.

Individual-responsibility appeal, as illustrated (on next page) in the approach a magazine editor used in a request for information from readers:

BROOKDALE FIRE DEPARTMENT
Brookdale, New Jersey 07023, Tel. 201-555-1111

February 15, 19--

Dear Neighbor:

For the past two years the Brookdale Fire Department has been named the "most effective" volunteer fire department in our state. Wouldn't you like to make it three in a row?

In its last annual report, the Fire Chiefs' Association stated that our community again suffered the least fire damage per capita throughout the state. Of course, this means that your home and your furniture and belongings are well protected from the dangers of fire. But it also means a lot more: It means that you, your spouse, and your children are well protected from the dangers of fire.

The men and women volunteers who sacrifice their time and risk their lives as fire fighters are ready to continue their efforts for all the residents of Brookdale. All they need is your support. To keep their equipment in excellent condition and to pay the expenses of maintaining their trucks and their firehouse, the volunteers of the Brookdale Fire Department depend on your contributions. To help them continue their superb work, send your dona-tion today. Use the enclosed postage-paid envelope, and please be generous.

Sincerely,

Martha Chambers

Martha Chambers, Director
Fund-Raising Committee

This persuasive request letter captures the reader's interest in the first paragraph. Then, through its use of the "you" attitude, it secures the cooperation of the reader.

You can assist us, yourself, and other readers. Will you?

Advertisers in PRACTICAL BUILDER often say, "What kind of advertisements do your readers like best?" These advertisers are interested in designing their advertisements so that they are more helpful to you. Naturally, before we can answer their question, we must learn the answer from you.

Personal-experience appeal, as illustrated in the recall of childhood memories in this excerpt from a letter trying to persuade the reader to donate money to help build a zoo:

> Remember the kick you got out of going to the zoo when you were a youngster? Seeing the strange animals and birds was quite a thrill, wasn't it? And the excitement of feeding time! Won't you agree that such experiences are long remembered by youngsters lucky enough to visit a zoo—and that they should be a part of every child's growing up and every grownup's reminiscing?

2. *After you select the strongest theme for your approach, follow through with a "you" attitude explanation of the reason for the request.* Effective explanations often contain two popular features:

a. Emphasis on an advantage to someone other than the writer—to the reader or the reader's company—as illustrated in this paragraph from a letter asking distributors of paper napkins to complete a questionnaire for the Paper Napkin Association, Inc.

> Your cooperation in this project will be of definite help to the paper napkin industry, as you can readily see. But it will be of even more benefit to your distributors because the results of the survey will be used by our members in developing better merchandising methods and better service to individual distributors.

b. Complimentary reference to the reader, as illustrated in this sentence from a letter asking a business executive to address a high school club:

> We know that any talk you give will be stimulating and helpful to our students.

3. *State the request in definite and specific terms* after you have prepared the way for it. Be sure the reader knows exactly what you want and how and when he or she is to respond. Notice how explicit this writer makes his request to a club member for her cooperation.

> Specifically, Diane, these are the things I am asking you to do:
>
> 1. Attend the monthly meetings.

> 2. Chair the Membership Committee. You are to form the committee. Please send a list of its members to the Executive Secretary by April 11. Submit a plan for this year's membership drive to the Executive Secretary by May 8. Your annual committee report will be due November 20.

> 3. Serve as adviser to the Education Committee. Your experience should be especially valuable to this committee, and I have asked its chairman to contact you directly.

> 4. Draft a cover letter for the attached questionnaire, which we will send to our membership this year. I leave the content of the letter up to you.

4. *Stimulate action with closing remarks suggesting that compliance will be easy and satisfying.* Doesn't this closing paragraph make listeners feel that supplying the information asked by a radio station will be simple yet worthwhile?

> You will find our questions easy to answer. We shall not use your name—no one will try to sell you anything. We have stamped the ballot—so no postage is necessary. But we <u>do need</u> your vote—so please fill in the few blanks on the enclosed ballot, fold it, seal it, and drop it in the mail.

5. *Reflect appreciation of and confidence in the reader's favorable response.* Sincere belief in people and an optimistic outlook shine through every paragraph of most successful persuasive letters.

Notice the positive tone in the following excerpts from persuasive requests.

> Your help is vital. The vote is going to be so close that a contribution of $10, $25, or $50 could make the difference.

> Your contribution will be warmly and gratefully received. I'll be eagerly awaiting your reply in the next few days.

> The enclosed questionnaire will take only a few minutes to check and mail in the return envelope. Because the information you can provide is urgently needed to complete our study for the benefit of all students, we would appreciate your returning the questionnaire by March 10—or sooner.

ASSIGNMENT: Complete Section A of the Worksheet for practice in improving poorly worded inquiries. Then try your hand at planning, composing, and typing inquiries and persuasive requests in Section B.

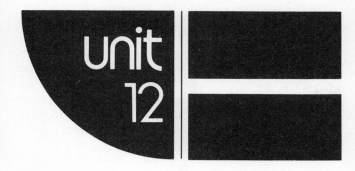

Writing Replies to Inquiries and Requests

People who write simple requests for information about products or services usually need prompt answers. And it is good business to send them the information as quickly as possible before they "cool off" and decide not to buy. For that reason, inquiries are usually answered the same day they are received. If an inquiry cannot be answered quickly, an explanation should be written to the inquirer, including the reason for the delay and the time when an answer may be expected.

ANSWERING "YES" TO INQUIRIES AND REQUESTS

When you answer an inquiry positively, you should do these things in your letter:

1. *Give complete and specific answers to the customer's questions.* In the opening paragraphs of your reply, take advantage of the opportunity to give the customer the information he or she wants most to have.

2. *Express appreciation for the inquiry.* Either directly or by the tone of your reply, tell the customer that you are glad he or she has written to you about one of your company's products.

3. *Try to hold the customer's interest by commenting favorably about the product.* The inquiry shows that the customer is interested. By stressing benefits of buying now, you encourage the reader to convert interest into action.

4. *Make the letter attractive, clear, conversational, and friendly.* Writing letters with these characteristics is probably becoming a habit with you as you learn to satisfy customers and build business through *effective* correspondence.

When inquiries are clear, concise, and specific, they are easy to answer. Here's a good example of a request for information from Ralph Ewing, one of Cameron Products Company's customers.

> Since completing your Cameron Fishing Rod Kit, I have heard many people comment on the appearance and quality of my new fishing rod. I believe that I can sell some of these fishing rods if I make them up.
>
> Could you supply me with just the rod blanks and the handles? What would the price be if I ordered six of each at a time? I would use my own sources for guides, ferrules, and thread.

Immediately after receiving Mr. Ewing's request, Cameron sent him the following reply. Since the company could answer all the customer's questions positively, the writer used the direct approach.

> You must have done quite a job assembling your Cameron rod if it is resulting in sales inquiries. Congratulations!
>
> Of course we will supply you with rod blanks and handles. The rod blanks will come to you sized for ferrules and with one coat of epoxy base finish for protection. We will also include the proper handle with each rod blank.
>
> Since the rod blanks and the handles join with ferrules specially designed for the purpose, we strongly urge you to use the ones we include in our kits. Their cost is minimal, and using them would save you considerable expense for special machining.
>
> Your cost for each rod blank with handle and (when needed) butt ferrule will be $10.41, including shipping charges. We can offer you these items at reduced prices if you order six of each at a time. The total bill for six rod blanks, handles, and ferrules, including shipping charges, will be $54.68. Please include payment with each order.
>
> We'll be looking forward to your first order for rod blanks and handles, Mr. Ewing. Until then, good luck and...
>
> Good fishing,

When you reply to a letter containing several questions, be sure to answer every question completely. You can help your reader by putting each answer in a separate paragraph. If the questions are numbered in the inquiry, number your answers to correspond, as the writer of the letter at the top of page 68 did in answering the inquiry on page 64. Since the writer had a positive answer for *every* question, numbering the answers was easy to do.

But if you don't have a positive answer for *every* question, don't follow the inquirer's order when you answer. You might find yourself beginning your letter with a negative answer! Answer the questions in the order that's best for you, starting with your most positive answer and working your way down to your weakest answer. Make full use of positional emphasis and subordination to help you.

Reread the inquiry on page 64; then read the following reply to that inquiry. Could this reply have been strengthened by putting the answers in a different order?

You can select Permaweave Draperies for your new home with confidence because they measure up on all the points about which you asked.

1. Permaweave Draperies can be washed. If they are washed in warm water with a mild detergent, their colors and sheen will remain bright and beautiful.

2. We recommend either washing or dry cleaning. This is really a matter of personal preference since Permaweave Draperies will look new either way.

3. Because of a new process used in dyeing, we are now able to guarantee Permaweave Draperies against fading or streaking after exposure to the sun for long periods. Extensive testing in our laboratories and the Better Homemaking Seal of Approval assure color fastness for even the dark greens.

We appreciate your interest and invite you to write again when you have other questions. Meanwhile, Argo's Furniture Center, in your city, offers you a wide selection of colors and patterns in Permaweave Draperies.

Answering a persuasive letter is easy, too, when you can say "yes" to the request. A smiling "Here it is" or "I'll be glad to" just about sums up the reply. Make your answer direct and uncomplicated. Follow these suggestions:

1. *Write a cheerful "yes" in the first paragraph.* "Yes" is the good news the reader is hoping for. Opening the letter with it will make the reader happy. If the request is granted grudgingly or with reservations, the reader may think he or she should not have asked the favor or may feel uncomfortable about accepting your help.

> The solution to the drop in membership is important to me too. I am glad you planned the conference, and I'll be there with the rest of you.

2. *Confirm details of the request and acceptance.* The confirmation can often be included with the acceptance in the first paragraph, as in this opening sentence:

> Yes, we would like to send you copies of our April Newsletter—and in fact we have.

Otherwise, the confirmation should follow in the next paragraph and should repeat enough of the request to make clear that the reader and the writer agree on the details. For example, a letter accepting an invitation to give a talk at a meeting should confirm the date, time, place, and perhaps the subject and length of the talk. Or if a contribution is enclosed, the letter should state the amount and purpose.

3. *Ask for any additional information needed to comply with the request.* For instance, a woman accepting an invitation to give an address at a convention wrote: "Can the room be sufficiently darkened and can a large screen be provided so that I may plan to illustrate my talk with color slides?" A man agreeing to act as coordinator of the annual Sports and Boat Show wrote: "Will you help me out with some of your expert advice? I

don't know just what the job of coordinating this project entails, but I'm eager to learn."

4. *Show special friendliness by giving something extra when the gesture seems appropriate.* If you give the reader more than he or she expects, the reader may feel glad about coming to you with the request.

The "something extra" may be an offer to do more than requested, as in these two examples:

1. A Boston University professor accepts an invitation to speak at a UBSA convention in Washington, with expenses paid but no fee, and offers to come at no expense to the nonprofit organization:

> Since I plan to make frequent business trips to Baltimore this summer, I shall be happy to drive over to Washington to appear before the afternoon session on June 19. Also, I'll bring along some display materials that may be helpful to those attending the UBSA convention.

2. A Chicago member sends his contribution to the Alumni Fund and asks:

> Shall I call the other Chicago members? I'll be glad to add a little personal persuasion to the fine letter you sent them.

Or the "something extra" may be an expression of interest and willingness to help further if asked, as in these two excerpts:

1. An accountant sends the data requested by a student and closes her letter with:

> Just write me if I can give you any more help. I certainly want that term paper to earn an A.

2. A business executive sends an author the charts and graphs requested, with permission to reproduce them, and closes her letter with:

> I hope I may have the opportunity to cooperate with you again. And please let me know when your book is published. I'm most interested in having a copy for my library.

ANSWERING "NO" TO INQUIRIES AND REQUESTS

You can be brief and to the point when you grant a request. But if you must say "no," take a little longer and deliver the bad news gently and tactfully. Try to let courtesy and thoughtfulness shine through your letter.

You do not really need to learn new principles to write a letter that says "no" graciously. Simply apply the principles of building goodwill and avoiding negative tone. Of course, these are the same principles that make a request persuasive. And a gracious refusal is very much like a persuasive request—when you say "no" persuasively, you ask the reader to accept your decision as the only fair answer under the circumstances.

You have already seen these principles applied to writing letters in which it was not possible to say "yes." Do you remember how tactfully a store said "not now" to the customer who asked it to stock petite sizes (page 50)? How a firm said "no" to a request from one of its dealers to purchase advertisements in two suburban telephone directories (page 55)? These letters had a common goal: to keep the friendship of the customer.

When you say "no" in a letter, consider these suggestions.

1. *Approach the letter as an opportunity to "talk it over"* and to give whatever encouragement you can—not as a plain "no." If you think, "I must decline this order or this invitation or refuse this request," you will probably write negatively. But you will probably write constructively if you think, "What can I do to encourage this person even though I can't do what the person asks?"

2. *Start pleasantly with a friendly buffer paragraph.* Suppose you receive a letter beginning, "It is my unpleasant duty to inform you that..." or "I'm sorry to tell you that we cannot grant your request..." Don't you immediately close your mind to whatever else the writer may say? Wouldn't you think that he or she is not interested in helping you, in building goodwill, or in keeping your friendship? The writer seems concerned only with getting a distasteful job out of the way. But suppose the letter begins, "Your proposal for a joint meeting of Phi Beta Lambda and Future Business Leaders of America is very interesting, Darin." Aren't you likely to read the rest of the message with an open mind?

3. *Tell the reader why you cannot say "yes."* In your explanation imply that you would rather say "yes" than "no." And try to compliment the reader in some way. The PTA president who received the following certainly felt that he had chosen a worthwhile film.

> Many parent-teacher groups throughout the state have enjoyed "Safeguard Your Children." In fact, it is our most popular film. Last March we had three additional prints made so that it would be available to more people, but even these are booked well in advance.

4. *Avoid a negative refusal.* Explaining *before* you refuse is best. And you need not bluntly say "no." If your letter does a good job explaining, the reader realizes that you cannot do what he or she asked—the "no" is inferred. If you feel you must, state your refusal—to be sure the reader realizes you are not putting it in negative terms. Sometimes limiting expressions, such as *only* or *exclusively,* may substitute for negatives such as *regret, apologies, cannot,* and so on. Notice how this actual business letter dwells on the negative and almost obscures the positive points.

> We are very sorry that your portrait has been damaged. This rarely happens to Pixie photos.

> I regret to advise we cannot hold negatives for a long period of time due to a lack of storage space; therefore, we will not be able to reprint your portrait. To compensate for this I am processing a refund in the amount of $5.95, which you should receive within the next twenty working days. I am also returning the damaged 5 x 7 portrait to you and a free coupon.

> Please accept our sincere apologies for this as we greatly value your patronage.

The following letter shows interest in the reader and tries to keep her business while refusing the request.

> We were happy to hear that your family was so pleased with your portraits. And we are sorry that one was damaged. Since our storage space is limited, however, negatives are destroyed about ten days after an order has been filled.

> We are returning the 5 x 7 portrait, along with a refund of $5.95. You should receive them in about three weeks.

> You may use the enclosed coupon for a complimentary 5 x 7 color portrait when Pixie Photos returns to Bridgetown on November 3.

5. *Give encouragement—and when you can, give help.* Sometimes you can take the sting out of a "no" with a helpful suggestion. For example, a department store representative, in declining an order for an article not carried by the store, often tells the customer where he or she can make the purchase. The reservations manager of a Chicago hotel, not able to make the reservations requested, suggested:

> If you can conveniently defer your arrival in Chicago until April 10, we shall be glad to reserve a double room for you and your wife. If you must be here on April 7, you might write for help to The Greater Chicago Hotel Association, at 105 West Madison Street.

6. *Close pleasantly with a look toward the future.* In your last paragraph, *do not look backward.* Do not say, for example, "We hope our inability to grant your request does not inconvenience you too much." This would leave your reader thinking how dissatisfied he or she is about your refusal. Also, *do not include an apology* in your last paragraph. Saying something such as "We are sorry that we couldn't send the information you requested" emphasizes what you *can't* do. Instead *put into* the last paragraph (a) a substitute suggestion, (b) an expression of your desire to cooperate further, (c) a wish for the reader's success, or (d) a pleasant off-the-subject remark.

Don't you agree that the following letter says "no" graciously to the applicant who asked Holiday Inns for a job?

> It was certainly a pleasure to meet you this week and have the opportunity to discuss career opportunities at Holiday Inns.

> Because of its position as the number one hotel chain in the world, Holiday Inns offers unique public relations challenges and opportunities. I think you would find the hotel industry an

exciting one to work in . . . and being associated with the industry leader would be an especially nice bonus.

Although there are currently no openings in Public Relations other than in Chicago and New York, I will keep your résumé on file. I wish you much success in your job search; and I'll be sure to give you a call if anything develops here at Holiday Inns that would fit your skills and abilities.

WRITING FORM REPLIES TO INQUIRIES

Form letters and cards are often used in business to reply to inquiries. These forms may be prepared in

connection with advertising campaigns to take care of the flood of inquiries expected.

The form letter below is used by GBC to reinforce the sales points for its products and to say that the reader will be contacted by a representative of the company who will give him or her full information. Note that the letter is natural and cheerful. Though obviously a form letter, it concisely covers the lines of products GBC makes. It does its job well: it prepares the way for the company's representative, it subtly reinforces the company's image of size and success, and it briefly describes the company's products.

The form post card on page 71 was prepared by the Sportcycle Center. Since duplicated cards were

 General Binding Corporation

THANK YOU . . .

. . . for your interest in one of GBC's fine family of products. I am certain that you will find one that fits your every need. The following briefly describes the major GBC machines, supplies, and systems and their potential uses in your organization:

PLASTIC BINDING SYSTEMS for office and plant for binding professional-appearing presentations and booklets that lie flat--stay flat.

THERM-A-BIND "invisible binding" systems for do-it-yourself-in-seconds publisher-quality paperback and hardcover-bound presentations.

COLLATING from desk top to automatic collators for the quickest, most accurate way to gather pages into the proper sequence.

LAMINATING with variable size laminators for sealing paper and other materials in transparent film for protection and enhancement.

PHOTO IDENTIFICATION SYSTEMS utilizing B & W or color photos to produce photo ID cards compatible with data collection and access control systems.

GBC OFFICE SUPPLIES & SPECIALTIES with custom imprinting service using all printing processes including:

      Cerlox plastic bindings and coversets
      Therm-A-Tape
      Therm-A-Binders & Therm-A-Cases
      Naplam laminating film & ID pouches
      Gebex LP and GBC Vinyl metal loose-leaf binders
      GBC custom index divider sets

and much more.

A GBC representative has been alerted to your interest and will contact you shortly with additional information and samples. If your requirements are urgent, please refer to the nearest GBC Branch Office (a complete list of branch offices is on the reverse side of this letter).

All of us at GBC welcome the opportunity to be of service to you.

Very truly yours,

Paul A. Jason
Senior Vice President

PAJ:jk

One GBC Plaza • Northbrook, Illinois 60062 • (312) 272-3700

Courtesy General Binding Corporation

GBC uses this form reply to inquiries in order to reinforce the sales points for its products and to tell the reader that a GBC representative will call soon.

sent to hundreds of inquirers, the message could not be personalized. But it is carefully worded to make each person feel that his or her request is welcome, and it invites the prospective customer to call to find out what is currently available, discuss the terms, and possibly place an order.

Dear Friend:

Thank you for your request for information about new and used Sportcycle models now in stock, including prices and terms.

For specific information, please call us on our toll-free number between 8 a.m. and 5 p.m. any weekday. Our toll-free number is 1-800-386-4307.

Sincerely yours,

Kelly T. Hymann

Kelly T. Hymann
Customer Relations Department

WRITING COVER LETTERS

Advertising leaflets, price lists, catalogs, checks, reports, and miscellaneous items are often sent to customers, dealers, and others. Sending one of these without comment would be a bit abrupt, like walking in without knocking. Writing a short, friendly cover letter to accompany each is both courteous and helpful. Usually the covering letter is mailed in the same envelope with the material. If the item is bulky, the cover letter may be attached to the outside of the package or it may be mailed separately.

In addition to being courteous and friendly, a cover letter actually helps both the reader and the writer. It tells the purpose for sending the enclosed material and points out pertinent details, so that the reader doesn't waste time thumbing through or reading pages that do not concern him or her—or just wondering what the material is all about. The writer can stress how the reader is to use the enclosure and can stimulate interest and prompt action. A cover letter also becomes a file record of the date and the reason something was sent or received.

A cover letter accompanying a shipment of merchandise is used to create personal contact with customers and lay the foundation for future sales. Just sending the merchandise would be enough, but the cover letter is that "something extra" that can help strengthen the business relationship between the company and its customers.

Mail order houses often receive requests for their catalogs, which are usually offered free in every advertisement. When people don't order the items featured in an advertisement but ask for the catalog instead, they need more selling. A letter does the job. Such letters are form letters but can be personalized to

the extent that the customers of a certain business have similar characteristics.

Here are suggestions for writing a cover letter for merchandise or literature.

1. *Start with a short, direct identification of the item being sent.* Referring to the reader's request for the item or explaining your reason for sending it may be enough to introduce the enclosure pleasantly.

2. *Stress the reader's use of the item.* The fact that *you are sending something* isn't important. The fact that *your reader can use or enjoy it* is important. Avoid the selfish-sounding "I am enclosing" and the obvious "You will find enclosed," "Enclosed please find," and "Enclosed is."

3. *Be specific but choose details carefully.* Arouse the reader's interest in the enclosure by referring to specific advantages he or she may gain from it. Mentioning page numbers and marked excerpts in a booklet can stimulate reading and encourage buying. Remember, though, that the letter is only one part of the message and should never overshadow the enclosure.

4. *Close with a forward look.* This closing is designed to foster friendly relations and future business.

Even when there seems no immediate possibility of a sale, try some sales promotion. And be sure to stress the service attitude.

ASSIGNMENT: Complete Section A of the Worksheet for practice in improving poorly worded replies to inquiries. Then plan, compose, and type replies to inquiries and persuasive requests in Section B.

Writing Order Letters and Acknowledgments

Buying and selling by mail is a service provided by large and small mail-order houses, large department stores, equipment and supply companies, and various other businesses. Doing business by mail is popular because of the convenience of shopping where and when one wishes, the detailed information available, the excellent guarantees and return privileges, and services such as installation. The usual disadvantage is, of course, that one sees only a picture of the product and cannot try it without buying—although the "15-day free trial offer" makes even that possible.

When order letters and acknowledgments are needed, they are easy to write because you have no problem in getting the interest of the reader (who is definitely interested in buying or selling) and you do not have to persuade the reader. You simply use a direct, good-news-first approach.

WRITING ORDER LETTERS

You will seldom find it necessary, however, or even desirable, to write a straight order letter. Many companies have their own purchase order forms, and individuals and small companies ordinarily use the printed order blanks provided by the companies from whom they order.

Order forms are easier to read than order letters. Also, important information is less often omitted from order forms, because these forms provide blank spaces for inserting all needed information.

You may occasionally use a letter to order goods or services (1) when you do not have an appropriate order form or (2) when you need to include explanations that will not fit a standard form. If you organize the letter like a typical order blank, your order will be easy to read and to fill.

A letter used as a substitute for an order blank should contain the basic elements included in the following order letter addressed to the shopping service of a large department store.

Please send me the following articles advertised in the June 10 *Shopper's News:*

2	#33 D 16072R	Perma-Pressed Bedspreads Twin–Royal Blue–at $16.96	$33.92
1	#33 D 16075N	Perma-Pressed Bedspread King–Navy Blue–at $39.96	39.96
3 pairs	#33 D 16080L	Perma-Pressed Draperies 54" x 96"–Light Blue at $27.92	83.76
		TOTAL	$157.64

Please charge these to my account, #059358204, and send them by parcel post to my summer address:

Route 2, Box 108
Rushville, Michigan 48675

I shall appreciate delivery of the draperies by Thursday, June 29, since the man I've hired to hang them can be here on Friday morning only.

In the letter you just read, note how all the order letter suggestions below have been followed.

1. *Start with a direct and definite request for the merchandise wanted.* "Please send" is a more business-like opening than "I want," "I need," or "I would like to have." An order that begins "Please send" becomes part of a written contract between the buyer and the seller.

2. *Give a complete description of each article ordered.* Such a description will distinguish each article from any similar article the company may stock. Include in the description the exact name of the product with a catalog number if possible. Also include, whenever needed, color, grade, size, weight, model number or designation, as well as special patterns, materials, or other distinctive features. If you cannot supply all distinguishing details, explain how you plan to use the article; then the person filling the order may complete the specifications.

3. *List the quantity or number of articles wanted for each item or class of items ordered.* Be sure to include *dozen, gross, pounds,* or whatever may be appropriate with the number.

4. *If you can, list the unit price for each article, the extension, and the total cost of all items.* ("Extension" is the cost for the quantity or number of each item ordered.) These figures help the clerk select the articles to fill your order and verify the amount of the payment or charge.

5. *List the items and descriptions in indented, tabulated form.* Use double spacing between items, to make reading and checking quick and easy.

6. *Identify the method of payment.* If the payment is enclosed, mention the amount and the form, such as check or money order; or you may specify c.o.d. Or you may want to charge it to your account, in which case include your account or credit card number. Be sure to add shipping charges and sales taxes that may be part of the total cost.

7. *Include the address to which the merchandise is to be sent if it differs in any way from the address in the heading of your letter.* In the order letter above, the address is given because it is not the address on the writer's charge account.

8. *State the method of shipment if you have a preference.* You may need merchandise in a hurry, for example, and be willing to pay the extra cost of Air Express. If you do not specify, the company will make the choice, usually between express and parcel post; extremely large or heavy items are sent by freight.

ASSIGNMENT: Turn to Section A of the Worksheet to see how well you can prepare orders.

ACKNOWLEDGING ORDERS

Companies try, of course, to ship merchandise as soon as possible, usually within one or two days of receiving the order. But it is a good idea to send a letter acknowledging each order on the same day the order is received, since delivery by mail is often made several days after shipment. As first-class mail, the letter usually reaches the addressee within two or three days and assures the customer that the merchandise is on its way (or gives reasons for a delay, if that is the case). And in addition to showing the customer that the company is efficient and reliable, the acknowledgment letter helps to establish a closer personal relationship between the company and the customer—a relationship that serves as a firm base for future orders.

Keep these general principles in mind when writing a letter acknowledging an order:

1. Write simply and clearly so that the reader will easily understand *every* statement.

2. Identify the order and give complete information about how you are handling it.

3. Express appreciation for the order subordinately—remember that the reader is interested in what you are doing about the order.

4. Close with a suggestion of continuing service.

Some companies acknowledge all orders received; others do not. A company that receives many orders from different customers or frequent repeat orders from regular customers—particularly from dealers—often just sends the goods without a letter. However, an acknowledgment with an explanation is usually sent if:

1. The merchandise cannot be shipped promptly.

2. A substitution, however minor, is made in any part of an order.

3. An order can be only partially filled.

4. There is any question about the precise interpretation of an order.

5. An order must be refused or cannot be accepted on the exact terms specified.

Firms that are particularly public-relations-minded often reply with *special appreciation* when:

1. A first order is received from a customer.

2. An exceptionally large order or an order for a new line of goods is received from an established customer.

3. There is reason to think that the customer who buys in small quantities may feel his or her orders are not welcome.

An individually dictated letter may be sent:

1. *When a special explanation is needed.* As you read the letter below, you will realize how hard it would be to confirm this order in a form acknowledgment.

Thank you very much for your letter of October 23 ordering 100 informals No. 130 engraved from the plate in our files for Miss Ann Louise Jones. This order will have our prompt and careful attention, and shipment will be made before Christmas.

We also thank you for the order for 100 sheets and 100 envelopes No. 45020, the paper to be stamped in the upper left corner from your monogram die and the envelopes to be stamped on the flaps from your address die. This is good form and is done quite often. We are, of course, stamping in blue ink to match the border.

It is a pleasure to serve you again. We feel you will be pleased with the informals and the stationery.

---

2. *When an order can be only partially filled.* The writer of this acknowledgment (of the order on page 72) gets off to a good start by first telling the customer what items *have* been sent.

You will have your 3 pairs #33 D 16080L Perma-Pressed Draperies, size 54″ x 96″, in light blue—at $27.92 per pair in plenty of time to hang them next Friday morning. They were sent out by parcel post this morning.

Your Perma-Pressed Bedspreads—2 twin-size in royal blue, at $16.96 each; and 1 king-size in navy blue, at $39.96—will reach you sometime next week. We expect a new shipment of these popular spreads in a day or two and will mail yours right out.

The charges on these items will appear on your next monthly statement.

We appreciate your order and invite you to shop by mail whenever we can help you.

Replying to an Order That is Filled Promptly

The acknowledgment of an order that is filled promptly should:

1. Identify the article or articles ordered.

2. Include details concerning the prompt handling of the order.

3. Express appreciation for the order.

4. Suggest continuing service.

5. Explain the terms of payment, when appropriate.

Since a letter acknowledging an order that is filled promptly will bring welcome news to the reader, use the direct approach in writing the letter. Begin with the first two elements listed above: identify the articles ordered (briefly) and give the details concerning the prompt handling of the order. Telling the reader what he or she ordered is hardly important information—unless he or she has two or more orders pending with you. Since the customer already has this information, you should make the necessary identification as concisely and as quickly as possible.

Since the reader really wants to know *when* you are going to send the merchandise, you should begin with this information. And since the identification of the order blends naturally with the details of shipment, you usually can cover both details in one sentence at the beginning of your letter. If necessary, you can add a few sentences in the first paragraph to provide more detailed information about the shipping.

Sending the merchandise promptly is the best evidence of your appreciation for the order, but you may write a courteous "thank you" that is not overdone. If you need to mention the terms of payment, you can generally combine the necessary statements with your expression of appreciation in a short paragraph.

Some resale of the merchandise being shipped is usually appropriate—and it helps reinforce one purpose of an order-acknowledgment letter: to set the stage for future orders. Reselling the merchandise will help make it easier for the reader to wait for actual delivery, and it will give you a logical and smooth way to promote the sale of related items. *Caution!* If you start selling something else before the reader has received the order you are acknowledging, you run the risk of appearing greedy. To be successful in using sales promotion material in an order acknowledgment, you must show a service attitude and write carefully.

The following letter acknowledges an order that was filled immediately.

You should receive the 30 bolts of Decorator's coordinating wallcoverings by the end of the week. They were sent by prepaid express yesterday afternoon.

Thank you for sending your check with your order . . . and thank you for your order.

We know your customers will be pleased with these fine wallcoverings, which are prepasted, vinyl-coated, washable, and dry strippable.

You may now choose from more than 50 patterns and colors that coordinate with our other home furnishings, as you can see in the enclosed brochure.

You may also wish to take advantage of our regular terms of 2/10, n/30 on future orders. If you will fill in and return the enclosed form, we will be glad to consider your credit application.

It's a pleasure to serve you, and we hope we shall have the privilege often.

Follow these suggestions when you reply to an order that is promptly filled.

1. *Get off to a good start.* Identify the order and give complete information about your handling of it. In the first paragraph, tell the customer when the article or articles should be received (or when they were sent)—

and remember that you send merchandise, *not* an order. Often you can identify the order by date, by number, or by a concise description of the article (for small orders). If the order includes more than one item, you may refer to an enclosed invoice covering the order; or you may itemize the order.

2. *Make the message clear and easily understood.* Use simple, direct language.

3. *Build goodwill.* Use a sincere and friendly tone. Assure the customer that you are handling the order promptly and efficiently. Express appreciation for the order. Show genuine interest in the customer and a desire to serve.

4. *Make the letter look inviting.* An attractive letter reflects the pride a company takes in everything it does. To project the best image of your company and of yourself, be careful to carry out this suggestion in all the letters you write.

Replying to an Order When Delivery Is Delayed

Even though it cannot fill all orders immediately, the farsighted company continues to acknowledge each order the same day it is received. Why?

Prompt and friendly acknowledgment of an order is even more important when delivery is delayed. The customer wants the merchandise and will be disappointed not to receive it soon. But disappointment most likely will become irritation if the customer has to wait and wait without hearing anything about the order.

When an order cannot be filled promptly, write the customer immediately to tell him or her when the merchandise should arrive and to explain the reason for the delay in shipment. The letter assures the customer that his or her order is important and that the company is doing everything it can to fill the order as soon as possible.

Notice how the basic elements of a successful acknowledgment are incorporated in the following reply to an order on which delivery is delayed.

Your choice of a Garnet sewing machine is one that many seamstresses are making. In fact, our sales of these sewing machines are at an all-time high.

But we've refused to compromise on quality to get increased production. That wouldn't be fair to you. We are insisting that the factory reject any sewing machine that does not automatically produce perfectly interlaced stitches.

Frankly, few sewing machine manufacturers meet this requirement, and our supplier is learning new ways of quality control and careful craftsmanship. Production is increasing daily, and we can promise you that your Garnet sewing machine will be shipped to you by August 11—sooner if possible. We'll hold your check for payment in full until we make shipment.

When you begin to sew on your Garnet sewing machine, you'll be proud to own for a lifetime this high-quality, precision sewing machine.

When you reply to an order on which delivery is delayed, follow these suggestions:

1. *Use an indirect approach that is pleasant and positive.* Start with a compliment or some point on which you and the customer can agree.

A negative opening, such as "We regret that we cannot fill your order at present," might put the reader in a gloomy mood for the rest of the letter. Saying something favorable about the merchandise in the opening paragraph is a good idea, because it represents the first step in persuading the customer that the product is worth waiting for.

2. *Give a specific reason for the delay and assure the customer that you will fill the order as soon as you can.* Don't write a general statement like "Our stock is temporarily depleted." The customer will have more confidence in your promise of quick service on future orders if you tell *why* your stock is low. The customer must not think these delays are usual.

3. *Express appreciation for the order (and the payment, if one was sent) and tell the customer when he or she can expect delivery.* By giving the customer the information he or she wants, you demonstrate your interest and desire to be of service.

4. *Close with a reminder of some good points of the merchandise.* By reselling the merchandise, you remind the customer that delivery is worth waiting for.

Replying to an Order That Is Incomplete or Not Clear

Even though most companies include order coupons in their advertisements and order blanks in their catalogs, some customers omit important information from their orders. Consequently, you may occasionally need to write to a customer to get "more information." This additional correspondence means, of course, a delay in shipment. And the letter unavoidably calls the customer's attention to the fact that he or she failed to send in a complete order. Thus the whole situation presents possibilities for bad relations with the customer or for a cancellation of the order.

Here's a letter which was sent to a customer who ordered six spoons (metal fishing lures) and 300 yards of 10-pound test monofilament fishing line but neglected to specify the color he wanted—clear, sea blue, or sand. Note that the letter uses an indirect approach to minimize the unpleasant aspects of the situation and subordinates the request for additional information to avoid emphasizing the customer's mistake. This letter did its job well: It saved the order.

The six Bass Spoons you ordered are among our best buys this season. They must catch fish or we wouldn't be sending so many out—even though the price is surprisingly low!

The new "Invisible" monofilament line you ordered is another popular item. It comes in Clear, Sea Blue, and Sand colors.

_____ Clear is the best general-purpose color.

_____ Sea Blue is for use in clear lakes and streams, especially on sunny days.

_____ Sand is for cloudy water and cloudy days. It's good for fishing in lakes and streams with light bottoms.

If you will check the color you want and return this letter to us, Mr. Borg, we'll get your 300 yards of 10-pound test line and your 6 Bass Spoons off to you the same day we hear from you.

We have fished with the new Invisible line ourselves—and it really does seem to disappear when it goes under the surface of the water! It's just what the doctor ordered for those days when the fish can see everything and you can't seem to get them to take a lure. Put one of your new Bass Spoons on the end of some of this line, and you'll have an unbeatable combination.

Follow these suggestions when you reply to an order that is incomplete or not clear.

1. *Start pleasantly.* Offset the customer's disappointment over the delay caused by his or her oversight. A pleasant opening acts as a buffer against the bad news that the customer must send more information before you can fill the order.

2. *Give the customer any help you can in making the decision, and avoid suggesting that he or she was careless.* Your job is to find out what you need to know to fill the order to the customer's satisfaction, not to blame anyone for anything.

3. *Tell the customer exactly how to send the information needed, and make it easy for him or her to send it.* A reply card or a return envelope often helps you get an answer.

4. *Close with a favorable comment about your merchandise or your service.* Make the customer feel that it is worthwhile to answer and to wait for delivery.

Companies, too, can send incomplete orders. But companies keep correspondence in files. This means that if you send a customer a letter asking for information he or she neglected to include in an order, the customer will reply and then put your letter in the files. And every time the customer handles that file folder, he or she may see your letter—and be reminded of his or her mistake!

The best thing is to get your letter back. Since the customer has to send you the necessary information, why not have him or her do it on your letter? That's what the writer above did, by having the customer check the color he wanted. Though it wasn't mentioned, a stamped, addressed envelope was furnished to make it quick and easy for the reader to answer.

This technique gets the needed information, retrieves a "bad news" letter from the reader's files, and makes it easy for him or her to answer.

Writing Form Replies to Orders

Many routine and special acknowledgments can be handled satisfactorily with form letters or cards.

A form letter may serve as a "cover letter" for an attachment that describes the order. The form letter is not addressed, it is printed in quantity, and it is used for many customers. Generally, such form letters thank the customer for the order, say what a pleasure it is to serve him or her, and then refer the customer to the attachment for specific information. The attachment may be a computer-printed description of the order plus the expected date of shipment and the method of shipping. Or, to simplify matters, the attachment may merely give the customer's order number and follow with shipping information.

When you do not have the exact item a customer has ordered, you may send a form message to the customer, with a clipping about the substitute item. The form acknowledgment shown in the left-hand column is part of a wraparound to hold the enclosed clipping; the back page of the form is the order blank mentioned in the message.

Such impersonal acknowledgments of orders are suitable for large companies doing considerable volumes of business and for inexpensive items. They are not used by yacht brokers and locomotive manufacturers, however!

Acknowledgment copies of orders received are common among companies doing business with other companies, but not with those selling to consumers. When an order is processed, the seller must type an invoice or a bill sooner or later. If it is done sooner, one extra copy can be made, marked "Acknowledgment— This Is Not an Invoice" or something of the sort. The acknowledgment copy is sent to the customer immediately. When the customer receives it, he or she knows not only that the seller has the order and is working on it but also how much is due and what the terms are. Often, the shipping date is shown too.

Acknowledgment cards with "filled-in" descriptions are particularly favored by large companies doing business with customers by mail, such as catalog houses and large department stores. Cards may be simply printed general acknowledgments sent to all customers; but most firms use printed form cards with space provided to write in the order or a description of it and the expected date of shipment, such as the card shown below. The card can be filled in and mailed quickly.

The description of the customer's order is written in the top space and the expected date of shipment in the bottom space.

LOWENSTEIN'S

THANK YOU FOR YOUR INQUIRY...

We have something similar to what you are looking for—a picture and a description of it are enclosed.

Also enclosed are an order form and a return envelope that will make it easy for you to let us know your decision.

LOWENSTEIN'S money-back guarantee insures your satisfaction.

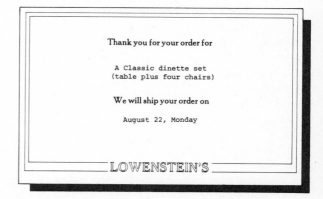

Thank you for your order for

A Classic dinette set
(table plus four chairs)

We will ship your order on

August 22, Monday

LOWENSTEIN'S

There is nothing wrong with a form acknowledgment so long as it reflects the same care in its preparation that the company is giving to filling the order. A poorly printed or mimeographed card can give the customer the impression that you are going to be as sloppy with his or her order. The cold, formal acknowledgment can make you seem cold, formal, and uncaring. You can use form acknowledgments successfully if you remember that no matter how many orders you get each day, every order is unique to the customer who sent it.

ASSIGNMENT: Sections B and C of the Worksheet give you practice in planning, writing, and typing replies to orders.

Writing Goodwill Letters

Most business letters have two purposes:

1. To do a specific job—make a sale, ask or give information, collect an account, transmit literature, etc.

2. To build goodwill.

As you learned in Unit 9, all letters should try to build and maintain goodwill. But we call "goodwill letters" those that have *only* one purpose: to promote a friendly feeling between the reader and the company. Goodwill letters are special because they are letters that *do not have to be written* (but should be). If such letters were not sent, no material change in the situation would result. But when someone takes the trouble to send a goodwill letter, valuable improvements in human relations result.

What is goodwill? A precise answer is difficult, for goodwill never reveals itself directly but only secondarily in terms of sales or other tangible results. Goodwill means the favorable attitude and feeling that people have toward a company. Basically, people feel that an organization is interested in them or is not interested in them. When they feel that the organization is interested in them, respects them, and considers their welfare important, then that organization has their "goodwill."

Goodwill messages are effective in all aspects of a company's business relationships. Progressive business

people realize that they can transact business without the personal touch of goodwill letters but that they cannot build good human relations without it. Goodwill letters to employees and other associates make the company's work go more smoothly. Goodwill letters to customers show interest—and that is the best way to keep customers. About two-thirds of all customers who stop buying at a department store drift away because of the store's indifference.

Those who receive goodwill letters from business firms appreciate them especially because they are unexpected. Business people seldom take time to write letters they don't have to write. So when they do, these people and the firms they represent are remembered as firms interested in people. And this kind of reputation pays off in more satisfied employees and customers and in more sales and profits.

Typical goodwill letters include:

Letters to say thanks.

Letters of congratulations.

Letters that announce, invite, or welcome.

Letters that maintain or reactivate business.

Letters that express get-well wishes or sympathy.

The letters in all five groups share one purpose: to gain the reader's goodwill by showing interest in the reader. They also share these characteristics: reader approval, friendliness, naturalness, enthusiasm, and sincerity. Of these, perhaps sincerity is the most important. To the reader, a goodwill letter that does not sound sincere becomes only lip service.

The goodwill letter you write will probably be successful when you can answer "yes" to the following:

1. If you were the reader, would you honestly like to receive this letter? A goodwill letter hits the target only when it strikes a welcoming response.

2. Will the reader feel that you *enjoyed* writing the letter and that you *mean* everything you wrote? If the reader detects a gushy, bored, or indifferent note, he or she may doubt your sincerity and interest.

3. Did you keep the spotlight on the reader? To make the reader feel important, put your company and yourself in the background and convince the reader you wrote the letter *just for him or her.*

4. Did you omit specific sales material? The reader will feel let down if your personal good wishes are only a prelude to a sales pitch.

Here is a quick-check reminder of the principles you should emphasize in writing a goodwill letter:

• Write sincerely and enthusiastically.

• Make the reader feel important.

• Keep the message as natural and friendly as a person-to-person chat.

WRITING THANK-YOU LETTERS

Just as you can find many occasions for writing personal thank-you messages, in business you will find many opportunities for writing thank-you letters to build goodwill.

Letters of appreciation are often sent:

1. To a new customer for a first order.

2. To an established customer for a particularly large order, or for the payment of an overdue bill, or for the last installment of a special-account purchase.

3. To an individual or an organization that responds to a special appeal, completes a spectacular job, or makes a suggestion that proves worthwhile to his or her company.

Occasionally (it should happen much more often) such letters are also sent:

4. To customers who order regularly and pay their bills as they come due.

5. To employees who do their work well but unspectacularly.

6. To individuals and organizations who cooperate on the everyday jobs but get little attention.

Anniversaries and holidays are also occasions for sending thank-you messages. Even though the new year's greeting from 24 Karat Jewelers was printed, the warm tone comes through.

24 **K**ARAT JEWELERS
1365 Chatham Road, Springfield, Massachusetts 01106,
Tel. (413) 555-3500

December 28, 19——

Dear Friend:

As the new year begins, 24 Karat Jewelers thanks you for your friendship and for the business you have given us during the past year.

The expansion of our store will be completed in a few weeks. We can then offer you the largest selection of fine jewelry in the city.

During the coming year we will do our best to serve you in every way.

We hope that the new year will be a happy and successful year for you.

Cordially,

Jason P. Buzanne

Jason P. Buzanne

JPB/mtb

Note the warm tone in this thank-you letter from 24 Karat Jewelers.

The following letter was written by a professor who wanted to encourage professional relations with the department members at another college.

I enjoyed visiting your campus and attending your excellent conference last weekend. That was my first visit in Georgia, and I was impressed! I got to know several "Georgians," and their congeniality reminded me of the people "back home in Arkansas!"

The small-group session on typewriting was especially helpful to me, since I teach intermediate and advanced typewriting. And Dr. Glover's workshop on trends in business education was very worthwhile. I am enrolled in a graduate course called "Issues and Trends in Business Education" this semester, so I was able to share several ideas with my class after the conference.

Thank you, Dr. Woodall, for inviting me to be a part of the conference, and please thank the other members of your faculty for making me feel welcome and for helping to make your conference very successful.

Have you ever worked as a salesclerk during the Christmas rush? If so, you can understand how pleased Bob O'Neill was to receive this letter of appreciation when he completed his temporary job. It was signed by the president of the company.

Thank you, Bob, for a job well done during your service with Fairmont's this past Christmas season.

Your enthusiastic cooperation has been an important factor in making this Christmas successful not only for the many customers who rely upon Fairmont's to help them play Santa, but also for the store.

Although your temporary employment with Fairmont's has ended, I hope that we may benefit from your services in the future. Please drop in at our Personnel Office at any time . . . you are always welcome.

You have already studied several letters of appreciation. An example of a letter that did not *have* to be written is the acknowledgment of an order for Decorator's wall coverings (page 74).

The company might have sent the merchandise without explanation but preferred to show interest in the customer by writing a thank-you letter. The letter was an unexpected goodwill gesture. The customer was probably surprised as well as pleased to receive the friendly message.

Suppliers and others are often sent letters of appreciation whenever they give exceptional service. The following is typical.

You really give your customers service, Mr. Steffen!

We were just about out of 10-quart SuperBags for our Brock vacuum cleaners when you arrived—in person and on a Saturday—with an emergency delivery for us. Because you did a "little more than was expected," many Brock customers will have their SuperBags earlier.

We appreciate such special cooperation. You confirm what we suspected: we're dealing with a company that *cares* about its customers.

Many companies use routine customer cooperation as an occasion to send a goodwill letter, as illustrated in the following letter to a new customer who has just made the final payment on a special 90-day account. The credit manager did not *have* to acknowledge the payment, which Mrs. Greene made on a visit to the store, but he showed interest and built goodwill by writing.

You took care of your special account in topnotch form! We appreciate the check for $98.50 that enables us to write "Paid in Full" and "Thank You."

Customers like you have made possible our growth and success during the past 49 years and will determine our future progress.

Of course, you are welcome to call on our credit department and other service departments whenever we can help. Won't you do this—any time and often, Mrs. Greene?

WRITING LETTERS OF CONGRATULATION

A message of congratulation or commendation is much like a message of appreciation. Each recognizes and expresses interest in a worthwhile achievement. A letter of appreciation says "thank you" and implies "well done"; a congratulatory letter says "well done" and implies "thank you." Read the sample congratulatory letter on page 80.

When your friends celebrate special events or receive honors, you like to congratulate them. In the same way, business people see opportunities for congratulatory letters on such occasions as anniversaries, graduations, births, marriages, new businesses or homes, promotions, elections, and various awards and rewards.

For instance, this brief congratulatory note was sent to an executive who recently became president of the company:

Congratulations on your recent promotion to president of the Wharter Company. I am sure that the business will grow and prosper under your capable leadership.

And notice the encouragement in the following letter sent to a new insurance agent who has just made her first sale.

When a new agent makes that first sale, it's important news. That's why I got a real kick when Bill Lowrie reported yours.

You've cleared the biggest hurdle. You've enjoyed the thrill every salesperson knows—the feeling of real accomplishment. You're off to a great start, and nothing can stop you now.

I expect to see you in Hartford next April for the Home Office Career School. Until then, here's to many "repeat performances" for you!

You should distinguish between goodwill messages and sales letters in which congratulations are used as an attention-getting gimmick for sales promotion. Emphasis is on goodwill when a leading dairy sends a beautiful baby diary to new parents and attaches this message: "Congratulations to the proud parents from Peerless Milk Service—the dairy that delivers the most delicious and most wholesome milk and milk products in town!" But on the other hand, emphasis is on sales promotion when a retail store sends the parents a letter that begins "Our sincerest congratulations on the new arrival in your home" and then plunges into specific sales talk about strollers or baby foods.

Certainly the architect who received the following sales message was not fooled into thinking it was a sincere, personal message simply because it began with:

Congratulations on being selected as architect for the new Post Office in Pittsburgh!

You, as chief architect, will be interested in specifying material that will be permanent and still economical. We assure you that CRANFORD'S pipe and plumbing supplies have both these qualities.

A letter like this one is unadulterated sales promotion with a gimmick opening and is not likely to build

---

BRADFORD SHIPPING COMPANY

516 Emerald Parkway
Tulsa, Oklahoma
74120

Tel. 918-237-9692

January 4, 19--

Ms. Alma Ribelow
Senior Vice President
Allied Oil, Inc.
One Allied Plaza
Tulsa, Oklahoma 74115

Dear Ms. Ribelow:

Congratulations on your being named to the Governor's Task Force to Study Equal Opportunities in Business, Industry, and Government. I was very pleased to read that Governor Poole has chosen you as one of the ten executives for this task force.

If anyone at Bradford Shipping could be helpful to you and to the other members of the task force, please do let me know. We should be delighted to be of service.

Sincerely,

Kenneth E. Quentin

Kenneth E. Quentin
Vice President
Personnel

The writer expresses the best wishes of his entire company in this congratulatory letter.

goodwill. A company's goodwill message should focus attention on the occasion that inspires it. If the writer seems more interested in his or her company than in the important event in the reader's life, the one who receives the letter naturally feels tricked.

Remember that when you write a letter on your company's letterhead, it is your company talking as well as you. Perhaps saying it is your company talking *through* you would be more accurate. Thus, when you write a congratulatory message on your company's letterhead, whatever good feeling is aroused in the reader's mind will be for your company as well as for you personally. Your company will be remembered (because you used its letterhead); don't spoil the good impression with an unnecessary sales pitch.

WRITING LETTERS THAT ANNOUNCE, INVITE, OR WELCOME

Goodwill announcements and invitations include:

1. Announcements of a new business, a new location, or an expansion or a reorganization of facilities. These usually include an invitation to visit.

2. Announcements of the appointment of a new company official or a new company representative.

3. Announcements of a new service or policy, often inviting the reader to use it. For instance, a store announces that it will be open an extra evening each

---

CAMTRO INDUSTRIES

1212 Elm Street
Dayton, Ohio 45426
Tel. 513-288-4562   **Office of the President**

September 19, 19--

Dear Karen:

   Welcome to CAMTRO INDUSTRIES! Beginning today, CAMTRO is
your company . . . a company made up of friendly people who are
willing and eager to help you with your new job. You are important to us both as an individual and as a member of a great team.

   To answer some of the questions you may have about your new
job and your new company, I have enclosed a copy of Camtro and
You, which will introduce you to the management team and tell
you about employee programs and benefits and various company
activities.

   As an employee of CAMTRO INDUSTRIES, you will have the opportunity to use your ability and initiative. You--and your work--
are important to the company and to our customers. I hope you
will find satisfaction and happiness in your work with us.

                              Sincerely yours,

                              Douglas A. Campbell

                              Douglas A. Campbell
                              President

DAC:bjc
Enclosure

A letter welcoming new employees helps foster their sense of "belonging" to the organization.

week; or a bank announces a new direct deposit plan, as in the example below.

As an employee of Louisiana State University, you can now have your paycheck deposited into your checking account automatically.

Arrangements have been made with Louisiana State University and First Bank of Louisiana to set up a direct deposit plan.

The plan is confidential and very convenient, because it deposits your paycheck directly into your checking account every payday. Of course, you'll still receive your paycheck stubs—even when you're away from school or out of town.

To make your paycheck deposits automatic, simply complete and sign the authorization card and return it in the enclosed reply envelope. That's it. We'll see that the university accounting office gets the card.

Welcoming letters are written for many occasions. These messages may be morale builders;* they may welcome new employees. Usually, they have a definite sales cast, such as letters welcoming new residents of the community, new subscribers, new or inactive charge account customers, and new dealers. These messages discuss company services and products and invite readers to visit but avoid specific sales promotion.

Letters welcoming new residents of a community can benefit both the receiver and the sender. Many retail stores and service firms use them regularly to build goodwill and gain new customers. A typical letter begins with a statement of welcome, comments favorably on the newcomer's choice of a place to live, mentions what the firm has to offer, and perhaps even includes an inducement such as a special discount to encourage the customer to come into the store.

New employees, too, may receive a cordial welcoming letter on their first day with the company. See, for example, the letter on page 81.

WRITING LETTERS THAT MAINTAIN OR REACTIVATE BUSINESS

Letters that follow up on customer response to products and services build goodwill because they show the company's interest in customers' reactions and its desire to improve its products and services. Such letters are often sent to customers whose accounts have been inactive for a long time. In this way, the company tries to find out why former customers are no longer using their charge cards—whether some failure on its part is

---

McALPIN APPLIANCE CO.

Dear Customer:

Our shipping department reports that your recent purchase has been delivered.

So that we may know whether you are pleased with your purchase or whether the merchandise needs further service or adjustment, please fill out and mail the attached card.

We appreciate your business and want to do everything we can to make sure that you enjoy shopping at our store and that you are satisfied with your purchases.

Sincerely,

Ashlea Wilson

Ashlea Wilson
Customer Service Dept.

	YES	NO
Was your visit to our store pleasant?	☐	☐
Was the sales representative helpful?	☐	☐
Did the delivery truck arrive on schedule?	☐	☐
Were delivery persons careful?	☐	☐
Did they place or install your appliance as you requested?	☐	☐

If you have suggestions for ways we can improve our service, please write them below.

_____
_____
_____
_____
_____
_____
_____

McAlpin shows its service attitude and helps to maintain its business by sending a follow-up questionnaire.

responsible for lost business. The company makes it easy to return the questionnaire by enclosing a postage-paid envelope. Or it may try to persuade customers to start using their charge cards again by reminding customers of the benefits and offering a free gift.

Occasionally a company will send out a checking letter to follow up a major delivery. Notice the service attitude expressed by the appliance company that sent the message on page 82. The double postal card makes the questionnaire easy to return.

WRITING GET-WELL WISHES OR SYMPATHY LETTERS

When someone you know, either as a personal friend or a business acquaintance, is ill, a letter from you will be appreciated. Gauge the seriousness of your tone by how sick the reader is. If the illness is not serious and there is no doubt about the recovery, you can send a humorous get-well card or a cheerful, happy letter. If the illness is serious or the person is getting over a major operation, then send a more subdued letter. That person will not be in a mood for jokes!

When you write to someone ill, be optimistic. Mention once at the beginning how sorry you are that the person is ill. From then on talk about his or her return to normal life, as the following letter did.

We were sorry to hear that you're in the hospital and hope that with rest and care you'll be up and about again soon.

Meanwhile, if there's anything we can do for you in a business way, just let us know. We wish you a speedy recovery and a quick return to the office.

Letters expressing sympathy or condolences are often the hardest letter-writing tasks. Because no other writing situations have as many negative aspects, people seldom write letters of sympathy and therefore get little practice in handling them.

The usual occasions for sympathy letters are death, serious illness, and business misfortunes (fire, robbery, etc.).

Letters of sympathy should be short because the more you write, the more you dwell on the reason for the letter, and the more you remind the reader of the loss or trouble. You don't want to be curt (and so seem unfeeling), but you should be concise.

You will be wise to limit your letters of sympathy to two paragraphs. The first paragraph expresses sympathy. The second paragraph is a calm and optimistic look toward the future. Here is an example.

We were all saddened to learn of the death of your president, Mr. James Mullens. We have enjoyed a close and pleasant business relationship with him for many years. Few banking executives earned greater respect and admiration.

But we know that his memory will be with you through this difficult period of adjustment and that it will be a comfort to you in the years ahead.

Notice how hard it would be to add another paragraph to the letter without being morbid.

Note one other thing. The letter uses the word *death*. The more you use euphemisms to avoid *die* and *death* and the dead person's name, the more you will string out your talk of the death, and the longer you will dwell on the reason for grief.

Letters of sympathy for business trouble should be handled much like any other letter of sympathy. Keep them short. In the first paragraph express your sympathy for the reader's misfortune. Be specific about what you can do. Then, if you have not done so already, look forward to a return to normalcy.

I was very concerned this morning as I was driving to work and heard over the car radio about the fire at your plant. For you at this season of the year, it is especially serious.

Can we help? We have some unused desks, typewriters, and offices that we can make available to you. If you would like to send some of your people over, they're welcome to work here as long as they need to. Call me and I'll set it up.

Meanwhile, I know you'll be busy with your plans to rebuild. I'm sure all your fellow members of the Chamber of Commerce can be counted on to help.

ASSIGNMENT: The problems in the Worksheet for this unit cover various goodwill letters that you may write.

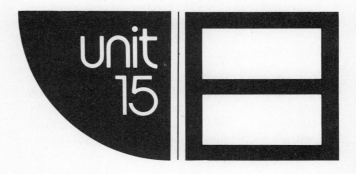

Writing Sales Letters

Sales letters have been an effective selling tool for many years—and for good reason. The cost of producing and mailing a large quantity of sales letters is often less than the cost of producing a radio or television commercial and buying time for it (or the cost of producing and buying space for a newspaper or magazine ad). Moreover, direct mail offers selectivity: the seller may select a mailing list according to the profession, geographic area, income, interests, and so on, of the people on the list. By selecting the mailing lists carefully, the seller is virtually assured of reaching a certain number of "qualified" prospects.

Direct mail sales letters do, however, have certain drawbacks. Because many people look upon all direct mail as "junk" mail, a sales letter may be discarded before it is read, even though it is well written and makes a spectacular offer. In addition, even a "successful" sales letter will usually draw a positive response from no more than 5 percent of the total number of people receiving the mailing.

Letters written specifically for direct-mail selling are not the only sales letters. The writer who acknowledges receipt of a large order will write a thank-you letter that will also resell the customer. The writer who introduces a new sales representative to a customer is preparing the way for that representative to call for an order. And the writer who tries to convince his or her boss to approve a project or an expense must sell the boss on the reasons why it should be approved. Therefore, every business writer must keep in mind these principles of writing sales letters:

1. *Know your products and services,* their advantages and disadvantages, why they appeal or should appeal to people—in fact, know as much as you can about them.

2. *Know your potential customers,* who they are, where they are, what their needs are, how to get through to them—in short, know everything you can about them.

3. *Know how sales are made,* what motivates people to buy, what appeals are likely to prove successful, how to get people to act.

4. *Remember the basics of effective writing,* especially in persuasive messages, and practice the techniques of clear communication that you have learned from this book and elsewhere.

You already know many of the things you need to know to write sales letters, and you will learn more from this unit as you look at sales letters that ask for an order. After you have completed this unit, you should continue to apply the techniques of sales writing as you pursue your occupation.

PLANNING SALES LETTERS

Before someone can sit down and begin actually drafting the letter, he or she must take six important steps. Until this initial planning is completed, it is virtually impossible to write an effective sales letter.

1. *Prepare a list of prospects.* First, you need a good mailing list. The obvious place to start is your company's own list of customers. This provides the nucleus of the mailing list for the letter. You can also buy lists from companies that specialize in compiling lists of names and selling them. For sales effectiveness, a good mailing list must contain the correct names and addresses of people or companies with common characteristics that make them a group of likely prospects for your product or service.

2. *Analyze the prospects in terms of the product.* Identify the characteristics that describe the most likely prospects for your product or service. From research and/or experience, build a "composite" prospect, someone who truly represents those on the prospect list. The sex, age, occupation, geographic location, financial situation, etc., of the "average" prospect determine what appeals will be used in the letter. The answers to these and many other questions help you discover the needs and desires of the prospective buyers.

You wouldn't, for example, try to sell a "Sixty-Five Plus" insurance plan to college students. Nor would you try to sell homeowners' insurance to apartment dwellers.

3. *Analyze the product in terms of the prospects.* What specific feature of the product or service makes it attractive or useful or appealing? What features should be emphasized? What features should be played down? (These analyses are usually made along with step 2.) Letters that present a product in terms of what prospective buyers think of it and how they can use it do more than make sales—they win satisfied customers.

4. *Decide on the Central Selling Point (CSP).* The central selling point should be the item of information that will help the prospect most in reaching a decision about buying. After analyzing the prospects and the product, build your letter around this central selling point. The CSP could be appearance, durability, comfort, convenience, price, or any other positive feature that you think would have the greatest influence on the reader.

5. *Make a plan for the letter.* The standard formula for any sales presentation is AIDA—Attention, Interest, Desire, Action. By promising a benefit, try first to get the prospect to read the letter. Then arouse interest by helping the prospect to imagine himself or herself successfully using the product or service. Next, try to convince him or her to desire it, to buy it. Finally, attempt to get the reader to act, to send in an order and a check. You will find, however, that many good sales letters do not follow a set pattern. Do not let the formula dictate the letter, but rather link the product with the prospects' needs and give sufficient factual information so that he or she can make an intelligent decision about buying.

6. *Build the CSP into the beginning of the letter.* To get the letter off to a fast start and to get the prospect

reading, the CSP and the promise of a benefit to the buyer should be woven together at the beginning, preferably in a headline or in the first sentence. (A headline is a statement set up in inside-address fashion to replace the inside address and the salutation—see the letter from GEICO, below. The beginning of a sales letter is critical. If the prospect doesn't read the letter, no matter how good the offer is, no sale will result.

WRITING SALES LETTERS TO CUSTOMERS

After you have planned the letter, follow these suggestions when you actually write a sales letter.

1. *Get the reader's attention and interest in the opening sentences.* The purpose of your message is to give the reader information he or she needs to buy and use your product or service. The reader must be listening—but won't be unless your letter captures the reader's attention and interest by telling him or her how to get something he or she wants.

Often you can capture the reader's attention *(a)* by arranging the first sentence as a headline—perhaps in all capitals or in color—or as a faked address block; *(b)* by presenting a humorous cartoon or striking color display; or *(c)* by attaching a simple gadget such as a coin, stamp, piece of string, or button. But some tricky openings are like the bang of a door. The noise gets attention, but the attention doesn't last unless the

(A capital stock company not affiliated with the U.S. Government)

GOVERNMENT EMPLOYEES LIFE INSURANCE COMPANY
WASHINGTON, D.C. 20076

THOMAS R. HEFNER, President

*Look at life insurance
the same way you look at
auto insurance!*

Consider the risk of driving a car without liability insurance. One serious accident could bankrupt your family. In fact, auto liability insurance is so important that in many states it is illegal to drive without it.

Living without life insurance can be risky for your family too. A serious accident or sudden illness could take your life—and with it your family's income. There's no law that says you must buy life insurance. Maybe there should be. If death takes your life, who will make the mortgage or rent payments? Where will the cash come from to pay college tuition costs? And, where will the money come from for groceries and clothing?

The enclosed folder describes life insurance plans that can provide the money to pay rent or mortgage...provide an income for food and clothing and make cash available for the education of your children. The folder also gives you an idea of how life insurance can do more than just protect your family. You'll see how some policies build guaranteed cash values...money you can use as an emergency fund to meet unexpected cash demands, pay college tuition expenses, or enhance your retirement income. In addition, you'll find out about GEICO Life's affordable rates, premium discounts, and other money saving features.

Mail the enclosed postage-paid card and we'll send you complete information and rates for the policies that interest you. Of course, there's no obligation on your part. We think we can provide you with the right policy, in an appropriate amount, at a premium you can well afford. Let us prove it! Drop the enclosed inquiry card in the mail today.

Sincerely,

T. R. HEFNER
President

Courtesy GEICO

Because the beginning of a sales letter is critical, GEICO uses a special headline to get the letter off to a fast start and to get the prospect reading.

person who hears the noise is interested in finding out why the door banged.

If you use an attention-getting device, be sure it leads right into the heart of the message. For instance, the cartoon may be a pictorial presentation of the Central Selling Point of the letter and the stamp may be introduced as "the postage needed to send for a Passport to Adventure." Remember, any unusual opening device should not call attention to itself; it should always point *toward the reader benefits you stress in the letter.*

Among sales-letter openings with sufficient "you appeal" to capture the reader's *interest*—not merely attention—these types are popular:

An answer to a problem, need, or desire of the reader. Almost all successful sales-letter openings are variations of this basic opening. It is usually a winner, because all of us are interested in finding answers to our problems. It is also a natural opening, because the answer offered is always the use of the product or service advertised.

A brochure featuring a picture of an electric clock set was enclosed with a sales letter that began:

> You can have this electric clock decorator wall ensemble without paying one cent of your own money!
>
> What room in your home could use this touch of elegance *plus* accurate electric timekeeping? In any room, its antique gold and white finish and ornately carved design will lend decorative drama. The swag ropes accent the gold and antique white finish for an added decorator touch.

A letter introducing a vacuum cleaner began:

> You can double your cleaning power *free* for 15 days with America's most advanced vacuum cleaner! We'll include a year's supply of bags *plus a valuable mystery gift free!*
>
> Want to revolutionize your cleaning methods? It's easy— with the amazing new...

An unusual headline, news item, or statement of fact. An obvious statement, like "spring is just around the corner," or "school will be starting again in a few weeks," lacks imagination and attracts no attention or interest, because the reader accepts it without questioning. But an unusual headline, news item, or statement of fact usually leads the prospect to read on to discover why it is true or how it applies.

> Every issue in government and politics has three sides— the *pro* side, the *con* side, and the *inside.*
> GOVERNMENT JOURNAL gives you *all* sides.

> ATTENTION: PEOPLE WITH SUBSTANTIAL MONIES IN SAVINGS ACCOUNTS, CERTIFICATES OF DEPOSIT, ETC.

> U R G E N T R E M I N D E R:
> The deadline is 12:01 a.m.

A thought-provoking question. A question with an obvious "yes" or "no" answer—like "Could you use more income?" or "Do you like people to laugh at you behind your back?"—is usually boring. But a question that challenges the reader to do some thinking is an excellent way to arouse interest in a message. Often, a question is better than a statement because it gives the reader a share in the idea. Instead of telling the reader, you ask him or her to think about it. And in answering, the reader may sell himself or herself on your idea. Naturally the idea, the answer to the question, involves the use of the product or service you are selling.

> MORE INFLATION AHEAD...
> WHAT CAN *YOU* DO ABOUT IT?

> WOULD YOU BE INTERESTED IN A MORTGAGE POLICY THAT PAYS OFF WHETHER YOU LIVE OR DIE??

> Most policies will, of course, pay off the remaining mortgage on your home if you die...but what if you live?

A clever quip or an adaptation of a familiar saying. A clever phrase, a play on words, or the quotation of a familiar saying usually gets attention. It has particular appeal if the interpretation suggests disagreement with an accepted idea. But clever opening sentences build interest only if they are closely related to the central selling point of the letter.

FROM A HART DRUG CORPORATION LETTER ABOUT COLD MEDICINES:
A HART TO HEART TALK
    ABOUT A COLD PROPOSITION

ON A LETTERHEAD IN WHICH THE COMPANY NAME—DARTNELL—APPEARS AS SKYWRITING:
Skywriting soon disappears...but withholding tax is here to stay.

An anecdote, a fable, or a parable. A story opening—if the story is a good one—usually arouses interest. It is effective as a sales letter opening if it is appropriate to the central selling point of the letter and doesn't overshadow the message itself. A story that seems to be dragged in by the tail obviously defeats its own purpose.

> As a youngster, did you ever toss a stone over a cliff or down a very deep well—then wait and wait to hear it land?
>
> We tossed a stone down your well, in the form of a quotation on the 14th of March, and it hasn't landed yet.

2. *Keep the message interesting and informative.* Skillfully build up the interest your opening sentences arouse. A sales letter that drags in even one paragraph usually means one more letter in a wastebasket. To keep the reader interested, use a language and style that is easy to understand and that can be applied to the reader's own situation. Your letter about a product or service succeeds when it leads the reader to say: "I didn't know this product (or service) would do that for me. I want (or need) it."

3. *Plan the message around the reader.* What the reader *thinks* a product or service will do for him or her influences the decision about buying. Often a prospective customer knows little or nothing about the product or service you offer and is not interested in it when he or she starts reading the letter. But the person is interested in self. The reader is on the outside looking in when he or she reads a lifeless description of a product's appearance, use, and durability. Bring the reader into the picture by showing how he or she can enjoy it in a special way or how it can save time, energy, or money.

Your sales letter *holds* the reader's interest if it gives information to help him or her live more happily or do a better job. Specifically, your message may appeal to one or more of the basic wants of people everywhere—such as the desire to be comfortable, healthy, and attractive to others; to have attention, praise, material possessions, relaxation, and enjoyment; to avoid pain, trouble, and criticism; and to protect one's reputation and family.

Your message may stress an appeal to reason, *the rational appeal,* or to desire, *the emotional appeal.* Most successful sales messages combine rational and emotional appeals. People seldom buy something just because they have a logical reason for buying it or just because they desire it. Usually their buying depends upon both reason and desire. You *need* a car for transportation. But you make decisions about style, color and other features on the basis of what you *like.* You buy jewelry or cologne and think you do it because of a sudden *desire* to have them. But don't you usually convince yourself that giving a boost to your morale is a logical *reason* for spending the money?

The important point about any appeal is that it is appropriate and adapted to the reader. Take a look at this excerpt from a sales message to a car owner:

> Every year many friends and acquaintances ask about an easy method of keeping a record of the cost of operating their automobiles and the approximate amount of taxes deductible from income taxes.

This appeal is to the car owner's *need* for the record and the *desire* for an *easy* method of keeping it.

One benefit that your product or service offers prospective buyers usually appeals forcefully to one group of readers. Make this benefit the *Central Selling Point* of a letter. As you develop this leading appeal, back it up with discussion of other benefits that may also appeal to the prospect. Suppose you are selling shoes. In one letter your CSP may be long wear, because you feel the customer is most interested in buying shoes that will last a long time. In developing this theme, you would certainly bring in such factors as good fit and comfort. In another letter your CSP may be style, because you feel the customer is especially interested in shoes that look good. While stressing that the shoes are attractive and

up-to-date, you may mention that they fit well, are comfortable, and keep their fine style and appearance with continued wear. In every letter, center the appeal around the reader's wants.

4. *Be sure your information is accurate and your interest in the reader is sincere.* Concentrate on facts, not opinions or puffery. Misinformation in a sales letter is unethical and can endanger the success of the message. The reader may be fooled by misrepresentation and buy once, but not twice. And most companies depend on *repeat sales* for their profits.

Sincerity in selling includes confidence that the service you offer will be useful, practical, and economical for the buyer. Your sales message will not reflect sincere interest in the reader unless you believe that *when you make a sale you will make a friend.* Remember that making friends is the key to making *repeat* sales.

5. *Forestall objections and procrastination.* Imagine yourself talking with, instead of writing to, the prospective buyer. Think of the reasons that might be given for not buying or for waiting until later to decide. Then answer those objections in your letter *before* the reader has a chance to think of them.

At times the reader may object or hesitate because he or she can't quite accept everything you say the product will do. So you must present *evidence* to back up your statements. Here are three kinds of evidence often used effectively in sales messages.

a. *A vivid picture of the use the reader can make of the product or service.* The most convincing evidence you can use in a sales promotion letter is undoubtedly a picture of the reader getting satisfaction from the thing you are selling. This is basically a problem-solving approach. You recognize a problem that the reader has. You present your product or service as a solution to that problem.

b. *An offer of a sample, a trial use, a money-back guarantee, or a don't-pay-unless-satisfied proposition.* Sometimes you can offer tangible evidence—a free sample or a trial use of the product or service—so that your reader can personally test the claims. Or you may convince the reader that all you say is true by giving a money-back guarantee or suggesting that he or she need not pay unless or until satisfied that the purchase lives up to the promises made for it. Notice how well the writer of the following excerpt from a sales letter understands the importance of evidence.

> Perhaps you are skeptical. It's natural for you to want proof about a sales claim. I want to prove mine by having you try the SAFEGUARD system in your own home without me around to put on any pressure. In short, you be the judge. Either the SAFEGUARD system is good—and will work well—or I get it back.
>
> You don't need to make up your mind now. Just mail the self-mailing card. In a few days the SAFEGUARD system will be there for you to try.

c. *Performance facts and endorsements by users.* Facts based on actual experiences with a product or service or testimonials of people who have tried them offer strong sales support. Both the performance facts and the testimonials are sometimes included in the letters. More often, though, the surveys and tests on which the facts are based, as well as authentic endorsements, are included in leaflets or other literature enclosed with the letters.

You realize, of course, that if your reader puts off until later the decision about buying, enthusiasm for the product may cool off. So, whenever you can, suggest the advantages of *deciding now.* Suppose you are trying to persuade a reader to buy an air conditioner in January. You think of two objections the prospective customer might make to acting promptly. He or she might say, "Why should I buy now—why not wait until summer when I'm ready to use it?" and "I just haven't that much money to spend right now." You wouldn't mention these objections in the letter, of course. But you can offset them before they are made by writing about (1) the reduced January sale price, which will go back to the regular price in February; (2) the prestorage plan, by which the air conditioner can be kept in storage until delivery and installation are requested; and (3) the special credit arrangements offered, so that payments can be spread over several months.

6. *Avoid high-pressure selling and knocking competing products.* Never try to force the reader to buy. Don't even tell the reader he or she needs what you are selling. Most people resent being ordered around. You will usually get better results if you tell what the product or service can do for him or her and then leave the decision of buying to the reader.

7. *Introduce the reader to the enclosure* (if you send one—and you usually do). You can make a brochure or other enclosure an integral part of your sales message if you keep two ideas in mind:

Refer to the enclosure only after you have given the reader sufficient information to interest him or her in reading the rest of the letter before making a decision about buying.

Refer to your enclosure actively by suggesting that the reader observe something interesting about it. "I have attached a reply card" sparks nothing. To spark a desire to do what you ask, say "All you have to do is check off your choices on the enclosed postage-paid reservation certificate, fold, seal, and drop it in the mail."

8. *Talk about price at the best psychological moment, and make the product sound worth the cost.* Naturally, somewhere in your letter you talk about the cost of the item you are selling. Few people decide to buy until they know the cost. If you feel the reader will consider the article a bargain at the price you offer it, stress the price—as good news—by mentioning it near the beginning of the letter. It may even be the Central Selling Point headlined in the opening sentences. But if you think the price may seem high to the reader, talk about

cost toward the end of the letter. Convince the reader that he or she wants the article before mentioning cost. And make the cost seem less by telling the reader at the same time how much he or she is getting for the money. Notice how cost is linked to benefits in these excerpts from next-to-last paragraphs of letters.

Teachers and parents have discovered the tremendous value of *Nature Magazine* in educating youngsters through the fun and reading found only in this fantastic nature-oriented magazine. It's filled with great pictures and stories about other children around the world, science and adventure, games and puzzles—everything a child loves. A gift subscription to *Nature Magazine,* 12 issues a year, is only $9.

Cook with this 21-piece set for 15 days. Fry with it . . . braise with it . . . boil with it. Try your old favorites and take a stab at something new. You're under no obligation. But if you're as delighted as I'm sure you will be . . . keep it—for just $9.63 a month for the next 12 months.

9. *Close with a request for action that is specific, easy, and rewarding to the reader.* The closing paragraph of your letter often is the key to getting the reader to act. He or she may think about buying the article mentioned in the letter but may not do anything about buying it unless the letter tells exactly what to do. Be specific; for instance, *(a)* tell the reader to fill out and send in the enclosed order form; *(b)* ask the reader to come into the store for a demonstration—after you tell where, when and what the demonstration will include; or *(c)* tell the reader he or she can invite a representative to call—after you give the representative's name, phone number, and office hours.

Whenever you can, mention a reason for acting at once. The longer the reader waits before acting on your suggestion, the less likely he or she is to act at all.

Even when the reader is interested in the product advertised and is convinced he or she wants it, a little push for action is usually needed. Your closing paragraph can become the push into action if it *(a)* suggests a specific thing for the reader to do; *(b)* makes it easy to do; and *(c)* gives a reason for doing it promptly.

These closing paragraphs from an effective sales promotion letter use a three-way call for action. Notice how the words in italics *(a)* ask for exact action; *(b)* make action easy; and *(c)* give a reason for acting promptly.

Just *check the enclosed certificate*—it is numbered and registered in your name—slip it into the postage-free reply envelope and drop it into the mail. *If it's inconvenient to include your check now, just charge it.* We'll bill you later.

Remember, this special offer is open for ten days only—and the sooner you subscribe, the better—for once your order is in, continuous service is guaranteed.

The following letter, too, uses a three-way call for action in its closing paragraphs.

Take just a moment to *jot your name on the enclosed prepaid order card, drop it into a convenient mailbox,* and we'll see that your Roll King is on the way in less than a week.

If you care to include a check or money order, we'll pay all express charges. Or, if you prefer, we'll send the Roll King c.o.d. Just check the appropriate box on the order card.

With a Roll King your next round will be the easiest and most enjoyable you have ever played!

Short closing paragraphs often combine the three persuasive elements in one or two sentences.

There's no need to bother with a check at this time—I'll be glad to bill you later—but do avoid missing a single exciting issue of TRAVEL by returning the postpaid card today.

You can't prepare an effective sales letter if you think of the recipients merely as names on a mailing list. Instead write to a group of people who are alike in at least one aspect—their need for your product or service. And the more attributes the members of the group have in common, the easier it is to relate your sales information to the individual reader's interests.

The letter below is a general sales letter about a product that is commonly purchased—a camera.

The IBM sales letter (page 90) was directed to executives, office managers, and purchasing agents. Notice that it is not a high-pressure sales approach but does ask for action in the last paragraph.

the F stop

112 Garvey Boulevard
Los Angeles, California 90024
Tel. 213-674-9292

June 2, 19--

Make The F Stop
Your First Stop . . .

. . . Whenever you need camera or photographic equipment.

Whether you want a highly sophisticated sound movie system
or a simple pocket camera, whether you're an amateur photographer
or a professional,

The F Stop

is for you!

Nikon, Minolta, Canon, Yashica, Hasselblad, Kodak--all these
famous brands and more are available at The F Stop. Every type
of camera, lens, film, and darkroom equipment is in stock at
The F Stop, because we have the largest inventory on the West
Coast.

The enclosed brochure describes some of the many items now on
sale at The F Stop. For an extra discount, just bring this
letter with you and you will get $10 off on any purchase over $30!
(Offer ends July 30.)

Sincerely,

Mario Fermi

Mario Fermi
President

This effective sales letter from The F Stop offers the reader a special discount just for bringing the letter to the store.

WRITING SALES LETTERS TO DEALERS

Before preparing a sales promotion letter to send to a prospective customer, ask yourself: How will this customer use the product or service I want him or her to buy? Then plan your letter to show the reader how, by using your product, he or she can have more fun, do a better job or do it more quickly or easily, or save money.

When the prospective customer is a dealer, you ask the same question. And because your answer is different, you use a somewhat different sales approach in a letter to a dealer than in most of the other sales letters you write.

You can stress two important reader benefits in sales letters to dealers:

1. *Turnover.* Naturally, a retailer is more interested in how much or how many can be sold in a short time than in any other fact about the product. No matter how much potential profit can be made on each item sold, an article is of no value to the dealer so long as it stays on the shelves. A sales letter to a dealer should stress how fast the product will sell and give facts to prove its popularity with customers like the dealer's.

2. *Markup.* After salability of the product, the dealer's next interest is markup, the difference between the price paid for the article and the price at which it is sold. (This is not profit, because there are other selling

```
                                         IBM


International Business Machines Corporation          Parson's Pond Drive
                                                     Franklin Lakes, New Jersey 07417
                                                     201/848-1900



                          September 5, 19--



        Mr. John E. Kaufmann
        Kaufmann and Sons, Inc.
        1319 East Otis Avenue
        Joliet, IL 60436

        Dear Mr. Kaufmann:

        NOW THERE'S AN EVEN BETTER REASON
        TO BUY THE IBM COPIER II . . .

        The compact IBM Copier II has always been responsive to everyday copying
        needs.  It's designed with the entire office in mind ... to give you
        quality copies, throughput speed, simple operation, and easy maintenance.

        And now you have an even better reason for buying an IBM Copier II--the
        new IBM Convenience Collator.  When you need several sets of multipage
        documents, a simple push of a button gives you assembled sets ready for
        distribution.

        Another good reason for considering the IBM Copier II is the pricing
        plan that guarantees a predictable monthly cost with no surprises.  You
        can count on a single, low per-copy cost and a fixed cost ceiling.

        The enclosed brochure tells you more about the features of the new IBM
        Copier II/Convenience Collator.  Please look through it.

        Then, if you'd like more information, just complete the enclosed reply
        card and mail it back in the envelope provided.  I'll have an IBM
        Marketing Representative call you, at your convenience, with full details.


        Sincerely,



        Jack Wirts
        Vice President-Sales

        ds 12
        Enclosure
```

Courtesy IBM

Note how this effective sales letter from IBM asks for action in the last paragraph.

expenses that must be deducted before the dealer makes any profit. But turnover and markup are important factors in determining the profit.) Your sales letter to a dealer should convince him or her that the difference between buying price and selling price is large enough to insure a worthwhile profit.

The opening paragraph of a letter to a dealer, like the opening paragraph of any selling letter, usually gets attention and interest if it tells the reader what the product or service can do for him or her. A successful opening often is a direct comment about the salability of and markup on the product, like the following:

A quick sale and a 60% markup is yours
When a customer spots
TRADITIONAL OFFICE FURNITURE
On your showroom floor!

Adapt the whole letter to the dealer. Talk about the customers' use of the article and the features customers will like. Talk prices and buying in terms of quantity purchases. Stress the ways in which you can help the dealer increase the sale of your products. The dealer aids you suggest often include your national advertising—which brings the customers into the store, asking for the articles advertised; mats for the dealer's newspaper advertising; display materials and suggestions; envelope stuffers, posters, catalogs, and other publicity items.

A variation of the dealer sales letter is seen in the following letter about a promotional package offered by Promotions Unlimited.

How do your customers react to the words "FREE" and "WIN"? The TREASURE CHEST (shown in detail in the enclosed brochure) will appeal to passersby because you offer them the opportunity to WIN it! All the prospective customer has to do is fill in his or her name and address on an entry blank and drop the blank into a box!

You get everything you need for a successful promotion in one package: the TREASURE CHEST containing prizes for the whole family; a giant colorful window poster; 1,000 entry blanks; and an entry box.

The cost? Only $49.95 each! The result? The TREASURE CHEST will bring shoppers inside your doors!

Take a moment to fill in the post-paid order card and drop it into the mail. Your TREASURE CHEST will be shipped the day we receive your order. If you're not completely satisfied, just return the package within 10 days, and you owe nothing.

If you enclose your check with your order, we'll prepay all freight charges.

WRITING REPLIES TO INQUIRIES AS SALES LETTERS

Sales promotion letters written in answer to requests for information about advertised products and

services are often called *invited* or *solicited* sales letters. You studied these letters in Unit 12.

The big difference between invited sales letters and other sales promotion letters is that you start invited sales letters with a direct answer to one of the questions asked. You do not need—and, therefore, do not use—an attention-getting opener. The reader is interested in the answers to his or her questions. You can best hold that interest by answering all questions directly and fully.

In invited sales letters you should, of course, stress the advantages to the reader of using the product or service. And you should close with a three-point request for action. For help in writing a sales letter in reply to an inquiry, refer to Unit 12.

Remember that every inquiry about your product or service is important since it opens a door for your sales message. So send that message promptly—the same day if possible. Make it an interesting, factual answer to all the questions asked and implied. Relate specifically and helpfully to the inquirer's needs.

WRITING COVER LETTERS AS SALES LETTERS

Cover letters are often successful sales messages and may be equally effective as answers to inquiries or as uninvited (cold turkey) sales letters. For a review of cover letters, reread "Writing Cover Letters," page 71.

WRITING SALES LETTER SERIES

A series of sales promotion letters may be sent to prospective buyers when the seller feels that one letter won't accomplish the job of selling the product or service. The two most frequent ways of using a sales letter series are described below.

1. Company executives prepare a number of sales letters, each one complete in itself and independent of any other letters or advertising plans. They send the first letter to a selected list of prospects. Then they continue to send letters to each prospect at intervals as long as they feel the prospect may still be in the market. Every letter in the series tries to get an order. This type of letter series, used chiefly for selling *inexpensive* merchandise, is sometimes known as the *wear-out series*.

2. Company executives prepare a number of sales letters, each one building on the one that preceded it. As they plan the letters, they decide the number of letters to be sent and the intervals—often 10 to 15 days—at which they will be sent. They plan to send the complete series of letters to each prospect and ordinarily do not expect an order until the prospect has received all the letters. Frequently the company coordinates this direct-mail advertising with newspaper, magazine, radio, and

TV publicity. This type of letter series, used chiefly for selling *expensive* merchandise, is sometimes known as the *campaign series.*

ASSIGNMENT: In the Worksheet for this unit, plan and prepare effective sales messages.

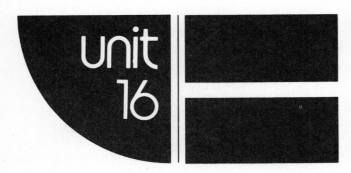

Writing Claim and Adjustment Letters

Every business occasionally receives letters from customers calling attention to the mistakes, defects, and dissatisfactions that are bound to occur, even in the best-managed organizations. Customers ask for adjustments when they are disappointed in a product which does not meet their expectations or in a service which is not adequately performed.

Such claims should not be called "complaints," a label that could lead to a bad company attitude toward its customers. Usually such letters are called claim letters or adjustment letters. *Complaint* connotes irritation, unpleasantness, and negativism. *Adjustment* is a more positive term suggesting fair resolution of the problem.

Consider these questions:

Would you rather have satisfied customers spreading good reports about your company than unhappy customers complaining about your products or services?

Can you satisfy an unhappy customer unless you know what is making him or her unhappy?

Unless someone tells a company that something is wrong, the company might never know it and the error could be repeated. Complaints and requests for adjustments are the best—and sometimes the only—source of information about what a company is doing wrong. They give the company the opportunity to discover, analyze, and correct defects in its products and services. That's why progressive firms welcome requests for adjustments from their customers—in moderate numbers.

And they always try to answer such letters promptly and graciously.

To keep the goodwill of their customers, adjustment executives try to solve customer dissatisfactions fairly, quickly, and tactfully. Business success depends on customer satisfaction. Whether a claim is granted or refused, the adjustment letter should be used to build and keep customer goodwill.

WRITING REQUESTS FOR ADJUSTMENTS

Here is a clear, complete, concise, and coherent request for an adjustment. Notice especially how the writer organizes his letter and the order in which he states the things he needs to say.

On December 2, I ordered a game table and four chairs from you and enclosed payment with my order (a copy of the invoice is enclosed).

When the table and chairs arrived on December 10, however, the vinyl tabletop and one of the padded seat covers were split.

I am returning the damaged table and chairs to you via United Parcel Service. They should arrive Wednesday. Will you please either send me a new table and chairs or refund my money.

Below is another well-written letter requesting an adjustment. This writer uses a different style and puts the elements in a different order, but the letter gets the job done just as well.

Please send me a new metal basket for my Small Frye deep fryer. After only two months of use, the plastic handle broke off the basket.

I am enclosing a copy of my receipt for the fryer. I checked the warranty, which guarantees material and workmanship for one year.

Follow these suggestions when you write a request for an adjustment:

1. *Assume that the company to whom you write wants to keep your goodwill and your business and will do the fair thing.* Don't show anger or disgust; don't argue or threaten; don't even try to persuade. Just tell your story calmly and clearly with confidence that you will be treated fairly.

2. *Present in logical order the details needed to give the reader a complete and unbiased picture on which to base the adjustment decision.* Include in your message *(a)* a description of the original transaction with all pertinent facts, such as date and place of purchase, from whom purchased, and terms of payment; *(b)* a sales slip or other evidence of purchase, if possible; and *(c)* a clear, concise explanation of the disappointment which brought about your request for an adjustment.

3. *Ask for the adjustment you think you deserve.* Tell the reader what you think should be done. If you are not sure what the adjustment should be, ask the reader to study the circumstances and determine the fair solution.

WRITING LETTERS GRANTING ADJUSTMENTS

Let's see how Bob Talley's request for an adjustment for a damaged boat cover was handled. Since the request is being granted, the letter begins with the good news.

Your new boat cover is being mailed prepaid today, Mr. Talley. It should arrive in a few days.

Thank you for returning the torn one. Since a mended cover might not be water-resistant, we are sending you a new one, so that you can keep that new boat well protected. You will notice that the new covers are now made of vinyl-coated nylon, which has proved superior to the polyester and cotton one you bought last year.

When you need boating accessories, you will find everything from anchors to boat trailers in our latest catalog. You can rely on our guarantee of high quality and "satisfaction or your money back."

Note the organization of the letter to Mr. Talley. First comes the news he wants to hear most: a new boat cover is on its way. Next comes the writer's appreciation for the customer's calling attention to the defect. Then the writer explains the change in materials, an explanation she owes the reader, and one that in this case can make the company look progressive and concerned. The final appeal for another sale is not out of place. The company has done what the reader wanted and left him satisfied.

Follow these suggestions when you write a letter granting an adjustment:

1. *In the opening sentence tell the reader that full adjustment is granted gladly.* Even if *you* feel that you are making a special concession, don't let the reader feel that you are doing him or her a favor. Instead, convince the reader that goodwill and friendship are more important to you than the money involved and that your company can always be depended upon to take good care of its customers.

2. *Be sure your message reflects sincere appreciation of the reader's request for adjustment.* Then the reader will know you are aware that writing the letter and waiting for the adjustment inconvenience him or her and that you welcome this opportunity to set things right. If possible, let the customer know how his or her letter has helped the company to improve its products or service.

3. *Stress the effort the company is making to prevent a recurrence of customer dissatisfaction.* Frankly accept the blame if the company is at fault and, without

censuring any employee, explain why a repetition of the mishap is unlikely.

4. *End the letter positively.* Don't make the error of ending with a negative phrase, such as "We hope you do not have any more trouble with your Weir Hedge Trimmer." The best ending of a letter granting an adjustment makes no reference to the incident that caused the adjustment. Instead, since the reader will be pacified, end on a note that implies future dealings. And don't overlook the possibility of doing some effective sales promotion for related products or at least some reselling of your company.

WRITING LETTERS DENYING ADJUSTMENTS

Sometimes you cannot grant an adjustment because the customer is wrong. Letters denying adjustments should help to rebuild customer goodwill while refusing to do what the customer asked—a difficult task.

You have already seen the effectiveness of the buffer-paragraph technique used to begin bad-news letters. You may wish to review "The Indirect Approach," pages 54 and 55, and "Answering 'No' to Inquiries and Requests," pages 68 to 70, for other special techniques to help you write effective bad-news messages.

The writer of the following letter realizes that she must sell Mr. Cortez on the company's position and try to keep him as a customer (after all, he did buy an expensive item by mail). Here's the answer to Mr. Cortez's request for repair or replacement of a humidifier.

You are right to expect high-quality merchandise from Ross Belk's, Mr. Cortez. And we try to give you the best for your money and to stand behind our products when they fail as a result of defects in material and workmanship, as our warranties state.

We appreciate your sending the humidifier to us for analysis. It appears that the humidifier was not cleaned properly as the instructions specified. After many hours of inefficient running because of the resultant scale buildup, the fan and belt wore out.

Our service manager estimated that cleaning the humidifier and replacing the fan and belt would cost $54. Please let us know whether you want us to repair it.

Since your humidifier is several years old and the other parts are becoming worn, you may want to consider buying a new one. With periodic cleaning and changing of the fiber pads, a new humidifier should give you even longer service than your old one did.

These suggestions will help you when you write a letter denying an adjustment:

1. *Start with the reader's point of view in your buffer paragraph.* Since the customer probably thinks he or she is right, try to coax—not force—him or her to accept the logical solution. Be sure the customer realizes that you understand the problem and that you will be fair.

2. *Convince the customer that the request is appreciated and has been given individual consideration.* This adjustment is important to the reader. In your letter, show that it is important to the company also.

3. *Present the explanation before the decision.* Stress what can be done and emphasize your purpose—to be fair to all customers. Don't blame and don't argue. Avoid unfriendly expressions, such as *your complaint, your error, you neglected, you claim, our records show, we refuse.* By a full, frank, and tactful presentation, lead the customer to accept your solution as the only reasonable one.

4. *Be courteous even when answering an angry or a distorted claim.* If you answer sarcastically, you may lose both your self-respect and your customer. Usually it costs less to keep the customer you have than to find a new customer to replace him or her.

5. *Try to leave the reader in a pleasant frame of mind.* A friendly but concise closing is even more important when the adjustment is not granted.

WRITING LETTERS COMPROMISING ON ADJUSTMENTS

You may decide to compromise on the adjustment because both the seller and the buyer share responsibility or because you are uncertain about who is responsible and want to correct the trouble to satisfy the customer. In the following case, the company tries to retain the customer's goodwill by repairing the product with no labor charge, even though the warranty has expired.

As a Rowe's customer, you *should* expect customer satisfaction because our pledge is based upon the terms of our sales agreements, including warranties.

Since your credit record shows that the one-year warranty on your Exer-Cycle is no longer in effect, it is too late to credit your account, Mrs. Vaughn. However, we will gladly repair your Exer-Cycle for you at the cost of the replacement parts, with no charge for labor. Our estimate for the parts is $9.95.

If you will please complete and return the enclosed authorization form, we will repair your Exer-Cycle and ship it back to you as quickly as possible.

When you write a compromise adjustment, follow these suggestions:

1. *Reflect pleasant cooperation in the buffer opening.* But don't imply that you are granting the request.

2. *State the facts and reasons thoroughly and courteously*—but don't oversell the reader and don't chide.

3. *Make the refusal clear but subordinate.*

4. *Follow with the counterproposal or compromise.* Let the service attitude show.

5. *Tell the customer what to do, but leave the decision to him or her.*

WRITING FORM LETTERS AS ADJUSTMENTS

The tone and style of the usual form letter reek of "mass production." Trite phrases, used much too often, sound insincere. Form letters are commonly used in adjustment correspondence; but even a form letter, carefully written, can stress personalized service and genuine concern for the reader.

Read the following two form letters, which are routine cover letters used by insurance agencies. Both are concise, clear, correct, and complete. But which letter would you, as the reader, prefer to receive?

Dear Madam:

This letter is to acknowledge receipt of your communication relative to your recent loss.

It is necessary that you fill out in detail the enclosed report-of-death statement immediately.

When corresponding on this claim, please refer to the claim number above.

Very truly yours,

Dear Mrs. Garrett:

I am sorry to hear of your loss and want to give your claim my immediate attention.

You can help me by filling out and returning to me the enclosed report-of-death statement as soon as it is convenient for you. I will work on your claim as soon as I receive it.

Please refer to the claim number above when writing to me. If I can help you, call me at 274-5655.

Sincerely,

The second letter is more personalized than the first and is not so brusque, even though it, too, is a form letter. For further illustration of this point, reread "Avoid a Formal Tone in Your Writing," pages 44 and 45.

ASSIGNMENT: The problems in the Worksheet give you a chance to demonstrate your understanding of adjustment correspondence.

Writing Credit Letters

Credit is the practice of accepting a customer's promise to pay in the future for goods delivered now. Over 90 percent of buying and selling in the United States is done on a credit basis.

The consumer buys merchandise on credit from the retail store, which is stocked with merchandise bought on credit from the wholesaler. The wholesaler's goods, in turn, are obtained on credit from the manufacturer, and the manufacturer purchases raw materials from suppliers, also on credit. The use of credit enables companies to buy materials, manufacture goods from those materials, and pay for the materials when they receive money from selling the merchandise.

CREDIT BUYING AND SELLING

Convenience is the major reason for buying on credit.

A personal credit account allows consumers to make their purchases more conveniently because:

1. They can buy now and pay later.

2. They do not have to carry cash with them or bother to write checks.

3. Exchanges and buying on approval are more convenient with credit transactions than with cash transactions.

Credit buying is convenient for retail stores that must sell the merchandise they have purchased before they pay their creditors for it.

To increase profits is the major reason for selling on credit.

Higher sales are stimulated by credit customers because they buy more merchandise of better quality on a regular basis.

Selling on credit, however, has some disadvantages:

1. Credit increases the cost of doing business because it creates additional work and other expenses in investigating accounts, in keeping records, and in making collections.

2. Capital that could be used for expansion, earning dividends, or other purposes is tied up.

3. Minor losses inevitably result from bad debts.

The seller cannot afford to extend credit to every customer who asks for it. The seller must, therefore, evaluate the financial stability of the individual or the company and decide whether the account would be more likely to increase sales and profits or to become an uncollectible account. The seller must find an acceptable balance between a too-cautious and an overly risky approach to credit extension.

BASES FOR EXTENDING CREDIT

The privilege of buying now and paying later is usually based on the credit standing or the credit rating of a person or a business. *Credit standing* means the reputation for financial responsibility. *Credit rating* means a credit bureau's appraisal—based on reports from creditors—of a credit standing at any one time.

Traditionally the *three C's—character, capacity, and capital*—form the basis for extending credit privileges.

Character refers to a sense of honesty and ethical dealings with others. It means meeting obligations and is evidenced by *willingness to pay.*

Capacity is the *ability to pay*. It is evidenced by income or potential income.

Capital refers to tangible assets in relation to debts. Capital also determines the *ability to pay* if the debtor does not pay willingly.

When evaluating the financial potential of business firms, credit managers frequently take into consideration a fourth C—*conditions*. This may refer to general business trends, local business influences, or a demand for particular products at that time.

INVESTIGATING CREDIT APPLICATIONS

To determine the character, capacity, and capital of applicants for credit, credit managers must obtain information directly from the applicant and from others, such as business firms, banks, and credit bureaus.

A form is typically used to obtain information from the applicant. Usually an applicant for a retail charge account comes into the store personally and fills out an application blank that the store provides. On the application blank the applicant gives such information as home and business addresses, personal references, a list of stores where he or she has charge accounts, and the name of the bank where he or she has a checking account.

The credit manager then has the credit bureau check the references that have been supplied or writes directly to the businesses and banks. Such correspondence is often done by means of form letters. They are letters of inquiry (see Unit 11) to determine whether the applicant satisfies the requirements of the three C's.

If the decision is made to approve credit for an individual or a business, then a letter extending credit privileges is an appropriate first step in establishing the credit relationship.

Businesses welcome the opportunity to offer credit privileges to those customers who are good credit risks. The credit approval is, then, a good news letter with a pleasant tone.

OPENING A DEALER CREDIT ACCOUNT

Grand Manufacturing Company, a manufacturer of stereo systems and accessories, does much of its business on a credit basis. Just as it buys most of its materials for manufacturing on credit, it sells the final products on credit too.

Grand has received a letter from Markham's Department Store asking that an attached order be filled on open account according to Grand's regular terms. The request includes credit references and information about the current financial condition of the store.

Grand's credit manager, Steve Jackson, then conducts a thorough investigation. He realizes that ultimately both Markham's Department Store and Grand Manufacturing Company will suffer if the store cannot pay for all the stock it buys on credit.

When Mr. Jackson writes to the credit references, he is careful to mark his inquiries "confidential" and to promise to keep all information received confidential.

Reports from the credit references, as well as the store's Dun & Bradstreet rating, are favorable. In fact, the investigation reveals that Markham's is a well-managed store in excellent financial condition.

Mr. Jackson writes the letter on page 97 to Markham's store manager, Joan Ellis, acknowledging the order and extending credit privileges. He explains clearly the terms of credit and encourages the new customer to use the credit privileges. The letter is typical in both content and organization of letters extending credit to a dealer.

New customers should be informed of credit terms and their meaning. Grand's terms to dealers are 2/10, n/30. The 2/10 means that if the dealer pays the bill within *10* days after the date of the invoice, the dealer can deduct a *2* percent discount from the total amount of the bill; the n/30 means that if the dealer does not take the discount, the full amount (the *net* amount) is due in *30* days. The bill, therefore, does not become *overdue* until one month after the date on which the dealer buys the merchandise.

OPENING A CONSUMER CHARGE ACCOUNT

Markham's Department Store opens charge accounts for consumers who measure up to the three C's of credit—character, capacity, and capital. These accounts differ in two aspects from the accounts through which the store buys from manufacturers and wholesalers:

1. Once a month Markham's sends each charge account customer a statement that lists purchases made on the account during the month, payments made on the account during the month, and the balance due. (Instead of a monthly statement, Markham's receives from its creditors an invoice after each purchase.)

2. The charge-account customer receives no discount for prompt payment. Instead, by a certain day of each month (or within a certain number of days of receipt of the statement) he or she is expected to pay either a specified portion of the balance or the entire balance due on the monthly statement. Markham's customers have 30 days to pay before their accounts become overdue; this time period varies with different stores, sometimes being as short as 10 days. (Most of the companies Markham's buys from offer discounts for prompt payment.)

Although the consumer charge account and the dealer's open account differ in respect to statements and terms of payment, the letters offering the dealer and the consumer charge account privileges have certain purposes in common:

1. To approve the credit cheerfully.

2. To express appreciation to the customer.

3. To explain the basis on which credit is extended.

4. To make clear the terms of the agreement and to stress the importance of prompt payment.

5. To encourage more buying.

6. To build goodwill as the foundation for successful company-customer relationships.

To accomplish these purposes, Markham's credit manager writes the letter illustrated on page 97 to a woman who has moved into the city recently and applied for a charge account.

From a psychological standpoint, this letter could be improved by deleting the talk about terms and payment. Such details, however, must be explained to the new charge customer; but they are, to the customer, the less pleasant parts of this business of credit and charge accounts. Notice that they are imbedded in the middle section of the letter, after the good news has been given and before the light sales promotion appeal and pleasant ending.

Many writers print the details of billing and payment on a card and enclose the card with the letter

GRAND MANUFACTURING COMPANY

1660 West Main, Portland, Oregon 97205, Tel. (503)555-7792

March 26, 19--

Mrs. Joan Ellis, Manager
Markham's Department Store
3842 Melrose Avenue
Dayton, Ohio 47382

Dear Mrs. Ellis:

The stereo systems and accessories listed on your order No. 2194 and on the enclosed invoice should reach you by Thursday. We have charged $720, the amount of the shipment, to your new account with the Grand Manufacturing Company. On the basis of your store's fine credit rating and reputation, we are happy to open this account and to welcome Markham's as a preferred customer.

Our regular terms of 2/10, n/30 apply, of course, to this and future orders. As you know, you can save $14.40 on your stereo systems if you send a check for $705.60 by April 5. The full $720 will be due by April 24.

You are acquainted, I believe, with John Robertson, who represents us in Ohio. He will be in to see you next week--and regularly after that. He will tell you how we cooperate with our dealers in local and national advertising and answer any questions about our many services to our customers. He will also bring catalogs and order blanks and assist you in placing your next order for Grand's fast-selling stereo systems and accessories.

Sincerely yours,

Steve Jackson

Steve Jackson
Credit Manager

SJ/dc
Enclosure
cc: John Robertson

MARKHAM'S DEPARTMENT STORE
382 Melrose Avenue
St. Louis, Missouri 63147
Tel. 314-555-3900

March 8, 19--

Mrs. Deborah Ruiz
212 Maple Avenue
Dayton, Ohio 47382

Dear Mrs. Ruiz:

Welcome to your place of honor among the many satisfied customers who say "Charge it, please" at Markham's. Your account is ready for use when you next visit our store. Our staff will do everything possible to make your shopping here pleasant and satisfying.

You will receive a monthly statement of purchases made shortly after our closing date, the 25th of each month. Then you may have until the 15th of the next month to pay your bill. From the fine way that you have handled charge accounts at other stores, we know that you will make prompt payments.

The enclosed "Charga-Plate," your personal identification, is the key to happy shopping. Markham's offers a wide selection of practically everything for you, your family, and your home--at reasonable prices.

We invite you, Mrs. Ruiz, to enjoy the convenience of your charge account to the fullest by taking advantage of Markham's many special services, such as telephone shopping with the help of Sara Friendly, our personal shopper; free parking at the back of the store; prompt and efficient delivery throughout the city and suburbs; and even a nursery for the preschool set.

Come in often to shop or just to browse around. You are always welcome at Markham's.

Sincerely,

Jack Walensky

Jack Walensky
Credit Manager

JW/dc
Enclosure

This letter acknowledges the first order from Markham's, extends credit privileges to the store, and explains clearly the terms of credit. Note, too, that it encourages prompt payment and talks about company service.

The letter granting credit to a consumer is similar to the one extending credit to a dealer. Note how this letter fulfills the six goals listed on page 96.

GRAND MANUFACTURING COMPANY
1660 West Main, Portland, Oregon 97205, Tel. (503) 555-7792

March 8, 19--

Mr. James Forrester, Owner
Phil's Music Shop
388 Sycamore Road
Louisville, KY 40201

Dear Mr. Forrester:

Your request for credit with Grand Manufacturing Company is a compliment to us. Thank you for completing and returning your recent application forms.

We are pleased to hear that your store is off to such a fine start. We are also pleased to hear the fine reports from your credit references. Our long experience in business has taught us that next to credit references, the most important factor affecting business success is cash on hand--especially for new stores. At Grand, we have always advised our customers to keep an average monthly cash balance that will be sufficient to cover salaries and expenses for at least four months. We know that within the next few months you will be able to increase your average cash balance substantially; therefore, Mr. Forrester, for your benefit and ours, we should like to suggest that you reapply for credit when your cash position is stronger.

In the meantime, if you were to cut your original order in half, you could reduce your cash outlay by about $450 and still take advantage of the 2 percent discount. If you agree with this practical suggestion, please use the enclosed form to reorder your merchandise. You will have your merchandise in your store--and selling--just four or five days after we receive your order and your check.

Very truly yours,

Steve Jackson

Steve Jackson
Credit Manager

SJ/dc
Enclosure

KENDALL
PLUMBING SUPPLY COMPANY
972 South Avenue
Seattle, Washington 98136
Tel. (206) 542-3535

November 12, 19--

Mr. Kenneth Jakway
Community Plumbing
12 Hardy Road
Pullman, Washington 99163

Dear Mr. Jakway:

Congratulations! Your application for credit has been approved, and we are pleased to welcome you as a Kendall credit customer.

Your first order will be ready for shipment Friday, November 16; a copy of the order plus an invoice will be included with the shipment. Please keep these papers for reference.

By the 20th of each month you will receive a statement listing all the purchases you have made as of our closing date, which is the 15th of the month. For the convenience of our credit customers, Kendall offers three different methods of paying for purchases. Each method is fully described in the enclosed Explanation of Credit Terms. Please do read this booklet carefully, and please call us whenever you have questions about the terms of credit. The members of our Credit Department will be delighted to help you.

Mr. Jakway, we have also enclosed our latest Kendall Catalog. In the catalog are several order forms and return envelopes that will make it easy for you to order from Kendall. With each monthly statement you will receive an additional supply of order forms and return envelopes. Of course, if you should run out of stock, please call in your order; we will rush it to you within five days.

All of us at Kendall look forward to serving you. We thank you for giving us the opportunity to show you why Kendall is well known for its high-quality products and for its excellent service.

Sincerely,

Cody Lee Peterson

Ms. Cody Lee Peterson
Manager, Credit Department

Enclosures
cc: Mr. Harold Gibbons
    Customer Service Department

This letter refuses credit for a valid reason. Nonetheless, it tries to persuade the customer to buy on a cash basis, and it encourages him to reapply for credit in the future.

This personalized credit letter will be more effective than a form letter in strengthening a credit relationship and building goodwill.

announcing that the account has been opened. This arrangement allows the letter to do its job of selling and building goodwill without having also to carry the less pleasant message about due date and payment. Endorsing the card is a useful way of maximizing the good aspects of the situation for the reader.

Many firms use form messages to notify customers of credit approval *and* explain monthly statements and add-on purchases; other stores believe, however, that a personalized credit letter such as the one on page 98 goes much farther in strengthening a credit relationship, building goodwill, minimizing collection problems, and increasing sales.

REFUSING CREDIT

When the decision has been made not to extend credit, the writer's objective is to explain tactfully why credit cannot be approved at present and to try to convince the customer to buy on a cash basis. The writer must include an optimistic note—namely, that the customer should reapply when his or her financial stability improves.

Occasionally a retailer who does not qualify for credit sends Grand Manufacturing an order for stereo systems and asks that an account be opened. Grand's credit manager writes the retailer a letter such as the one on page 98. This letter is a reply to an order for $1,600 worth of stereo systems on regular terms.

A credit investigation shows that Mr. Forrester, formerly a sales representative for a large music supply house in Louisville, has invested all his savings in this new store. Mr. Forrester is alert and promising; his reputation and standing in the community are excellent; but his capital is extremely limited. Mr. Jackson fears that the new shop will be in serious difficulty if Mr. Forrester buys more stock on credit. Thus, instead of approving credit at this time, he tries to persuade Mr. Forrester to cut his order in half and pay cash less 2 percent discount for the stereo systems he wants to order.

The goal of this letter is not to discourage credit buying but to convince the customer that ordering on a cash basis now will be advantageous to him. He is encouraged to apply for credit again when his financial stability improves.

STIMULATING CREDIT BUYING

One purpose of selling on credit is to sell more goods. An additional responsibility of a credit manager, then, is to write combined goodwill-sales letters to credit customers who buy regularly and pay promptly. An active account is an advantage to the company as well as to the customer. Both benefit when it is satisfactorily maintained.

Notice the technique of deserved praise which is evident in the following letter (see also Unit 9).

Dear Mrs. Ferguson:

Thank you for promptly paying the monthly statements we send you. We appreciate your cooperation in keeping your account in such good shape.

You should be proud of your fine credit record, Mrs. Ferguson. It's a pleasure to have you as a customer, and we want to continue to give you the kind of service you deserve.

We're here to help you whenever you visit us.

Cordially yours,

ASSIGNMENT: The problems in the Worksheet give you practice in writing the types of credit letters which you have studied in this unit.

Writing Collection Letters

You have seen how a credit manager selects the dealers and customers who can buy on credit and how carefully the letter opening each account explains the privileges and responsibilities of credit buying. Naturally you are interested in what happens when a retailer or a customer doesn't pay for the merchandise on time.

MINIMIZING COLLECTION PROBLEMS

Actually, the credit manager is more interested in what can be done to keep customers paying on time than what can be done to collect overdue bills. To minimize collection problems, the credit manager starts building good business relations with each dealer or customer as soon as a new account is opened. The credit manager uses his or her wide experience in credit work to help the retailers with their own collection problems. And the credit manager works with the sales department to be sure that dealers are not urged to overstock.

The wise credit manager writes thank-you letters to dealers and customers who regularly take advantage of cash discounts and pay their bills on time. This co-operation simplifies the credit manager's collection problems. More than half of the dealers pay within 10 days and earn the 2 percent discount. More than 80 percent pay within a 30-day period so that their bills never become overdue, and more than 90 percent pay within 60 days. Over the years, companies with good credit programs lose through bad debts less than one-half of 1 percent of their volume of credit sales—less than 1 cent out of every $2.

The credit manager plans collection letters carefully, although a letter may be sent to only one out of ten active accounts. The manager knows that the longer the account is overdue, the less likely it is to be paid. He or she also realizes that the sooner the customer pays back bills, the more likely that customer will be to buy from the company again, since most people do not try to shop where they have overdue bills. The credit manager, then, watches the accounts and sends collection messages promptly when bills are not paid on time.

A *series* of collection messages is prepared for use as needed. Every message is not sent to every dealer or

---

THE GREENHOUSE
Wholesale Florists
3317 Winchester Road, Clearwater, Florida 33518, Tel. (904) 555-2944

May 1, 19--

Mr. and Mrs. Frederick Lenhardt
Plaza Flower & Gift Shop
504 Balfour
Clearwater, Florida 33516

Dear Mr. and Mrs. Lenhardt:

Thank you for your response to our inquiry.

We are happy to accept your suggestion. The
arrangement to pay $75 a month until your account
is current will be fine with us.

Your first check for $75 has already been
applied to your account; as of April 30, your
balance is $375. Your next payment of $75 will
be due on the 15th of each month from May to
September.

If I can help you further, please call me.

Sincerely yours,

W. D. Geralds

W. D. Geralds
Credit Manager

WDG/dc

To minimize collection problems, the writer of this letter accepts the creditor's suggestion to pay $75 a month until the balance is paid.

customer whose account is past due; but the letters, and the intervals between them, are adjusted to individual customers and their payment records. The credit manager is careful, also, to stop the form-letter series as soon as a customer responds—even if the customer merely sends an explanation or a promise to pay (see page 100 for a personal letter that follows a customer's response).

PREPARING THE COLLECTION LETTER SERIES

The collection series described below is typical of the series used in many companies to collect delinquent accounts. Each of the first three reminders is sent as a printed form, because receiving a personal collection letter about a payment not seriously overdue often disturbs a conscientious customer. Each of the later messages is typed individually, with personalized inside address, so that the customer feels it was written just for him or her.

Gentle Reminders

Some companies use three impersonal messages to open the collection series. These gentle reminders imply that the customer has overlooked payment and indicate that the company expects a check but is not yet greatly concerned about the account.

The *first reminder* is a printed, end-of-the-month statement that lists purchases with dates and balance due.

The *second reminder* is another printed statement. A penned note on this statement may call it to the customer's attention by saying, "We haven't received payment of your recent invoice. If it's on its way now...thanks! If you haven't sent it yet, please do so today!" Or a slip such as the one shown below may be enclosed.

The *third reminder* may be a printed letter sent without personalization, or it may be an incidental reminder included in a personalized letter that is mainly concerned with something else. Notice that at this stage the message emphasizes reselling and sales promotion and subordinates the request for payment.

Dear Dealer:

Garden tools are selling sensationally these days. And the more active your account with us, the greater your share of the profits.

When you mail your payment of $82.50, due June 30, we suggest you send another order in the enclosed envelope.

More of the helpful displays, such as the one included in your recent shipment, are available upon request. If there is any other way we can help you sell Pond garden tools, just let us know. We are glad to be of service to you.

Cordially yours,

Request for an Explanation

The fourth message in this collection series is a personal letter asking why the payment has not been made. It is sent only to customers who do not reply to the gentle reminders and who normally keep their accounts up to date. This letter assumes that something out of the ordinary has happened to delay payment. The credit manager asks for a check, of course, but stresses the idea that if there is a reason for the delay, an explanation would also be welcome. This letter is friendly, shows confidence in the customer, and indicates a willingness to meet the customer more than halfway if he or she is in trouble.

ANCHOR LIFE INSURANCE COMPANY
328 BENNINGTON DRIVE, LANSING, MICHIGAN 48917   TEL. (517) 542-6000

Please . . .

. . . Don't forget the payment that is now due!

As you know, your Anchor insurance policy is designed to protect your family from financial difficulty when you are gone. Because missing a payment can cancel this protection, we urge you to send us the amount due as soon as possible.

Please don't delay! Keep your policy working for you and your family by sending us your payment before the cancellation date.

A gentle reminder such as this one may be sent with a duplicate statement.

Dear Mrs. Patton:

I would like to talk with you about the circumstances that have caused your bill for $287.40 to become two months past due. We have had no answer to our reminder notices of November 10 and December 15.

Because you have been a good customer of Buntyn's and have always paid promptly, I am wondering if you are having some temporary difficulty that prevents you from paying now.

We would like to have your check, Mrs. Patton; but we also want to keep your friendship. So will you please send either your check or an explanation in the enclosed envelope today?

Sincerely yours,

Notice that the following letter to a dealer is addressed to the individual in charge rather than just to the company. Items underscored in the letter show how it is personalized for different customers.

Dear Mr. Crider:

Can you help us out? We are wondering about the circumstances that have caused your bill for $359 to become two months past due.

Since you have always paid promptly, there must be a good reason for the delay this time. Won't you clear up the question in my mind by sending your check or a frank explanation.

Can we help you, Mr. Crider? You can be sure that we will cooperate with you in any plan that will enable you to keep on buying and selling our fine products regularly and profitably.

Your check? Your explanation? Your plan? Please send one of these soon in the enclosed envelope marked for my confidential attention.

Sincerely,

Firm Appeal (or Appeals) for Payment

The next step in a collection series is to make a firm and persuasive appeal for payment. Sometimes the credit manager sends one letter; sometimes he or she sends several letters at close intervals to impress on the customer the seriousness of the situation and the urgent need for immediate payment. The credit manager never makes a selfish appeal by suggesting, for example, that the customer should pay because the company needs the money. Instead, the manager tries to convince the customer that it is to the customer's own advantage to pay the full amount owed. The appeal may be to the customer's pride or sense of fair play. The following letter is typical of the firm appeals that credit managers send to dealers.

Your credit reputation is very good, Ms. Haskell, and I feel sure you are interested in keeping it that way.

Have you ever thought that your credit standing is much like an insurance policy in that it protects you against loss—loss of the convenience of buying on credit, loss of an adequate and varied stock, even loss of sales and goodwill? And that it doesn't cost you a cent, because paying your bills is the way to insure a good credit standing?

By sending your check for $303 for the bags bought almost four months ago, you will insure the privilege of continuing to replenish your regular stock and make seasonal and special orders without having to enclose a check each time.

Perhaps you need more fine luggage for your customers right now. How about sending your order for them along with the $303 to put your account in good shape? In fact, why not do it right now while it is fresh in your mind?

Keep that credit reputation good...don't let your insurance lapse...and we can continue to send you merchandise.

The appeal on page 103 is directed at the customer's pride in his or her credit reputation and sense of fair play.

Last Call for Payment

The final message in this collection correspondence is an appeal to the customer to pay so that the company need not turn over the delinquent account to its collection agency. The credit manager dislikes to use this last-call letter and sends it only after the customer has not responded to the firm appeals.

In this letter, the efforts that have been made to collect the account are reviewed. The customer is given one more chance to save a good credit standing by sending payment before the deadline—usually five to ten days from the date of the letter. Even now the credit manager tries to keep the friendship of the customer by stressing interest in playing fair.

Your credit reputation is important to you, Ms. Haskell.

For some time now, we have been writing to you in an effort to clean up that balance of $303, explained in the attached statement. So far you have not sent us either a check or an explanation, although six separate messages have called the debt to your attention.

Can't we still settle this account between ourselves in a friendly way? If you send your check for $303 now, you can continue to buy luggage and accessories on our regular terms. The agreement with our collection agency, however, does not allow further delay. We must turn your account over to the Wholesale Credit Bureau for collection unless it is taken care of within ten days.

The choice is yours. If your check reaches us by *November 16,* your credit standing with us will still be good; and our friendly business relations will continue.

Please mail your check for $303 today. Protect your credit reputation.

Sincerely yours,

The following suggestions will help you write successful collection letters:

1. *Even collection letters should be written as business-building messages.* Your goal is to collect the money *and* keep the customer.

2. *Make collection letters persuasive.* Don't try to force the customer if he or she hasn't the money or isn't willing to pay. Instead, try to persuade the customer that he or she (or the company) will benefit by paying promptly.

3. *Be fair, courteous, and tactful.* Avoid a harsh or demanding tone. Even with long overdue accounts, depend on persistence and firmness rather than sarcasm or abuse.

4. *Appeal to the customer's interest in keeping a good credit rating, to a sense of fair play, and to pride and self-satisfaction in paying debts.* Avoid threats, apologies, and implications that something could be wrong with the products you sold. Avoid also a selfish appeal—the suggestion that the customer should pay because your company needs the money.

5. *Have confidence in the people to whom you write.* Assume that the customers are honest and will pay their bills if they can. Sometimes you can express confidence by asking that, when the customer sends payment, he or she include another order.

6. *Don't backtrack in your collection series.* For instance, if you suggested in the reminder stage that the

---

Robert Greene & Sons, inc.
202 Market Mall   Wichita, Kansas 67202   Tel. (316) 601-7800

February 28, 19--

Mr. Leland Nelson
1444 Mill Avenue
Wichita, Kansas 67216

Dear Mr. Nelson:

Your good credit reputation enabled you to purchase a
$98.61 suit from us over two months ago. We were glad
to place your name on our credit list at that time;
and we made it clear that accounts are due on the 10th
of the month following purchase. When you bought the
suit, Mr. Nelson, you accepted those terms.

Your credit reputation is a valuable asset. We want
you to keep it that way because of the advantages it
gives you. You have enjoyed a liberal extension of
time; but to be fair to our other customers, you must
pay the amount that is past due.

Won't you please send us your check for $98.61 today?

Sincerely,

ROBERT GREENE & SONS, INC.

James R. Greene

James R. Greene
Credit Manager

JRG/dc

By directing this letter at the customer's pride in his credit reputation and sense of fair play, the writer makes a firm appeal for payment.

customer might have overlooked payment, don't mention overlooking in the inquiry stage.

7. *Be sure to state the amount the customer owes in each collection message you send.* As a rule, also indicate in each just how long the bill has been unpaid.

8. *When a customer writes you about a past-due account, answer with a personal letter.* And don't send any more form letters from the collection series.

ASSIGNMENT: The Worksheet problems will help you check up on what you have learned about collection correspondence and give you practice in writing collection letters.

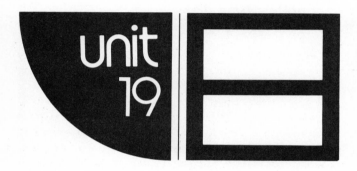

Handling Routine Correspondence

A secretary or an administrative assistant who can screen the boss's incoming mail and handle routine correspondence is a welcome asset to the busy executive. By relying on a secretary or an administrative assistant to write some correspondence, the executive is freed to spend valuable time on other activities.

Secretaries play a vital role in the correspondence activities of any company, since virtually all correspondence flows through their hands. A capable secretary may write some letters without the help of the executive; an administrative assistant writes even more.

Ability to write effective letters is an important asset for secretarial advancement. In fact, when the executive is promoted, he or she often arranges to take the secretary along to the new assignment.

Letters and memos that secretaries and administrative assistants may be given the responsibility to write include the following:

1. Requests for information.

2. Answers to routine inquiries.

3. Acknowledgments.

4. Referrals.

5. Transmittals.

6. Travel-related communications (reservations and appointments).

7. Invitations and replies to invitations.

8. Follow-up letters.

9. Meeting notices.

10. Instructions to other office personnel.

11. Messages of appreciation, congratulation, or sympathy.

You have already studied many of these types of letters. By adapting the principles you have already learned, you should soon be composing messages to take care of routine office situations.

When writing a letter, the secretary must decide whether to send it over the secretary's signature or over the employer's signature. For the writing style, the secretary uses his or her own style or the employer's, whichever is appropriate. In letters signed by themselves, secretaries refer to their employers in the third person—"Ms. Murray suggested" or "Mr. Cook requested." Below the space for the signature, type your name and (on the line below) the title "Secretary to Ms. Murray" or "Adminstrative Assistant."

When writing for the employer's signature, try to write the message much as the executive would write it. Follow the executive's writing style and make the message sound like one of his or hers. Write the message in the first person, of course, using "I" or "we" instead of "Ms. Murray" or "Mr. Cook." If you sign the executive's name, add your own initials below.

Ms. Jacqueline Murray
SR

ACCEPTING CORRESPONDENCE RESPONSIBILITIES

Whether the employer is in the office or away, a competent secretary shares in the responsibility for improving correspondence routines. An alert secretary will find countless ways to help in this task. Any secretary can start out by accepting at least these five basic responsibilities.

1. *The secretary should check incoming letters for discrepancies in dates, facts, and figures.* Suppose, for instance, the secretary receives a letter that mentions the date of a monthly meeting as Wednesday, June 14. The secretary automatically consults the calendar to verify the time and finds that Wednesday is the 15th. He or she must then check further and write for clarification. If the secretary finds that these meetings are regularly held on Wednesday rather than Tuesday, the letter might tactfully ask: "Am I correct in putting this meeting on the calendar for Wednesday, June 15?"

2. The secretary should note in the tickler file all promises of further correspondence made in outgoing letters. For example, the secretary who writes a letter mentioning that his or her employer will write the addressee again in a few weeks to arrange a meeting would immediately enter a reference in the tickler. Then at the appropriate time the secretary would call the letter to the employer's attention and proceed with arrangements for the appointment.

3. The secretary should confirm appointments, invitations, and similar telephone and in-person conversations in writing to avoid misunderstandings. Embarrassing and costly mixups can occur when the time, place, and other details agreed upon orally are not confirmed by letter.

4. The secretary should recognize the importance of the time element in writing letters of appreciation and congratulation and other goodwill messages and should work with the employer to make these letters timely. The secretary should maintain an up-to-date check of newspapers, broadcasts, telecasts, and trade journals and talk with the employer about items that suggest occasions for goodwill messages.

5. The secretary's responsibility for careful proofreading is most significant when he or she writes and mails letters without the employer's dictation or personal signature. Errors in typing, spelling, and word usage that the secretary fails to detect are sent along to the reader uncorrected and unappreciated. They reflect unfavorably on the secretary, the employer, and the company.

PREPARING ROUTINE COMMUNICATIONS

The following examples of correspondence are typical of those that are written on the secretary's own initiative or at the employer's request.

Routine Information Letters

By reviewing Units 11 and 12 (pages 63 to 71), you will easily recall the principles for writing clear, concise inquiries, requests, and replies. Secretaries are often called upon to prepare letters giving routine information like the following exchange written by a secretary with Clement Safety Equipment and a secretary with the Roanoke Rapids (North Carolina) Chamber of Commerce.

Dear Sir or Madam:

Will you please let me know the opening and closing dates of the Fall Festival this year. A group of our representatives would like to include a day at your famous festival during a conference trip to Washington, D.C.

Sincerely yours,

Dear Mr. Brady:

Our Fall Festival this year opens on Thursday, October 14, and ends on Saturday, October 23. We have added your name to our mailing list to receive all special announcements concerning the daily parades, shows and concerts, and other attractions. We believe your representatives would find our Fall Festival an enjoyable part of their trip.

Sincerely yours,

Acknowledgments

A simple letter to write and one that is frequently written by the secretary during the employer's absence is the acknowledgment. When letters must be held for the employer's attention, the secretary sends a short, direct acknowledgment explaining why an answer is delayed and when it may be expected. Be careful not to obligate the employer or to give out confidential information about why he or she is out of town. Such a letter might read like this:

Dear Mrs. Amato:

We have received your letter of May 14 asking Mr. Jennings to speak at your meeting on June 20.

Mr. Jennings is out of the office this week. As soon as he returns, I shall bring your invitation to his attention.

Sincerely yours,

The secretary also writes acknowledgments of remittances, packages, requested information, and other messages or materials received. These acknowledgments should be direct, concise, and courteous. They should include the details needed to identify the items received, since they become a record for the files. A form message may be useful for many similar acknowledgments.

Not all remittances need to be acknowledged. A canceled check is usually considered a receipt. A remittance accompanying an order is confirmed when the order is acknowledged or the merchandise sent to the customer. If a remittance is received separately, however, the secretary may acknowledge it in a brief letter expressing appreciation, mentioning the amount, and telling how it has been applied.

Dear Miss Webber:

Your postal money order for $25, received today, has been credited to your account.

We appreciate this prompt payment, which reduces your account balance to $18.75.

Cordially yours,

A secretary should also acknowledge, with thanks, information or material sent in response to a request by either the employer or the secretary. But judgment is needed in determining when to express appreciation for unrequested items. Simple and sincere thank-you acknowledgments should be written for gifts and favors extended to the secretary or the employer and for congratulatory and other goodwill letters sent to them.

Dear Mr. Baldwin:

You were most generous to send copies of your interesting booklet, *Writing What Comes Naturally,* for all the members of our office staff.

Your common-sense discussion of letter writing—with clear, refreshing style and clever illustrations—will certainly be helpful to our dictators and secretaries.

Sincerely yours,

Many letters the secretary writes while the employer is away are "stopgap" letters. So are the letters written to explain that more time is needed to prepare a complete answer. Often a person asking for information does not realize that it might take several days and several departments to get the facts together for a reply. The thoughtful secretary sends a short note—usually over the employer's signature—to explain a delay of this kind.

Dear Ms. Cohen:

You can expect the information you asked for in a few days. In order for my report to be helpful to you, I must get facts and figures from both the accounting and the personnel departments.

I am glad to cooperate with you on this project and expect to send a complete answer to your letter by the end of the week.

Cordially yours,

The secretary may sometimes prepare a form letter to take care of delayed replies. A company handling property insurance, for example, knows that time is needed to process a claim for damages and make a complete report to a client. The secretary builds goodwill by acknowledging each claim on the day it is received. The acknowledgment may be a card reading:

We have received your recent notice of loss and assure you that it is now having our careful attention. You will receive a complete reply soon.

More complex acknowledgments are discussed in "Acknowledging Orders," pages 73 to 77.

Referral Letters

Executives often receive letters that can be more satisfactorily answered by someone else. If the person to whom the letter is referred is not in the same office or, for any other reason, cannot reply immediately, the secretary may write a referral letter. Below is a short, courteous letter a secretary wrote for her employer's signature when told, "Tell this customer we're referring her letter to the dealer."

Dear Mrs. Blalock:

Your question about needed service on your Record-a-Call can be best answered by our Centerville distributors.

I am therefore referring your letter to Mr. Harold Fife, manager of the Service Department at Mitchell's. He will probably call you soon.

Cordially yours,

Transmittal Letters

Review the discussion of "Writing Cover Letters" (Unit 12, page 71) for suggestions and samples on writing letters to accompany information or articles. The transmittal (or cover) letters the secretary writes may be as simple as this one from a secretary to a dealer.

Dear Mr. Estes:

Here are the advertising mats you requested.

We appreciate your interest in promoting Chain Link Security Fencing in Circleton's newspapers.

Sincerely yours,

Invitations and Replies to Invitations

Formal invitations and answers to formal invitations follow an established pattern. To prepare a formal invitation or write a reply to one, the secretary should refer to an up-to-date book of etiquette (one of the "must" reference books in the office) for correct wording and arrangement. Replies to formal invitations are customarily written in longhand on semisocial or social stationery—not on business letterheads.

A secretary should adapt informal invitations and replies to the situation and to the personality of the writer. Mr. Allen's secretary sent the following invitation to members of a committee of the Campus School for Special Education as part of a project to raise money.

Dear Mr. London:

Mr. Allen is asking the members of the Planning Committee of the Campus School for Special Education to meet with him for lunch on Tuesday, April 8, in Room 201 of the Neeley Building, at 12 noon. He hopes you can come.

Mr. Allen would like the committee to discuss specific suggestions for a benefit show to be staged in May.

Will you let us know by Monday morning whether you will be able to attend the luncheon and meeting?

                    Sincerely yours,

The secretary should also be sure to confirm all the details when accepting an invitation for the boss.

Dear Mrs. Turello:

I appreciate your asking me to speak at your Associated Travel Agents meeting in Philadelphia on Tuesday, March 3. I shall be delighted to do so.

As you suggested, I have made a reservation for Tuesday night at the Holiday Inn on Union Avenue. Since my plane (Delta Flight 593) is scheduled to arrive in Philadelphia at 4:05 p.m., I should have plenty of time to check into the hotel before the meeting begins at 7 p.m.

I look forward to seeing you on March 3.

                    Very truly yours,

Follow-Up Letters

A secretary may be expected to follow up (1) on information or articles that were requested or promised

and not received promptly or (2) on enclosures that were omitted from correspondence. These follow-up letters are direct and courteous and carefully identify the item called for.

Dear Mr. Pratt:

May we have the committee report on proposed changes in dealer contracts. I believe the report was promised for last Friday, March 6. Mrs. Whitney must have it by March 11. She plans to use it as a basis for a sales conference discussion on the 14th.

                    Sincerely yours,

Dear Ms. Petroski:

Do you know what happened to our copy of the Treasurer's Report for the ABCA Association? It was mentioned as an enclosure in your letter of April 30 but was not in the envelope when the letter reached us.

We shall appreciate having this report when you track it down.

                    Sincerely yours,

Meeting Notices

The people who are to attend a meeting should be notified at least ten days in advance so that they can arrange to attend. However, the notice should not be sent so far in advance that the recipients forget about it. For very large meetings, more advance notice and a later reminder are required. A reply card or a reservation coupon may be enclosed.

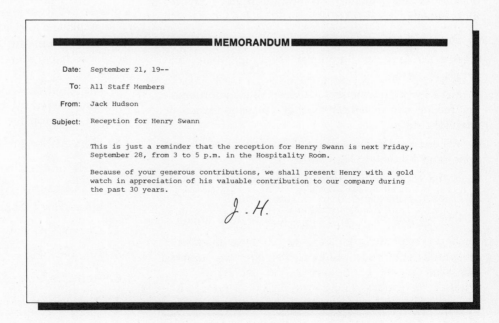

In-company communications such as this concise, informal memo are frequently written and signed by a secretary.

Informal meeting notices may be little more than announcements in letter form, written in a friendly tone. A post card may also be used.

Dear Members:

The next regular meeting of the Snow Lake Property Owners Association will be held at the Snow Lake Community Center at 6 p.m. on Monday, May 17.

Mr. Frank McAvoy of the Miller County Sheriff's Department will share with us some interesting ideas on security and protection on Snow Lake.

A family barbecue is planned following the meeting. We hope you will be able to attend.

Sincerely,

In-Company Communications

Frequently the executive will ask the secretary to write notes or memos to other people in the organization. Tone is important even in these informal messages because even though the secretary signs the message, others will react to it as if the employer had written it.

The memo on page 107 is an example of a concise, informal message written by a secretary.

EVALUATING YOUR WRITING

All communications, no matter how simple or informal, deserve careful planning, preparation, and review. As you glance at the finished product, answer these questions:

1. Does it look attractive?

2. Are the language, grammar, spelling, typing, and details accurate?

3. Have I written concisely yet given all the information the reader needs without further correspondence or telephone calls?

4. Will the reader know exactly what I said, what I want done, and how and when to do it?

5. Is the tone positive rather than negative?

6. Does the message focus on the reader?

7. Does it present a favorable image of my company?

If you can answer "yes" to all these questions, congratulations! You have written an effective business message!

ASSIGNMENT: The Worksheet problems give you opportunity to plan and prepare routine letters and memos.

unit 20

Writing Letters About Employment

How do you look for a job?

This major question faces students as they prepare for the end of their schooling and start looking toward the world of work.

If you do not take definite steps to prepare yourself, a diploma or a degree is certainly no assurance that a job will be awaiting you.

In a recent survey employers were asked what students can do to make themselves more hireable. Employers urged students to take business courses and technical courses and to acquire business experience through summer or part-time jobs. The cooperative or work-study program was recommended. They indicated that students need to develop more definite career goals, a better knowledge of business and how it works, and more flexibility in the types of work they would consider. A willingness to relocate or travel is helpful. The employers also stressed the importance of meeting the requirements for entry-level jobs, having a strong academic background, and mastering communications skills.

The employers also ranked those areas in which students needed the most improvement to succeed on the job. The top ten areas were:

1. Concern for productivity.

2. Pride of craftsmanship and quality of work.

3. Responsibility and the ability to follow through on an assigned task.

4. Dependability.

5. Work habits.

6. Attitudes toward company and employer.

7. Ability to write and speak effectively.

8. Ability to follow instructions.

9. Ability to read and apply printed matter to the job.

10. Ambition, motivation, and desire to get ahead.

Job hunting is hard—but you can make it easier if you take the time to do some advance planning and careful preparation. You will also need a résumé (which will be reproduced) and a letter of application (one for each specific job you apply for).

Most personnel managers prefer that the job candidate write a comprehensive application letter and enclose with it a separate résumé (also called a "data sheet"). This combination gives the applicant an opportunity to explain in detail how his or her qualifications fit the job for which he or she is applying. And it reveals a great deal about the applicant's personality.

You will find this two-part message effective in applying for a job. A prospective employer is interested not so much in what you can do right now as in what kind of a person you are, how well you work with others, how you will respond to on-the-job training, and what you will be able to do for the company in five, ten, or more years. The employer can judge these points best from a letter in which you interpret the facts that you have listed on your résumé.

The main thing is to sell a product—yourself—to a customer—the prospective employer. Your résumé and letter of application should, therefore, be planned much like a sales campaign.

Your customer is the company to whom you are applying. The product you are selling is your services. You can offer the company your willingness and ability to do the work required. Your ability depends on your background, personality, training, work experience, and attitude toward the job.

Before you can sell these benefits to an employer, however, you must discover your own traits, attitudes, and skills. Try to get a complete and objective picture of yourself as an applicant by standing back and looking at yourself as though you were another person, by studying your qualifications as though they belonged to someone else.

The first step is to take inventory of yourself—your experience, education, personal qualities, special interests and abilities, and so on.

Jot down everything: part-time, temporary, and even volunteer work; subjects you did best in; activities in and out of school; hobbies. Don't worry about getting these in any special order just yet. Simply writing them down will help you think about what you have to offer a prospective employer. It will also give you clues about the kind of work you should be looking for.

Of course, at this stage of your working life no one expects you to be able to list a long line of accomplishments. But you do have some selling points, and you should make the best of them by emphasizing them positively.

ASSIGNMENT: Complete Section A of the Worksheet.

PREPARING A RÉSUMÉ

Once you have had a good look at yourself, you're ready to take the next step: Prepare a written summary of your background—your résumé. *Always* prepare your résumé *before* you start to write the application letter that will accompany it. Putting together your résumé should help you organize your thoughts about yourself and see yourself realistically in relation to the job you want.

For this summary, you rearrange the notes you've already jotted down. Pick out the key points and present them in a way that will give an employer a truthful and persuasive picture of who you are and what you can do. The résumé is a helpful job-hunting tool, especially for the person who finds it hard to talk about himself or herself in an interview. Having it all down on paper in a well-organized summary will help you, and it will focus attention on your strong points. Also, it's something you can leave behind as a reminder of who you are and what you offer.

You'll probably be asked to fill out a regular application form too. But the résumé, if you do it right, is more likely to catch the employer's eye and help him or her gain a quick and favorable impression of you. A good résumé must be tailored to suit you and your background as well as the specific type of job for which you are applying.

The following guidelines will help you decide what to put in your résumé, what to leave out, and what form and tone to use. These suggestions—based on the likes and dislikes of many employers—will help you prepare an effective résumé.

Start With a Personalized Heading

Begin with your identification: your full name, mailing address, and telephone number. These should stand out at the top of the page. Be sure the telephone is one at which messages will be taken during business hours. It is not necessary to type a heading such as "DATA SHEET" or "RÉSUMÉ" (it will be obvious).

Make the Résumé an Easy-to-Use Summary

Include pertinent details of your training, experience, personal background, and references. Arrange it so that the employer can review at a glance the important facts about you and your preparation for the job. These facts should be tabulated—listed in columns, *not* explained in sentences and paragraphs. Group them under clear, concise headings—with everything about one subject under one heading. Then, if the employer is interested in your education, for example, he or she can find under "Education" or "Training" all the facts about your high school, college, and special education. By underscoring group headings (see the résumé on page 112) or typing them in capitals (see the résumés on pages 111 and 113) you make it easier for the reader to spot the information he or she needs.

Keep the Entire Summary as Objective as You Can

Your résumé should be a record of facts, not opinions or interpretations. Remember that the selling is done in the letter; limit the résumé to a description of yourself, your abilities, and your training. Try using a telegraphic sentence style: "Responsible for setting up and maintaining central filing system for regional office." It isn't necessary to say "*I was* responsible for...";; the meaning is clear. This style is obvious, but it has the virtue of conciseness.

Save Space, but Don't Crowd the Résumé

The résumé is probably the first glimpse a prospective employer has of how you do things. Make it attractive, uncluttered, neat, and correct. Use plain white paper, 8½ x 11 inches. Leave sufficient white space around and between columns so that all information stands out and is easy to read. Center all the headings, or use all side headings. Arrange all the data on one page if you can without crowding. If you need to include more details than will fit on one page, arrange the information attractively on two sheets. On the second page be sure to include your name at the left margin and "Page 2" at the right margin, or use some similar heading style.

Your résumé should be as long as necessary to do effectively the job it needs to do—but no longer. And before you have it copied, proofread it very carefully for typing errors, misspelled words, and inaccurate details.

Stress the Qualifications That Seem Most Important to the Job

Usually you will emphasize either your education or your work experience by placing this section near the top of the résumé. When you compare the qualifications of the applicants whose résumés are shown on pages 111 and 112, you can easily understand why Elizabeth Davenport lists her education first and Steven Martin stresses his work experience.

Many applicants dilute the effectiveness of their résumés by listing personal details first. Since most employers will be more concerned about details of your training and experience, do not overstress personal details by placing them in the most conspicuous position.

Include All Facts You Consider Useful in Evaluating Your Qualifications

Better to add a few extra details than to omit one helpful item. On your résumé you may list either your age or date of birth (not both); military status; leadership and leisure activities; and special honors and accomplishments. Include full details of any personal or educational facts directly related to the job for which you apply.

List All Pertinent Work Experience

Work experience is usually the key part of a résumé—even for students who may not yet have had any full-time jobs. Emphasize what you *have* done. List part-time jobs such as baby-sitting, delivering newspapers, and mowing lawns. If you have had little work experience, list work that you were not paid for, such as volunteer work.

No job is so menial or meaningless that you did not learn something of value from it. A baby-sitter is wholly responsible for the life of a helpless human being. A newspaper delivery route offers good training in meeting a schedule whatever the weather, in managing other people's (the newspaper's) money, and in selling. Mowing lawns means caring for other people's property, running an expensive machine, and being reliable in your service. All three jobs offer experience in dealing with people too.

If you have had many different jobs, you might choose to omit the less-important part-time jobs.

The work experience section should begin with your present or last job, and work in "reverse chronological order"—the last one listed should be your *first* job.

Give Concise but Complete Facts About Each Job

Include positions held, names of supervisors, company names, complete addresses, brief descriptions of your duties, and dates for each job.

Present the work in the best light you can. The key word is *responsible*. It is better to say, "Responsible for filing and finding both correspondence and customer orders" than to say, "Did some filing." Don't overlook the opportunity to present yourself as well as you can.

List All Formal Education

Begin with your present or most recent school and work backward to high school. Give the names of the schools with the dates attended, year(s) graduated, degrees, majors, and relevant courses.

```
                          Steven Wayne Martin
                          3323 Winchester Road
                          Glasgow, Kentucky 42141
                          Telephone (606) 555-7225


E X P E R I E N C E

June 1978          Mando's Italian Food, 4023 Summer Avenue, Glasgow,
to present         Kentucky.  Work as cook six nights a week (about
                   45 hours a week).  Also responsible for closing
                   restaurant Mondays through Thursdays.

July 1976          Red Apple Inn,  611 Madison Avenue, Glasgow, Kentucky.
to May 1978        Worked as a waiter (about 25 hours a week) while
                   attending State Technical Institute.

June 1974          U.S. Army, Fort Polk, Louisiana.  Attained rank of
to May 1976        sergeant.  Supervised training for a company of 500
                   men.  Received Honorable Discharge and Good Conduct
                   Medal.

September 1973     Oscar's Grocery, 4070 Willow Street, Neon, Kentucky.
to May 1974        Performed general grocery duties, including stocking
                   shelves, arranging displays, and serving customers.

E D U C A T I O N

September 1976     State Technical Institute, Glasgow, Kentucky.  Received
to May 1978        Associate of Science degree in Motel/Restaurant
                   Management.

September 1971     Memorial High School, Neon, Kentucky.  Received diploma.
to June 1974

A C T I V I T I E S   Photographer for college yearbook.  President of high
                      school senior class.  Captain of high school basketball
                      team.  ROTC officer at Memorial (two years).

P E R S O N A L       Date of birth:  April 22, 1956
                      Health:  Excellent

R E F E R E N C E S   Mr. James P. Lucchesi, Owner    Ms. Lena Jensen, Manager
                      Mando's Italian Food             Red Apple Inn
                      4023 Summer Avenue               611 Madison Avenue
                      Glasgow, Kentucky 42141          Glasgow, Kentucky 42141

                      Mr. William B. Champion
                      Division Head
                      General-Vocational Technologies
                      State Technical Institute
                      Glasgow, Kentucky 42141
```

By listing his experience first, this applicant stresses his work experience in his résumé.

ELIZABETH ANN DAVENPORT

Permanent Address: School Address (until May 31):

401 Kay Street   Box 44
North Little Rock, AR 72417   State University, AR 72467

(501) 555-2045   (501) 555-2218

Education

Bachelor of Business Administration Degree, Arkansas State University,
     May 1978.   Major: Marketing   Minors: Finance and Economics
     Completed all courses in major field with 4.0 GPA.

Diploma, East High School, North Little Rock,
     May 1975.   Salutatorian of graduating class.
     Received academic scholarship to ASU.

Experience

Sales Clerk, Campus Boutique, 618 University Avenue, Jonesboro, AR 72501,
     September 1977 - present.
     Employed part-time (20 hours a week) as salesperson of junior
     clothing, under supervision of Ms. Wanda Brown, Manager (501) 555-5513.

Activities

Arkansas State University:
     Alpha Kappa Psi (professional fraternity)
          Member, 1976-1978

     Phi Beta Lambda (national organization for business students)
          President, 1977-1978

     Alpha Omicron Pi (social sorority)
          Pledge Class President, 1975-1976; Social Chairperson, 1976-1977

East High School:
     Future Business Leaders of America
          Vice President, 1974-1975

     Student Council
          Member, 1972-1975

Personal Data

Age: 21   Health: Excellent   Marital Status: Single
Hobbies: Reading, camping, swimming, and skiing

References

Dr. Robert Ferralasco, Professor   Mrs. Sally Rice, Chairperson
Division of Marketing   Business Department
College of Business   East High School
State University, AR 72467   North Little Rock, AR 72202
(501) 555-2030   (501) 555-3592

Knowing that a prospective employer will find her education more impressive
than her work experience, this résumé writer listed her education first.

Résumé

JOYCE M. KRAMER

405 Churchill Street   Age: 20
Blancoe, Iowa 51523   Health: Excellent
(515) 555-2098

                          EDUCATION

DeSoto County Junior College, Middleton, Iowa, 1976-1978
  Associate of Arts Degree, 3.82 GPA
  Major: Secretarial Administration
  Special Skills: Typing - 75 words a minute
                  Shorthand Dictation - 100 words a minute

  Business Courses Completed: Typing, Gregg Shorthand, Business Machines,
                    Records Management, Data Processing,
                    Accounting, Economics, Business Law,
                    Business English, Business Correspondence

  Activities and Honors: Phi Theta (college scholastic honor society)
                    Phi Beta Lambda (business students' organization)

Central High School, Blevins, Iowa, 1973-1976
  Ranked fifth in graduating class
  Activities and Honors: National Honor Society
                    Gregg Shorthand Award
                    Future Business Leaders of America

                          EXPERIENCE

First National Bank, 501 Union Avenue, Middleton, Iowa, 1976-1978
  Part-time Secretary to Mr. James Brown, Vice President of Marketing
  Duties: Typing, taking dictation, filing, answering telephone

LeBonheur Children's Hospital, 848 Adams Avenue, Blevins, Iowa, 1974-1976
  Candy Striper volunteer
  Duties: Attending patients, under supervision of Miss Mary Greene,
          Head Nurse

                          REFERENCES

Dr. Carolyn Bowlin, Chairperson   Mr. Edward Jamison, Instructor
Department of Secretarial Administration Department of Accounting
DeSoto County Junior College   DeSoto County Junior College
Middleton, Iowa 52638   Middleton, Iowa 52638
(515) 555-2958   (515) 555-2960

Together with the application letter at the right, this résumé will help the applicant to compete successfully for the job she wants.

Application Letter

                                        405 Churchill Street
                                        Blencoe, Iowa 51523
                                        June 18, 19--

Mr. Hugh M. Brown III
Personnel Manager
BSM, Inc.
343 Oak Street
Omaha, Nebraska 68108

Dear Mr. Brown:

    Because of my college training in secretarial administration
and my work experience, I believe I can be the SUPERSECRETARY for
whom you advertised in yesterday's Omaha Star.

    Just two weeks ago I completed, with honors, the two-year
secretarial administration program at DeSoto County Junior College--
a program that was both practical and thorough.

    My typing speed is now 75 words a minute; I can take shorthand
dictation at 100 words a minute. Besides specific skills, the
business courses I took at DCJC have given me an understanding of
the business world and its functions.

    I learned to apply these skills to an office situation during
my employment at First National Bank of Middleton. During the two
years I was at DCJC, I found my job in the Marketing Department of
the bank very enjoyable. And I believe that my work background
will enable me to adapt quickly to your office routine.

    Office work is a challenge to me. I look forward to new
responsibilities, and I would like to put my abilities and skills
to work for BSM, Inc.

    When you have reviewed the enclosed resume and contacted my
former employers and teachers, I hope you will write or phone me
and suggest a time when I may come to your office for an interview.
(My phone number is (515) 555-2098.)

                                        Sincerely,

                                        Joyce M. Kramer

                                        Joyce M. Kramer

Enclosure

The writer prepared this effective application letter for a specific job. Note that her letter has an interesting opening, a convincing presentation of her qualifications, and a strong closing.

```
                              P.O. Box 37
                              Neon, Kentucky 41840
                              September 6, 19--


     Mr. Robert L. Jones
     Personnel Manager
     Consolidated Freightways
     1942 Parkway Avenue
     Detroit, Michigan 48236

     Dear Mr. Jones:

     With a recent college degree in accounting and several years of
     work experience, I am confident of my ability to do excellent
     work as a junior accountant.  I am applying for the job that
     Consolidated Freightways advertised in the Detroit Herald.

     The past three years' experience in the trucking industry has
     increased my knowledge of the transportation field.  Working
     in an office has increased my awareness of operations, finance,
     and budgeting.  In addition, through my reading I have also become
     familiar with many of the Interstate Commerce Commission's regula-
     tions.

     Since your company leases over 90 percent of its equipment,
     proper accounting methods for leases are vital to Consolidated
     Freightways' accurate financial reports.  The attention to
     detail and accuracy which I have developed can reduce costly
     accounting errors for you.

     The enclosed resume will also give you a description of my
     activities and a list of references.  Will you write me or phone
     (606) 555-3327 to tell me when I may come in and talk with you?

                              Sincerely yours,

                              Rickey Lee Savarin

                              Rickey Lee Savarin


     Enclosure
```

Notice how the writer of this application letter adapts his work experience to
the job for which he is applying.

2802 Highland Street
Santa Fe, NM 87501
July 1, 19--

Mr. Cameron L. Faulkner, CLU
Anchor Life Insurance Company
Albuquerque, NM 87123

Dear Mr. Faulkner:

Because of my college training and experience in insurance
sales and management, I believe I can be an aggressive salesperson for Anchor Life Insurance Company.

I believe that my studies in insurance and related business
courses have helped prepare me for your intensive training
program. Your life insurance policies are very popular, and
I am confident I can boost the company's sales record even
higher.

My summer employment with Globe Life and Accident Insurance
Company of Santa Fe taught me a great deal about human relations
as well as the finer techniques of selling. As a result of this
experience, I am eager to prove that I can build sales and goodwill for Anchor Life.

Will you let me put my education, work experience, and personal
characteristics to work for you? I am single and willing to
travel or relocate. I can start to work for Anchor Life following my graduation on August 20.

After you have reviewed the enclosed resume, I would like to
come to your office for an interview. My telephone number is
(505) 594-6855; or you may write me at the address above. I
look forward to meeting you and your sales force.

Sincerely,

William N. Burkett

William N. Burkett

Enclosure

This application letter shows confidence and highlights the writer's related
experience in insurance. In addition, it has a strong, effective closing.

List Your References in an Easy-to-Read Arrangement as the Last Item on the Résumé

Name as references only people who know you well enough to report on your work habits and on the quality of work you do in school or on the job. Include both school and job references when you can. Ask permission before naming any person as a reference. Use a courtesy title (*Mr., Miss, Ms., Mrs., Dr.,* and so on) before each name. Follow the name with the person's title (Manager, Accounting and Collection Department; Professor of English; Sales Manager; Transcription Supervisor). Give a complete mailing address (business rather than home address) for each reference. Don't forget to give a telephone number for each reference. Many people would rather telephone than write a reference. Not only is it faster, but one can also tell a good deal from the reference's tone of voice as he or she describes you.

Omit Certain Details

On most job-application forms you will see these words: "Federal law prohibits discrimination because of race, color, religion, age, sex, or national origin." Remember those words!

Remember, too, as you prepare your résumé, to avoid mentioning your race or religion. (Many people still prefer to list their birth dates, even though they are not required to do so.) In addition, do not indicate your political preferences.

On your résumé, make no mention of the salary you want or expect to receive. Leave salary discussions for the interview. Also, do not include the reasons why you left a job you had or want to leave a job you now have. Don't give excuses for not having a job! Avoid the negative.

PREPARING A LETTER OF APPLICATION

An application letter may be the most important letter you will ever write, because it may determine the course of your life—at least for a time. An effective application often leads to an interview, the interview to a job offer, and the job to a satisfying and successful career.

As you may have guessed, an application letter is difficult to write well. You cannot expect just to sit down and write a winning application. Such an important letter must be planned, written, and possibly rewritten several times before it is ready to mail. The time you invest in planning and writing your application will be spent wisely.

Never copy a letter that someone else writes, no matter how successful it was for that person. A letter borrowed from a textbook or some other source does not allow your personality to show. Let's suppose you do copy an application letter you like, and it wins an interview for you. Isn't the employer going to be disappointed when he or she talks with you and finds out that you are an entirely different person from the one the employer pictured while reading the letter?

Plan and write your own letter in your own style. To be successful for *you*, an application letter should reflect *your* personality, *your* attitude toward life and work.

An application letter is your personal sales letter. Prepare to write it in much the same way that you prepared to write the sales promotion letters in Unit 15. Review that preparation to see how each step works out as you get ready to write an application for a job.

Prepare a Mailing List of Prospective "Buyers"

One way to obtain names of prospective buyers for your mailing list is to study various companies that have employees who do the kind of work you plan to do. After comparing these companies, you can select the ones where you feel you could be happy working. You can then write an application (called a *prospecting application*) for the purpose of interesting the personnel directors of these companies in your qualifications and in your request for an interview. When you write more than one prospecting application, type each letter individually and address each to the person in charge of employment at the particular company.

A more popular way to obtain names for your list is to locate companies that are advertising suitable job openings. You can then write an application (called an *invited application*) to each prospective employer for a job which you know is open and for which you are qualified. You can readily find out about such job openings through *(1)* help-wanted ads in newspapers, magazines, and trade journals; *(2)* school placement services; *(3)* public or private employment agencies; or *(4)* relatives, friends, or acquaintances who tell you about vacancies.

Study the Company and the Job

You must understand both the company and the job for which you apply before you can tell an employer how your personality, training, and experience make you a good choice—or *the* choice—for that job. The more you learn about company policy and job requirements, the more interesting and convincing you can make your letter.

Determine What You Can Do for the Company

To secure attention and interest, write about doing something for the reader. Avoid overusing *I* and *my*. Just as sales executives do, consider your qualifications in terms of what a particular job requires. Only then can you give the employer any practical reasons for buying your services.

Remember that you are in competition with many other people who are trying to sell their services. Yet you hope the employer will ask you to come in and talk about the job. If your application is to stand out from the others, it must highlight the specific qualifications that would make you a valuable employee in the company. Every reply to an advertisement for a typist will probably mention the applicant's ability to type. To make your letter stand out, find out what kind of typing ability is needed and then determine what you can offer. You might learn, for example, that typing reports containing statistics is part of the job. If this is a requirement for which you are prepared, you won't just say that you can type; you will tell the employer that you can set up statistical material in attractive form and type reports rapidly and accurately.

Decide on the Central Selling Point to Be Featured

In the letter you may mention all your important qualifications for the job, but you can't stress them all. Ask yourself: Of all my qualifications, which one would be most important in the job for which I am applying, which one will appeal most to this employer? It may be your experience in similar work; your ability to get along well with people; your college training; or a special skill, such as the ability to take rapid dictation and transcribe accurately. This most important qualification becomes your Central Selling Point, around which you build your letter.

Make a Plan for the Letter

Ordinarily the purpose of writing an application letter is to obtain an interview. The letter, therefore, should be persuasive. It should convince the employer that you are so well qualified that he or she will want to talk with you and find out more about you before making a choice among the applicants for the job opening.

Plan the content of a letter that will capture the employer's attention and interest, convince him or her that you have the qualifications to do an outstanding job for the company, and persuade the employer to invite you to come for an interview.

Objectives of an Application Letter

To interest the employer in you as an applicant—and to obtain an invitation to a personal conference—aim to accomplish these four purposes in your letter.

1. *Show the employer you know how to write a superior business letter.*

Type your letter on a good grade of white 8½- by 11-inch stationery. Check balanced placement and arrangement of the letter on the page; appropriate heading, inside address, salutation, and closing lines; correct, clear, and easy-to-understand words and sentences; and accurate grammar, punctuation, spelling, and typing.

2. *Show him or her you understand the requirements of the job for which you apply.* If you are answering an advertisement, read it thoroughly and know exactly what it tells you about the job advertised and the qualifications wanted. If you are not answering an ad or if the ad does not give details, determine the job requirements by applying what you have learned in school, at work, or in talking with people who have done similar work. For example, if you are applying for a job as a stenographer, think of all the tasks a stenographer usually performs in an office—taking dictation, transcribing, handling telephone and office calls, filing, working with co-workers and a supervisor, and the like—and the abilities and personality traits that are necessary to handle these duties successfully.

3. *Show the employer you have the qualifications needed to fill the job.* The applicant's qualifications are the heart of an application. The employer is looking for someone who can do the work that needs to be done and who will do it well. Explain in detail just how your background, personality, training, and experience will help you to do the job well. If you are answering an advertisement, be sure to give all information requested and to show that you have every requirement suggested in the ad. Cover all the requirements in the letter itself; don't depend on the résumé to take the place of a thorough application letter.

Explain your qualifications in specific terms. It is not enough to say, "I can operate several office machines." Explain that you have transcribed mailable letters from machine dictation, that you can use automatic typewriters, and so on.

Toward the end of the message, call attention to the résumé enclosed. Then the employer will review your qualifications as revealed by both the letter and the résumé.

4. *Show him or her you are more interested in helping the company than in getting something for your own benefit.* Be sincere and enthusiastic when you talk about working, serving, and cooperating. You certainly won't sound as though you are interested in service to the company if your letter is filled with questions about salary, raises, vacations, pension plans, sick leave, and overtime pay. Leave these matters for the interview.

Desirable Features of an Application Letter

Perhaps the best way to be sure the application letter accomplishes all four objectives is to develop it in three parts: (1) an interesting opening that will get the employer's attention; (2) a convincing presentation of your qualifications; and (3) a strong closing requesting action.

1. An Interesting Opening. The opening must, of course, get the employer interested in your qualifications—interested enough to read on. If the job has been advertised, you can get the reader's attention by mentioning in the first sentence of the letter the source of your information about the vacancy. The openings below were written by applicants who learned of job opportunities from other sources.

> From the MSU Placement Office I learned that you are looking for a top-flight salesperson who can also give outstanding field demonstrations with Holtz farm equipment.

> Mrs. Martha Kendall, Director of the School of Medical Records Administration at the University of Maryland, brought to my attention your need for an Assistant Administrator in your Medical Records Department. Mrs. Kendall is confident that my college preparation and my experience in the Medical Records Department of Giles County Hospital will enable me to meet all the requirements of this job.

If you write a prospecting application for a job that is not advertised, you often get attention and interest:

a. By summarizing your qualifications for the kind of job you would like to have with the company.

> As a secretary in your purchasing department, I could rapidly and accurately take your dictation (80 wpm) and type your letters (65 wpm). I believe I would thoroughly enjoy working with my office associates and furthering Concord's goodwill with other companies both in the office and by phone.

> With my college background, accounting and selling experience, and ability to get along with people, I believe that I could do a good job selling Burroughs Office Machines.

b. By referring to the company's reputation, progress, or policies.

> The recent expansion of Roosevelt Refining Company's research and production facilities, as reported in *Chemical Engineering*, suggests a possible opening for chemists.

> As a recent college graduate certified to teach history and social science, I would like to have the opportunity to contribute to the continued growth and success of the Randolph County School System.

c. By suggesting your attitude toward the kind of work the company engages in.

> Retailing means to me the challenge of meeting people and selling them on a product, an idea, a principle, or a goal.

2. A Convincing Presentation. To be convincing, the presentation of your qualifications must be related to the work to be done and backed by evidence. Study the following excerpts and the three successful applications on pages 113 to 115 so that you may adapt your qualifications to individual job requirements.

Avoid vague, unconvincing expressions such as, "I have a good personality," "I am intelligent," "I am dependable," or "I am interested in working with people." You can portray your personal traits more convincingly by presenting the evidence and letting the reader draw the conclusions. Notice how this applicant tells the employer he is a hard worker.

> After delivering newpapers seven mornings a week while in high school, I'm not afraid of the long hours of work that always occur during rush periods. Hard work doesn't bother me either, since I enjoyed three busy summers assisting my father on construction jobs.

Interpret your training in terms of the work to be done. The courses you take and the school activities you participate in are not nearly so important to an employer as the lessons these experiences teach you. In your letter, instead of listing courses and extracurricular activities, try to point up ways in which you can do a better job for the company because of something you learned in school. Notice how the successful application letters on pages 113 to 115 and the following excerpts stress outcomes rather than action.

> **APPLICANTS FOR FIELD REPRESENTATIVE FOR TIMELY CLOTHES, INC.** My college courses in clothing construction and design and in salesmanship have given me a fairly broad knowledge of the makeup of men's and women's fashions and many pointers about selling that I could put to good use for Timely.
>
> In my basic college courses—including psychology, humanities, social science, and public speaking—I gained a broader understanding of human behavior and learned to think on my feet and win people to my point of view.

> **APPLICANTS FOR A JOB IN RETAILING** Among other extracurricular activities, I worked on the advertising staff of the college paper and had the opportunity to meet and talk with most of the merchants in Weston. Through this experience I learned about business problems and about what the public expects of a retail store.
>
> Since I have held several part-time jobs and participated in many outside activities while in college, I learned the value of budgeting my time and getting important things done first. This knowledge should be helpful in your busy office.

Adapt your work experience to job requirements. In the application letter, discuss work experience in terms of what you have learned from it. The employer is interested in how your previous jobs prepared you to do good work for his or her company. Use the application letters in this unit and the following excerpts to help you adapt your work experience to the job for which you are applying.

APPLICANT FOR JOB AS SALES REPRESENTATIVE As a successful book sales representative for Lawrence Publishing Company, I have learned to get along with people in the most difficult selling situation—in the customer's home. This job also taught me time management, which is very important to a salesperson working outside an office.

APPLICANT FOR JOB AS SECRETARY IN PURCHASING DEPARTMENT OF A MAJOR MANUFACTURER I am familiar with purchasing terms and the overall structure of a manufacturing firm. Working as a secretary in the purchasing department of the Bohn Aluminum Corporation also gave me a good background in buying policies and practices. This experience would enable me to process your orders quickly and accurately.

3. *A Strong Closing.* The application letter, like any other sales letter, should have an action ending. Close the letter with a specific request for action—usually that the employer name a time for a conference with you about the job—and give the reader a good reason for inviting you for an interview. When you apply for a job far from your home, the company may suggest an expenses-paid trip to its personnel offices, a closed-circuit television interview, or a conference with a representative in your vicinity. In the successful applications on pages 113, 114, and 115, each applicant asks for an interview and adds a statement about the contribution he or she can make to the company.

The references listed on the enclosed résumé will be glad to confirm that I can meet the high requirements of financial consultant for United American Bank. Please call me at (701) 458-4932 or write to me at the above address to tell me when it would be convenient for you to talk with me.

I can start to work for Southwestern Life Insurance Company after my graduation on August 20. I would like to have an appointment to meet and talk with you at your convenience. My telephone number is (392) 584-4951; my address is given above.

Give Your Letter a Final Check

When you have completed an application letter, decide whether it is the best letter you can write by asking the following questions.

1. Does the letter show that I know how to apply the principles of writing *effective* business letters?

2. Will my opening paragraph interest the employer in my qualifications?

3. Does the letter make clear that I understand the requirements of the job?

4. Does the letter emphasize that I have the personality, training, and experience to fill the job?

5. Does the letter indicate that I am interested in what I can do for the company?

6. Do I ask for specific action in the closing paragraph—and motivate the reply that I want?

COMPLETING THE APPLICATION FORM

An applicant for a job is often asked to fill out an application blank—usually when he or she comes for the interview. Application blanks vary in length, content, and organization from company to company; but all ask for basic information about personal characteristics, education, and employment—many of the same details included on a résumé. Before you complete the application blank in Worksheet 20, study the suggestions below so that you will be familiar with such forms.

When you fill out the application form, (1) read directions carefully, (2) give the exact information asked for in each space, (3) take care not to skip any item, and (4) complete the form neatly and accurately with pen, *not* pencil. If you are asked to complete the form at home, try to *type* the information. Remember that this form becomes a permanent part of your employment record with the company if you are hired.

WRITING FOLLOW-UP AND THANK-YOU LETTERS

Few job commitments are made at the first interview. The employer usually "screens" applicants (that is, narrows the field down to a few applicants), then calls the better ones in for another interview before making the final selection.

After an interview in which you are not told definitely whether you have the job, write a follow-up letter expressing appreciation for the interview and continued interest in the job. You may need to include in your letter something you did not get a chance to tell the employer in the interview. If you were asked to complete and return an application blank, fill it out and send it with your follow-up letter. At the top of the next page is the thank-you note Joyce Kramer sent after her interview with the personnel manager of BSM, Inc.

Dear Mr. Brown:

Thank you for talking with me personally about the secretarial job in your Customer Service Department.

Enclosed are the completed application form and the second résumé copy that you requested.

You can reach me at my home telephone (302) 555-2098. I hope you will let me put my abilities and skills to work for BSM, Inc.

Sincerely,

Write a similar thank-you letter if you have been told that your application will be kept on file for consideration when a job opening fits your qualifications.

You may write a second follow-up letter, after waiting a reasonable time, if you hear nothing more from the employer. Often you can make this second follow-up more effective by providing additional information, such as a change of address, graduation from school, or completion of a temporary job.

Sometimes a follow-up letter will spark a response when you have had no reply to your original application for several weeks and feel that the employer has overlooked it. In this letter you should mention the date of the previous application, the job for which you applied, and your availability for an interview. In it you may summarize and give additional information about your major qualifications but need not enclose a résumé.

If you are offered the job, you have several thank-you letters to write. Did someone tell you about the job opening? Did someone give a favorable report of your qualifications or in any other way help you to get the job? Did someone write you a note congratulating you and wishing you success on the new job? All these people deserve simple, sincere messages of appreciation.

REQUESTING INFORMA-TION ABOUT JOB APPLICANTS

When an employer writes to one of the references given on a résumé to ask for information about the applicant, the letter follows the form of a direct inquiry (see Unit 11). The employer should mark the inquiry "Confidential" and ask questions that will obtain the facts and opinions that he or she needs.

The person who answers a request for information about an applicant should also mark the response "Confidential." The reply should be a report of facts that will give an accurate picture of the applicant rather than a biased recommendation. And opinions should be clearly separated from facts. A former employer should not say, for instance, "Miss Dudiak will make you an excellent secretary." But the employer might say, "Miss Dudiak did superior work in my office, and I believe that she will make you an excellent secretary."

ACCEPTING AND REFUSING JOB OFFERS

If you receive a job offer by mail, write an acceptance or a refusal just as soon as you can. If you accept, say so in a short, enthusiastic letter. If you cannot accept, say "no" so graciously that you leave the door open for future employment with the company.

Notice the happy—not gushy—tone of Joyce Kramer's acceptance.

Dear Mr. Brown:

I am happy to accept the secretarial job in the Customer Service Department of BSM, Inc. Thank you for choosing me.

As you suggested, I'll report at nine o'clock on Monday morning, July 6. I am looking forward to the challenge of office work at BSM, Inc.

Sincerely,

ASSIGNMENT: In Section B you will utilize the self-analysis you made for an employment application. You will gain experience in preparing a résumé, writing letters about employment, and filling out an application form.

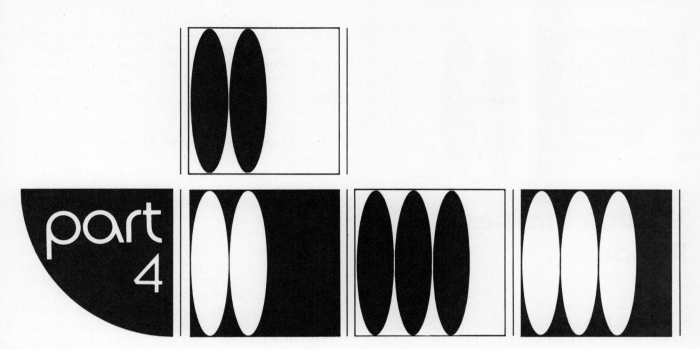

Principles of Report Writing

Business reports are written to communicate facts, ideas, statistics, and trends. Within the organization reports travel upward (to the top executives), laterally (between people of equal rank), and downward (directives to subordinates). Reports may also be sent to people outside the organization (for example, to consultants, customers, government agencies, etc.).

The flow of information and ideas is vital to business operations. As the modern business world becomes even more sophisticated and complex, accurate, reliable, objective reports become essential to efficient company operations.

Business reports are of many types, ranging from brief memos to nearly book-length reports on complex subjects. A report may be a brief financial statement, or it may be an involved analysis of highly technical and intricate experiments.

A report may be informal—giving facts and opinions in the first person ("I suggest...") and in conversational language and style. Or it may be a formal, objective report—written in the third person ("It is suggested...") in formal language and style, and supported by facts that have been assembled and validated by standard research techniques.

Report format is somewhat flexible, as you will see in Unit 21. Memorandum forms may be used for informal reports that are a few pages or shorter in length. Longer reports require a more formal format.

Managers and supervisors rely heavily on all types of information they receive through reports as the basis for sound decision making. A company that is considering a major change or an expensive proposal will need a detailed report that is based on the results of research and experiments. Routine or periodic reports—submitted at regular intervals, such as weekly or monthly—are common types of short business reports, often submitted on printed forms.

Whatever the length or type of the report, composing and transmitting an informative, useful message should be the goal of every report writer.

unit 21

Writing Business Reports

This unit examines three common types of business reports: informal memo reports, formal business reports, and minutes of meetings.

INTEROFFICE MEMORANDUMS AS REPORTS

Interoffice memorandums (called *memos*) are used to communicate with other employees. Memos are reports if they are written in answer to a request for information, to report progress, to make recommendations, or merely to state facts.

At the beginning of your business career, you will probably be more directly concerned with interoffice memorandums than with any other type of report because the memo is popular for routine, in-company communication.

Appearance, Style, and Tone

Just as the informal interoffice memo is different in appearance from a letter, it is also very different from the lengthy, complex report. You will see excerpts from a long, formal report later in this unit. For a review of accepted practice in typing memos, turn to "Interoffice Correspondence," Unit 3, page 13.

An informal memo may also differ in style and tone from a letter or a report written to someone outside the company, because the writer of the memo is often more interested in presenting facts and letting the reader form his or her own judgments than in persuading the reader. Although the memo writer does not forget about tact, courtesy, and friendliness, he or she assumes that the reader—a member of the writer's own company—will take it for granted that the company's interests are being served and thus will need little persuasion.

Not all interoffice memos are informal, however. Some business executives prefer objective, third-person writing in office communications. They think that facts and recommendations can be evaluated best when they are presented impersonally.

The tone and style of the memo often depend primarily on the writer, the person or persons addressed, and the nature of company business. The

---

MEMORANDUM			
To:	Carl Thompson, President	**From:**	Susan O'Meara, Chairperson
			Ethics Committee
Subject:	Code of Ethics Flier	**Date:**	June 10, 19--

As you requested, the members of the Ethics Committee and I have revised the Code of Ethics Flier that we distribute to all employees each year. A copy of the revised manuscript is enclosed.

Like last year's flier, the revision discusses Conflicts of Interest, Outside Employment, and Relations With Suppliers. All the committee members agreed that we should also include two new topics: Confidential Information and Payments to Others.

Please let me know your opinion of this revised Code of Ethics.

SO

An informal tone is appropriate for the subject of this brief memo report.

tone is influenced by the writer-reader relationship and by the personalities of both; for example, a memo prepared by the president of a company as a directive may sound informal and conversational if the president prefers it that way. A long report written to the president will probably be written in the third person for a more formal effect, as you can see on page 124.

The subject also helps to determine the tone. A report of financial condition would, of course, be more formal than the brief memo report on page 122.

Content and Organization

No rigid rules govern the content and organization of interoffice memos that function as reports. The memo report should follow the form best suited to its particular function. The memo below is an example of a request (or a directive that gives instructions). The memo on page 124 is an example of a report; notice the pattern it follows.

Commonly, the main idea is presented in the first paragraph; the middle paragraphs contain supporting details; and the ending consists of conclusions and/or suggestions for future action (recommendations).

Occasionally, however, you may decide that the indirect approach would be a better plan; for instance, if you are presenting conclusions or recommendations which you know the reader will be opposed to, you may be wise to start off slowly, by giving the details and facts leading up to them.

One of the most common and effective techniques of memo organization is to itemize the information. A report that contains complex facts and ideas will be easier to read if items are separated into paragraphs and enumerated. Too, numbering paragraphs helps the writer to write concisely and to organize carefully, as you can see by reviewing the memo on page 124.

A memo containing statistical information should present the information in tabulated form for easier reading, as in the memo on page 124.

Gathering Information

Because the office-memo type of report is often needed quickly, gathering the information for it is frequently more casual and less scientific than for the longer, more professional report. Longer, analytical reports may require more complex methods of collecting facts, such as library research, questionnaire surveys, observation, and experimentation. If you are asked to collect data for a less formal type of report, however, make the process as thorough and the results as factual as your limited time allows.

Now suppose you receive from your employer the memorandum shown below requesting a short report comparing the company's present janitorial costs with the cost of contracting with an outside firm for the service. How will you go about gathering data for the report?

First, you read the request carefully to make sure you know exactly what information Mr. Benedetto is asking for. Since his memorandum is clearly written and you understand what you are to do, you need not telephone him for further explanation.

You decide to start with your company, by finding out the yearly costs of salaries and fringe benefits for the

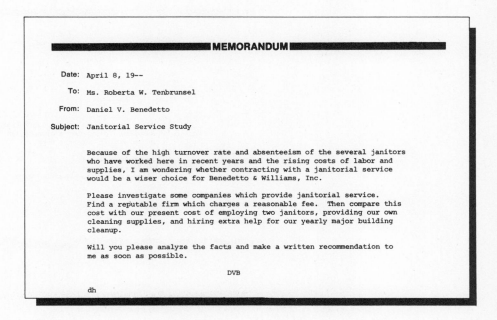

MEMORANDUM

Date: April 8, 19--

To: Ms. Roberta W. Tenbrunsel

From: Daniel V. Benedetto

Subject: Janitorial Service Study

Because of the high turnover rate and absenteeism of the several janitors who have worked here in recent years and the rising costs of labor and supplies, I am wondering whether contracting with a janitorial service would be a wiser choice for Benedetto & Williams, Inc.

Please investigate some companies which provide janitorial service. Find a reputable firm which charges a reasonable fee. Then compare this cost with our present cost of employing two janitors, providing our own cleaning supplies, and hiring extra help for our yearly major building cleanup.

Will you please analyze the facts and make a written recommendation to me as soon as possible.

DVB

dh

This request memo is really a directive that gives instructions.

```
                    M E M O R A N D U M


     TO:       Mr. Daniel V. Benedetto, President
               Benedetto & Williams, Inc.

     FROM:     Roberta W. Tenbrunsel

     DATE:     April 16, 19--

     SUBJECT:  Janitorial Service Study


     Purpose - To save Benedetto & Williams, Inc., approximately $1,000
     per year in janitorial expense, I recommend that we contract
     janitorial service instead of providing the service ourselves.

     Cost and Savings - The yearly cost of contracting janitorial
     service would be about $12,480.  Present yearly expenditures for
     employing two full-time janitors, hiring extra personnel, and
     purchasing cleaning supplies total about $13,522.  Using a
     janitorial service would save the company about $1,042 per year.

     Procedure - McDaniels Janitorial Service, a reputable firm based
     in Atlanta, would supply the needed janitorial service for $240
     a week.  MJS would be responsible for providing both the personnel
     and the cleaning supplies necessary to do the job.  This also
     includes our annual major clean-up.

     Cost Breakdown - The following compares the present cost of
     providing our own janitors and cleaning supplies with the cost
     of contracting with McDaniels to provide this service:

          Yearly salaries for two janitors
             (including fringe benefits) . . . . . . . $12,502

          Approximate cost of hiring extra
             personnel for yearly major clean-up . . . .   450

          Approximate annual cost of cleaning supplies .   570
                           Present Annual Expenses . $13,522
          Yearly cost of McDaniels Janitorial Service . 12,480
                           Savings Effected . . . . . $ 1,042

     Conclusions - Benedetto & Williams, Inc., would enjoy the following
     benefits if we used McDaniels Janitorial Service:

          1.  Present yearly cleaning expenses would be reduced by
              about $1,000 as shown above.

          2.  Increased costs caused by high turnover in the janitor
              positions would be eliminated.  The two men presently
              employed as janitors could be transferred to the shipping
              department to fill the vacancies there.
```

```
     Mr. Daniel V. Benedetto          2          April 16, 19--


          3.  Total responsibility for janitorial work would rest on
              McDaniels, including assigning and training employees
              and providing cleaning supplies.

          4.  Restrooms, hallways, and offices would be cleaned daily
              by dependable and trained help.  A major building
              clean-up would be scheduled once a year.

     sw
```

Note the content and the organization of this report, which was written in
response to the request on page 123.

two janitors, cleaning supplies, and the annual major cleanup.

Next, you look in the Yellow Pages and begin phoning janitorial services. They give you general information about their services and an estimate of the fee which would be charged for cleaning your building. After studying this information, you narrow down the choices to three firms which are well-known for dependability and which give you low cost estimates.

You set up appointments with representatives from the three firms to come and inspect your building and estimate what the charges would be. After the inspections have been completed, you select the firm which you believe would give your company the best deal. Now it is time to analyze the facts you have gathered from your company and from the janitorial service. You are ready to compare the costs, draw conclusions, and present your recommendation to Mr. Benedetto.

Writing the Report

You must determine the best way to report your findings. Remember that Mr. Benedetto expects your report to be factual and reliable. You will, of course, present the facts with absolute fairness and accuracy. You must also be careful not to mix your own opinions with the facts you report. Reserve your comments for your conclusions and recommendations.

THE EXPANDED ROLE OF THE PERSONNEL MANAGER

OF THE GARY L. TAYLOR COMPANY

Prepared for

Mr. Dennis R. Cooper

Vice President

By

Sue Ann Steelman, Personnel Manager
The Gary L. Taylor Company
Santa Monica, California
May 14, 19--

A formal report requires a title page such as this one.

Mr. Benedetto requested a "written recommendation" and gave you a relatively short time in which to prepare it. You feel, therefore, that the two-page memorandum shown on page 124 will do the job properly.

This memorandum report is well done from two points of view: (1) The information is presented in an orderly, easy-to-read fashion. (2) The report represents extra work because you not only make the recommendation Mr. Benedetto asked for but also take the time to present the facts clearly and show him a concise but complete comparison. In writing reports, as in other phases of a job, remember to do a little more than is required. You and those around you will benefit from your extra effort to produce a comprehensive, well-written report.

FORMAL BUSINESS REPORTS

The term *formal* in relation to business reports normally refers to the length, general appearance, and organization of the report rather than to its language. Representative of the more formal presentations are analytical reports on which important business decisions depend. A large corporation considering the purchase of a smaller company—with hundreds of thousands of dollars involved—will, for example, require an exhaustive report or a series of well-organized reports before making a decision. Similarly, a company considering a change in technical processes to effect savings in production costs will require a long, formal report

CONTENTS

A Table of Contents helps the reader to understand the organization of a formal report.

containing an objective appraisal of various aspects of the situation, backed by appropriate statistics.

The typical formal business report demands thoroughly documented, objective, and detailed preparation. This process, like the preparation of other business reports, starts with the *recognition of a problem* that needs solving. The second step is *planning the attack and collecting the data,* often by such popular methods as investigative observation, directed surveys, controlled experimentation, and library research. The final steps are *organizing and interpreting the assembled facts* and *writing the report.*

Its organization and mechanical makeup greatly influence the readability of a business report. You can get an idea of one typical method of organizing an analytical report by studying the sample Table of Contents on page 126.

The more formal business reports usually include ten major parts, some of which may be optional according to the nature and purpose of the report.

1. *Title page.* (See sample on page 125.)
2. *Letter of transmittal.* (Review the discussion of cover letters in Unit 12, page 71, and in Unit 19, page 106.)
3. *Table of contents.*
4. *Summary or synopsis.* Condensation of the complete report in a few paragraphs with emphasis on conclusions and recommendations.

THE EXPANDED ROLE OF THE PERSONNEL MANAGER

OF THE GARY L. TAYLOR COMPANY

The Why and How of This Report

Purpose

The purpose of this report is to acquaint the management of the Gary L. Taylor Company with the duties and responsibilities of the Personnel Manager.

In recent years, the Personnel Manager's areas of responsibility have been greatly expanded as the result of the company's growth and the passage of certain legislation.

It is believed that a better understanding of this role by those closely associated with it will promote better intracompany relations and will present to the public a more positive image of the company.

Scope and Methods

This study was confined to the specific areas of responsibility of the Personnel Manager of the Gary L. Taylor Company.

Special emphasis was given to the newer problems which the Personnel Manager faces, relevant guidelines for their solution, and the impact of these issues on the company as a whole.

A review of current related literature including journal articles and special reports which pertained to the subject was included.

An example of the first page of text of a formal report.

5. *Introduction.* Statement of the purpose, research methods, and scope of the report.

6. *Text.* Body of the report, which contains the facts and figures—with interpretations—that support the conclusions and recommendations. (See page 127.)

7. *Conclusions.*

8. *Recommendations.*

9. *Appendix.* The supplementary material (often graphic or tabular) not incorporated in the text.

10. *Bibliography.* A list of publications consulted.

Your company may have its own correspondence manual which will show you how reports are to be typed. If your office does not have such a handbook, consult a secretarial reference book for proper report format.

MINUTES OF MEETINGS AS REPORTS

Minutes are reports of meetings. They provide official records of meetings. Minutes of business meetings usually follow the conventional pattern given below.

When minutes are very lengthy or complex, brief, specific sideheads may be typed at the left to indicate the main topics covered. For more details about writing minutes, consult a secretarial handbook.

ASSIGNMENT: To put your knowledge of business reports into practice, turn to the Worksheet for this unit. You will gain experience in gathering information and in presenting it in informal report style.

MINUTES OF THE MEETING

of the

W E S T   S I D E   I M P R O V E M E N T   A S S O C I A T I O N

November 16, 19--

Presiding: Alicia Alonzo

Present: Grace Albertson   Michael Nash
            Thomas Borowski   Regina Owens
            Elaine DeSantis   Paula Petrak
            Shirley Feeney   Martha Shaw
            Maria Jimenez   Robert Talley
            Arthur Klein   Cecilia Trentacoste
            Fred Lenari

Absent: Cindy Anderton, Brian Hickey, Karen Mateyak

The regular meeting of the West Side Improvement Association was called to order by Mrs. Alicia Alonzo, president, at 7:30 p.m. on November 16, 19--, at the Civic Center, with 13 members present. After the roll call, the minutes of October 19 were read and approved.

The report of the treasurer, showing a balance of $541.35, was read and placed on file.

Mr. Fred Lenari, chairman of the Nominating Committee, reported that a slate of nominees for next year would be presented at the December meeting.

Plans for cooperation with other civic organizations in a city-wide snow-removal project were discussed informally. Several worthwhile suggestions were made. It was then moved by Mrs. Shirley Feeney that a committee be appointed to consider the suggestions and report at the next meeting. The motion was seconded and carried. The president announced that she would appoint the committee within a week and notify the members.

Mr. Steven C. Robbins, city attorney, addressed the meeting on "A New State Charter." He was given an ovation and vote of thanks for his presentation of this subject.

The meeting was adjourned at 9:30 p.m.

Respectfully submitted,

Robert Talley

Robert Talley, Secretary

Approved, December 21, 19--

Minutes of meetings, which provide official records of meetings, are generally typed as shown here.

reference
section

GRAMMAR

The ability to use the English language competently is an enviable skill in the business world. Speaking and writing clearly, coherently, and effectively is a goal of every business executive. The words you use in conversation, in the office, and in business letters must be well chosen so as to convey your meaning accurately. You therefore need to know which word to use—and when and why.

Studying and practicing the rules of grammar will help you to make fewer errors in your writing—and to recognize and correct your errors *before* you mail a letter or submit a report.

When you put together even two words that make a complete thought, you have formed a sentence. *I work* expresses a complete thought. The subject is *I* and the predicate is *work*. Every sentence must have a subject and a predicate. The subject must contain a noun or a pronoun. The predicate must contain a verb.

Words classified according to their use in the sentence are called parts of speech. The parts of speech are nouns, pronouns, verbs, adjectives, adverbs, prepositions, and conjunctions.

G-1. Nouns

A noun is the name of a person *(Gloria)*, place *(New York)*, thing *(chair)*, idea *(beauty)*, or attribute *(courage)*.

Nouns may be proper *(Gloria)* or common *(chair)*, concrete *(furniture)* or abstract *(modern)*, or collective *(family)*.

The gender of a noun may be masculine *(boy)*, feminine *(woman)*, common *(child)*, or neuter *(piano)*.

G-1-a. Plurals of Nouns. The number of a noun indicates whether it is singular or plural. To form the plurals of most nouns, follow these rules:

1. Add *s* to the singular *(order, orders; decision, decisions; price, prices)*.

2. Add *es* to a singular that ends in *s* (or an *s* sound), *sh* or *ch*, *x*, or *z* *(business, businesses; loss, losses; tax, taxes)*.

3. Change *y* to *i* and add *es* for words ending in *y* preceded by a consonant *(company, companies; copy, copies)*.

4. Add only *s* for words ending in *y* preceded by a vowel *(Monday, Mondays; attorney, attorneys)*.

5. Add only *s* for words ending in *o* preceded by a vowel *(ratio, ratios; patio, patios; studio, studios)*.

6. Add *es* to most nouns ending in *o* preceded by a consonant *(hero, heroes)*. Some exceptions are *memo, memos; zero, zeros*.

7. Add *s* to the singular of most nouns that end in *f, fe,* or *ff (belief, beliefs; brief, briefs; proof, proofs; bailiff, bailiffs)*. For certain other nouns, change the final *f* or *fe* to *v* and add *es (half, halves; self, selves; wife, wives)*.

8. A few plurals are formed irregularly *(foot, feet; child, children; woman, women)*. If you are not sure of a plural form, consult a dictionary.

9. For a hyphenated or a two-word compound noun, change the chief word of the compound of a plural form *(account receivable, accounts receivable; sister-in-law, sisters-in-law; notary public, notaries public)*. If the compound is made up of a noun and a preposition, change the noun (not the preposition) to the plural *(passerby, passersby)*. If the compound does not contain a noun, form the plural on the last element of the compound *(trade-in, trade-ins)*. Compounds written as one word usually form the plural at the end *(letterhead, letterheads)*.

10. Add *s* to most proper nouns *(Buzan, Buzans; Romano, Romanos; Gary, Garys)*. But add *es* to a proper noun ending in *s* or an *s* sound *(James, Jameses)*. Plurals of titles and personal names are formed as follows: *the Misses Shelton* or *the Miss Sheltons; the Doctors Wilson* or *the Doctor Wilsons*.

11. Some nouns have the same form in the singular and the plural *(Chinese; deer; corps; politics)*.

12. Certain nouns are always singular *(athletics; economics; mathematics; music; news)*.

13. Certain nouns are always plural *(credentials; pants; goods; proceeds; statistics)*.

14. Plurals of words from other languages that have been incorporated into the English language should be looked up in the dictionary *(analysis, analyses; parenthesis, parentheses; criterion, criteria)*. Some of these words have both a foreign and an English plural; in fact, there may be a difference in the meaning of each plural form, so be sure to look up such plurals in your dictionary.

15. Add *s* to form the plurals of most abbreviations (*Dr., Drs.; no., nos.; dept., depts.*). The abbreviations of many units of weight and measure, however, are the same in both the singular and the plural (*oz.* for both "ounce" and "ounces"; *ft.* for both "foot" and "feet"). A few single-letter abbreviations form the plural by doubling the same letter (*p.* and *pp.* for *page* and *pages*; *f.* and *ff.* for *following page* and *following pages*). The plurals of capital letters, abbreviations ending with capital letters, figures, and symbols are formed by adding *s* (*Bs, Ph.D.s, 3s, &s*) unless the omission of the apostrophe would cause misreading (*A's, I's, U's*). The plurals of words referred to as words are formed by adding *s* or *es* unless the plural form would be likely to be misread or would be unfamiliar (*ands, dos, don'ts* but *which's* and *or's*). Add an apostrophe plus *s* to form the plural of uncapitalized letters and uncapitalized abbreviations with internal periods (*i's, c.o.d.'s*).

G-1-b. Possessives of Nouns.

1. Add an apostrophe and *s* to form the possessive of most singular nouns (*woman's* coat; *manager's* office; *boss's* desk; *Charles's* vacation).

2. For singular nouns that end in *s*, if adding the apostrophe and *s* makes the word hard to pronounce, add only the apostrophe (Ms. *Billings'* idea; *Jesus'* teachings).

3. Add only an apostrophe to regularly formed plurals (*employees'* vacations; *ladies'* handbags; *presidents'* portraits).

4. Add an apostrophe and *s* to irregularly formed plurals (*men's* suits; *children's* toys).

5. Add the apostrophe and *s* to the final member of a compound noun (her daughter-in-*law's* car; the editor in *chief's* responsibilities; the *secretary-treasurer's* report). It is usually preferable to recast a sentence to avoid the plural possessive of a compound noun ("the decision of all the editors in chief" is better than "all the editors in *chief's* decision").

6. To indicate joint ownership of two or more nouns, form the possessive on the final noun (MacLaren and *MacLaren's* clients). But if separate ownership is meant, make *each* noun possessive (the *secretary's* and the *treasurer's* reports).

7. To indicate the possessive of a singular abbreviation, add an apostrophe and *s* (the Harris *Co.'s* offer; Mr. Hugh Miller, *Sr.'s* resignation); of a plural abbreviation, add only an apostrophe (the *M.D.s'* diagnoses).

8. Restrict the use of the possessive to persons and animals. Do not use the possessive form to refer to inanimate things; use an *of* phrase (the format *of the letter;* the provisions *of the will*). Some exceptions are expressions of time and measure (*today's* market; two *weeks'* vacation; ten *dollars'* worth of supplies) and personification (the *company's* assets).

G-2. Pronouns

A pronoun is used in place of a noun, to avoid repetition.

> The chairperson has studied the recommendations and agrees with *them.*

G-2-a. A pronoun must agree with its antecedent (word for which it stands) in number, person, and gender.

> One of the women left *her* keys on the desk.

G-2-b. Demonstrative pronouns (*this, that, these, those*) should plainly refer to a specific antecedent. Do not use *this* or *that* to refer to the thought of an entire sentence.

> VAGUE: Our shipping department had several workers absent. *This* accounts for the delay in sending out yesterday's orders.

> CLEAR: Several workers in our shipping department were absent. Their absences account for the delay in sending out yesterday's orders.

G-2-c. Relative pronouns (*who, whom*) do not agree in case with their antecedents. Their grammatical function in the sentence determines their case. A relative pronoun usually introduces a clause. To determine the correct case of the pronoun, rearrange the clause in the order of subject, verb, object. Disregard any parenthetical clauses.

> She is the one whom I believe the committee will choose. (Disregard the parenthetical clause *I believe* and the normal order of the clause is *the committee will choose whom.* The subject is *committee*, the verb is *will choose*, and the object is *whom.*)

G-2-d. Compound personal pronouns (*yourself, myself*, etc.) are used for emphasis. They reflect the action of the verb back upon the subject but are never the subject. A compound personal pronoun should not be used in place of a personal pronoun.

> He told me that himself. (Emphasis.)
> She gave herself time to get to the airport. (Reflexive.)

G-3. Verbs

A verb states a condition or implies or shows action. A sentence must contain a verb to be complete. When the complete verb is a group of words, it is called a *verb phrase.* A verb phrase has one principal verb and one auxiliary verb (the auxiliary may include more than one word). The common auxiliary verbs are forms of the verbs *to be* and *to have.*

> He *works.* He *has been working.* (Auxiliary: *has been*)

G-3-a. Verb Tenses. The tense of a verb tells when the action of the verb takes place.

> They want. (Present.)
> They wanted. (Past.)
> They will want. (Future.)
> They have wanted. (Present perfect.)
> They had wanted. (Past perfect.)
> They will have wanted. (Future perfect.)

1. The tense of the verb in a subordinate clause must agree with the tense of the verb in the principal clause unless the subordinate clause expresses a general truth.

> He *announced* that all employees *were expected* to attend.
> She *saw* a movie which *is* not *recommended* for children. (General truth.)

2. In a sequence all the verbs should be in the same tense unless any expresses a general truth.

> I *went* to the university, *registered* for five courses, and *returned* home at about 2 p.m.

3. Do not use the present tense for past events.

> He *came* to me and *said,* "I can explain the error."
> **NOT:** He comes to me and says...

G-3-b. Agreement of Verb With Subject. A verb should agree with its subject in person and number.

> Three sales representatives complete their training today.

1. Singular subjects connected by *either . . . or, neither . . . nor* require singular verbs.

> Either a refund or a credit memorandum *is* acceptable.

2. When *either . . . or, neither . . . nor* connect subjects differing in number, the verb should agree with that part of the subject that is nearer to the verb.

> Neither the retailers nor the wholesaler *is* liable.
> Neither the wholesaler nor the retailers *are* liable.

3. When such expressions as *together with, as well as, including,* separate the subject and the verb, the verb agrees in number with the real subject.

> The catalog, together with the special sales brochures, *is* ready.

4. When the subject is a collective noun that names a group or unit acting as a whole, use a singular verb.

> The company *is* liberal in its promotion policies.

But when the group or unit is considered to be acting separately, use a plural verb.

> The committee *were* still discussing the issue.

5. When a noun, singular in form, is used as the subject to indicate quantity (*some, all, none, part*) or when a fraction is the subject, use a singular verb when a

singular sense is meant and a plural verb when a plural sense is meant. Whether the plural or the singular sense is meant is usually indicated by the object of the prepositional phrase used with the subject.

> None of the catalogs *were* shipped today.
> All of the event *was* televised.
> One-half of the students *were* absent.
> One-tenth of the population *are* Orientals. (Exception.)

6. When the subject is *a number,* the verb must be plural. When the subject is *the number,* the verb must be singular.

> A number of secretaries *are* being honored.
> The numbers of complaints *is* not surprising.

7. When the name of a business firm includes *and Associates* or *and Company,* use a singular verb.

> Boyle, Rickman and Associates *is* opening new offices.

8. When the subject is a group of words, such as a slogan, a title, or a quotation, use a singular verb.

> "Sell the sizzle not the steak" *is* a well-known saying in the restaurant industry.

G-3-c. Verbal Nouns. Participles ending in *ing* are often used as nouns and are called gerunds. A pronoun modifying a gerund should be in the possessive form.

> I shall appreciate *your* sending the check promptly.

G-4. Adjectives

An adjective describes or limits a noun or a pronoun. An adjective construction may be a single word, two or more unrelated words, a compound, a phrase, or a clause. It may precede or follow the noun or pronoun.

> Five *new electric* typewriters are needed.
> The secretary *for whom we advertised* is hard to find.
> Samantha, *dressed all in black,* arrived first.
> The *loss-of-income* provision is explained below.

An adjective may be modified only by an adverb, not by another adjective.

> The child is *extremely* (adv.) agile (adj.).

G-4-a. Comparison of Adjectives. To express different degrees or qualities, descriptive adjectives may be compared in three forms: *positive, comparative* (two things compared), and *superlative* (three or more things compared).

> Jean's grades are *high.* (Positive.)
> Jean's grades are *higher* than mine. (Comparative.)
> Jean's grades are the *highest* in the class. (Superlative.)

To form the comparative and superlative degrees, follow these rules.

1. To form the comparative of most adjectives, add *er* to the positive: tall, *taller*. To form the superlative, add *est* to the positive: tall, *tallest*.

2. For irregular adjectives, change the form of the word completely (*good, better, best*).

3. For adjectives of two syllables, the comparative is formed by adding *er* or the words *more* or *less* to the positive, and the superlative is formed by adding *est* or the words *most* or *least* to the positive: *likely, likelier, likeliest*; OR: *likely, less likely* (or *more likely*), *least likely* (or *most likely*). Adjectives of three or more syllables are always compared by adding *more* or *most*, *less* or *least* (*more* efficient, *most* efficient).

4. Some adjectives state qualities that cannot be compared (*complete, correct, level, round, perfect, unique*). However, these words may be modified by *more nearly* (or *less nearly*) and similar adverbs to suggest an approach to the absolute.

5. The word *other* must be used in comparing a person or a thing with other members of the group to which it belongs. Our new model is selling better than any *other* we have developed.

G-4-b. Compound Adjectives.

A compound adjective is made up of two or more words used together as a single thought to modify a noun.

A compound adjective should be hyphenated when it precedes the noun if the compound:

1. Is a two-word one-thought modifier (*long-range* goals).
Exception: Very commonly used compounds are not hyphenated: *high school* teachers; *real estate* agent.

2. Is a phrase of three or more words (*up-to-date* report).

3. Is a number combined with a noun (*fourteen-day* period).

4. Has coequal modifiers (*labor-management* relations).

5. Includes irregularly formed comparatives and superlatives (*better-selling* items; *worst-looking* letter).

6. Combines *well* with a participle (*well-educated* executive).

A compound adjective that follows the noun should also be hyphenated when it:

1. Is a *well* compound that retains its one-thought meaning (*well-read, well-to-do*; BUT NOT: *well known, well managed*).

2. Is made up of an adjective or a noun followed by a noun to which *ed* has been added (*high-priced, left-handed*).

3. Is a noun or an adjective followed by a participle (*time-consuming, air-cooled, strange-looking, ill-advised*).

4. Is formed by joining a noun with an adjective (*fire-resistant, tax-exempt*).

Consult the dictionary for compounds composed of common prefixes and suffixes (*audiovisual, postscript, self-*addressed, *interoffice, mid-*July, business*like*).

Do not hyphenate a foreign phrase used as a compound modifier (*per capita* consumption, *ad hoc* ruling, *ex officio* member).

Do not hyphenate a two-word proper noun used as an adjective (*Latin American* conference, *Western Union* telegram, *Supreme Court* decision).

Consult a secretarial handbook for compound adjectives commonly used without hyphens (*real estate, income tax, social security, life insurance*).

G-5. Adverbs

An adverb explains, describes, or limits a verb, an adjective, or another adverb.

> Does this machine work *efficiently*? (Modifies verb.)
> It is *very* efficient. (Modifies adjective.)
> We drove *quite* carefully on the ice. (Modifies adverb.)

G-5-a. Place an adverb as close as possible to the word it modifies. Its position may alter the meaning of the sentence.

> He met her *only* today.
> He met *only* her today.
> *Only* he met her today.

G-5-b. Verbs of the senses (*look, taste, feel, smell,* etc.) and linking verbs (forms of *be, become, seem,* and *appear*) are usually followed by an adjective which describes the subject.

> The meat smells *bad*. (Adjective, modifies *meat*.)
> He looked *happy*. (Adjective, modifies *He*.)
> I feel *bad*. (Adjective, modifies *I*.)

But to describe the action of the verb, use an adverb.

> She looked *happily* at him. (Adverb, modifies *looked*.)
> He felt *carefully* for his key. (Adverb, modifies *felt*.)

G-5-c. Adverbs that are negative in meaning should not be used with negatives.

> She *scarcely* had time to finish the report.
> NOT: She *hadn't scarcely* time to finish the report.

G-6. Prepositions

A preposition is a word used to connect a noun or a pronoun with some other word in the sentence.

> He asked *about* the current financial condition *of* the store.

G-6-a. The noun or pronoun following a preposition is called the *object of the preposition*. A preposition and its object, called a *prepositional phrase,* may be used as a noun, an adjective, or an adverb. The object of a preposition must be in the objective case.

> She sat between *him* and *me.*

G-6-b. Do not use superfluous prepositions.

> Where has he gone?
>
> **NOT:** Where has he gone *to?*

G-6-c. Do not omit necessary prepositions.

> She is interested *in* and excited *about* the trip.
>
> **NOT:** She is interested and excited about the trip.

G-6-d. Certain words are always followed by certain prepositions.

> He is angry *about* the mix-up. (Angry *about* something.)
>
> He is angry *at* me. (Angry *at* a person.)

If you are unsure, look up the word in a dictionary or a reference manual.

G-6-e. Ending a sentence with a preposition is acceptable for emphasis. Short questions often end with prepositions.

> These are the questions I want answers *to.*
>
> Which files are you finished *with?*

G-7. Conjunctions

A conjunction is a word that connects words, phrases, or clauses.

G-7-a. A conjunction may be *coordinate* or *subordinate*. A *coordinate* conjunction connects words, phrases, or clauses of equal grammatical construction. A *subordinate* conjunction connects dependent words, phrases, or clauses to the main, or independent, clause.

> Ten applications have been received, *and* more are still coming in. (Coordinate.)
>
> We have not received the desk, *although* we ordered it six weeks ago. (Subordinate.)

G-7-b. *Correlative* conjunctions are a type of coordinating conjunctions used in pairs to connect two or more words, phrases, or clauses. They should immediately precede the words, phrases, or clauses that they connect, which should be parallel in form.

> You may order *either* now *or* when our sales representative calls.
>
> **NOT:** You may *either* order now *or* when our sales representative calls. (Note that *now* and *when* are in parallel form; both are adverbs.)

G-7-c. Do not use prepositions such as *without, except,* and *like* to introduce a subordinate clause.

> The package looks *as though* it has been tampered with.
>
> **NOT:** The package looks *like* it has been tampered with.

Using Words in Sentences

To convey your meaning successfully in letters or in conversation requires expertness in putting words together. A successful letter is made up of strong, well-constructed sentences and paragraphs.

G-8. Kinds of Sentences

A sentence must contain a subject and a verb (predicate) and express a complete thought. A *simple* sentence contains a subject and a predicate. A *compound* sentence contains more than one independent clause. A *complex* sentence contains one independent clause and at least one dependent clause in either the subject or the predicate. A *compound-complex* sentence contains two or more independent clauses and one or more dependent clauses.

> **SIMPLE:** The vice president left yesterday and will return on Thursday. (This simple sentence contains two verbs joined by the conjunction *and.* A simple sentence may also contain two or more subjects joined by conjunctions.)
>
> **COMPOUND:** The survey has been completed, and the results will be available in a few days.
>
> **COMPLEX:** Results of the survey, which has just been completed, will be announced tomorrow.
>
> **COMPOUND-COMPLEX:** Our Chromex model aroused much interest, and we believe it will appeal to a new market because its price is lower than that of any other model.

G-9. Sentence Fragments

A group of words that does not express a complete thought is not a sentence. Occasionally such an incomplete thought may stand alone for emphasis. Experienced writers sometimes use this device—but sparingly. In business correspondence, this technique is generally limited to sales writing.

> Capricorn Island. *The* place to spend your vacation this summer.
>
> Please check these figures carefully and return them to me as soon as you have finished.
>
> **NOT:** Please check these figures carefully. Returning them to me as soon as you have finished.

G-10. Run-on Sentences

A sentence containing two or more complete thoughts loosely strung together without proper punctuation is called a *run-on* sentence. The remedy for this sentence error is either to place each complete thought in a separate sentence or to retain the several thoughts in a single sentence by the use of proper subordination and punctuation.

> **RUN-ON:** The meeting had to be canceled and the chairperson asked me to notify each of you and she regrets any inconvenience this cancellation may have caused you.

> **BETTER:** The chairperson asked me to notify you that the meeting had to be canceled. She regrets any inconvenience you may have been caused.

G-11. Sentence Length

The length of the sentences in any written message is an important factor in catching and holding the reader's interest. Monotony can be avoided by varying the length of the sentences. However, very long sentences are only suitable for business letters if they are used sparingly and if they are carefully constructed.

In letter writing, as in cooking, too much of anything is not good. Avoid too many short words, too many short sentences, too many long words, too many long sentences. Avoid also too many similar sounds or too many sentences of similar construction.

G-12. Sentence Rhythm

To achieve good sentence rhythm, learn to place words carefully in the sentence. Vary the length and emphasis of the sentences. Use—but do not overuse—intentional repetition of sounds, words, and phrases.

Cultivate an ear for the sound of a sentence. Read your sentences aloud, emphasizing the important words. If the sentences sound awkward, choppy, or involved, rewrite them until they are pleasing to listen to.

Constructing Paragraphs

Combining sentences into paragraphs requires an understanding of the work a paragraph should do in any written message. A paragraph is made up of one or more sentences that together make a single point or relate to one aspect of a central theme.

G-13. Topic Sentence

A paragraph should usually contain a topic sentence that summarizes the main idea of the paragraph. The topic sentence is usually at the beginning of the paragraph, but it may be at the end or in the body of the paragraph. In business letters made up of short paragraphs, the topic sentence may be only implied.

G-14. Transition

One paragraph should lead naturally into the next, to guide the reader from one central thought or point to the next. To achieve this continuity, use transitional words or phrases, such as *however, therefore, for example, in addition, as a result.*

G-15. Paragraph Length

A paragraph may be of any length as long as it treats only one point or one aspect of the central thought. Business communications, particularly sales and advertising letters, tend to have fairly short paragraphs so as to keep the reader's interest. Technical communications often contain longer paragraphs.

G-16. Paragraph Rhythm

Like sentences, paragraphs should be pleasing to the ear when read aloud. Avoid a succession of very long or very short paragraphs. Vary the placement of the topic sentence. Avoid starting successive paragraphs in the same manner, such as with a participial phrase.

G-17. Unity, Coherence, and Emphasis

In addition to applying the fundamentals of grammar, a good business writer will be sure to observe the principles of unity, coherence, and emphasis.

G-17-a. To secure *unity,* include only relevant material and exclude all that is irrelevant. Ask yourself, "Is this word, this sentence, this paragraph essential to the development of my main thought?"

G-17-b. *Coherence* is the result of an orderly presentation of your message. Main points should follow each other in logical order. To achieve coherence you should plan your message carefully before you begin to write.

1. One enemy of coherence in the sentence is the *misplaced modifier.* Be sure to place every modifier where it clearly modifies the word it is intended to explain or qualify. Put phrases as close as possible to the words they modify. Placement of participial and infinitive phrases need special care in order to avoid the dangling modifier with its often ludicrous distortion of meaning.

> A few questions occurred to me after I had read the report.

> **NOT:** After reading the report, a few questions occurred to me.

2. Another enemy of coherence is *unclear antecedents.* Be sure every pronoun has a clear antecedent.

> The statements should be checked for errors, and *the errors* should be neatly corrected.
>
> **NOT:** The statements should be checked for errors, and *they* should be neatly corrected.

G-17-c. *Emphasis* means giving the important points in your message special prominence to show the reader that they are important. Ways to achieve emphasis include:

1. *Position.* Put the important word, phrase, or clause at the beginning or the end of a sentence, of a paragraph, or of the whole message.

2. *Proportion.* The most important point in the message should usually occupy the most space. Don't clutter a letter with trivial details.

3. *Repetition.* You gain impact by careful use of the same construction. Like all good things, intentional repetition should not be overdone.

> By using this new vocabulary builder, *you will discover how to* find the right word and *how to* avoid hackneyed words. *You will discover how to* increase your word power and *how to* put that power to profitable use.

4. *Balance.* You gain emphasis by balancing words, phrases, clauses, or sentences. But don't strain for this effect or your writing will sound forced.

> The more words you know, the better you can express your ideas.

If you heed the following warnings, you will not weaken the emphasis you intend in your messages:

1. Avoid generalizations and other vague expressions.

> **POOR:** As a rule, we ordinarily make an exception for such circumstances as yours.
>
> **BETTER:** Your circumstances merit our making an exception.

2. Change passive constructions to active whenever possible.

> **WEAK:** Your check must be mailed to us immediately in order to avoid legal action.
>
> **STRONGER:** To avoid legal action, you must mail your check to us immediately.

3. Eliminate general, unemphatic sentence openings.

> **POOR:** There are several new features planned for our next issue.
>
> **BETTER:** Among the new features in our next issue will be...
>
> **OR:** Featured in our next issue will be...

4. Watch the placement of transitional expressions. They are usually more effective after rather than before an important word, phrase, or clause.

> If you have a particular problem, however, please write to me about it.

PUNCTUATION

P-1. Period

The period is used at the end of a declarative sentence (one that makes a statement) and at the end of an imperative sentence (one that gives a command).

> Half a million people are employed by this company. (Declarative.)
>
> Take these books to the library. (Imperative.)

P-2. Question Mark

The question mark is used at the end of an interrogative sentence (one that asks a question). Even if the question is part of a declarative statement, the question mark is used. Even though a question does not form a complete thought, it may be set off if it logically follows the preceding sentence.

> How should we introduce our new product? on a television show? at a press conference?

Do not use a question mark at the end of a courteous request; use a period.

> Will you please send us your latest price list.

P-3. Exclamation Point

The exclamation point is used at the end of an exclamatory sentence to indicate strong feeling, surprise, or enthusiasm. An exclamatory sentence is seldom appropriate in business messages except in sales and advertising letters.

> Yes! You can save $100 *today only!*

P-4. Comma

A comma indicates a short break in thought within a sentence. Used properly, a comma ensures clarity by conveying the writer's exact meaning. Commas are not, however, to be used in a sentence simply because a speaker might normally pause. Rather, commas are to be used according to well-established rules. For a fuller discussion of comma usage, consult a handbook of English grammar and usage.

P-4-a. Separate the principal clauses of a compound sentence by a comma before the coordinate conjunction (*and, but, or*).

> New units will be organized, and new supervisors will be promoted to handle the increased business.

P-4-b. Set off nonrestrictive elements by commas. A nonrestrictive element is not essential to complete the meaning of the sentence.

The annual report, *which is published in April,* shows our financial condition. (Nonrestrictive.)

P-4-c. Do not use commas to set off a restrictive element, that is, one which limits the meaning of the sentence.

The bank cannot honor checks *that are improperly signed.* (Restrictive.)

P-4-d. Use a comma after an introductory participial phrase. (Avoid overuse of this construction in letters.)

Having committed ourselves to this plan, we are not backing down now.

Use a comma after an introductory dependent clause.

Since this report is due tomorrow, I must finish it tonight.

Use a comma after an introductory prepositional phrase unless the phrase is very short or very closely connected to what follows.

In the five years following our merger with Dynamo Sales Corporation, our sales increased 50 percent.

P-4-e. Use a comma after an introductory inverted phrase or clause.

Because it was improperly signed, the check was not honored by the bank.

P-4-f. Parenthetical (or interrupting) words, phrases, and clauses should be set off by commas.

We, *like all unions,* must protect the interests of our members. (Interrupting phrase.)

We cannot, *as you will agree,* make such an exception. (Interrupting clause.)

P-4-g. Transitional words, phrases, and clauses should be set off by commas.

We must, *therefore,* change our plans.

Therefore, we must change our plans.

P-4-h. Set off appositives by commas. An appositive has the same meaning as the word or phrase it follows.

Ms. Brown, *the new manager,* telephoned today.

P-4-i. A comma is used to set off a direct quotation from the rest of the sentence.

The speaker said, *"I agree with your recommendation."*

P-4-j. A comma should precede and follow such expressions as *for example, that is, namely* when they introduce explanatory words or phrases.

Homonyms, *that is,* words that sound alike, are often confused.

P-4-k. A comma should precede *such as* only when it introduces a nonrestrictive expression. When *such as*

introduces a restrictive expression, do not use a comma.

Office supplies, *such as* typewriter ribbons, letterhead, and carbon paper, are requisitioned weekly. (Nonrestrictive.)

An office *such as* this is every executive's dream. (Restrictive.)

P-4-l. Items in a series should be separated by commas. If each member of a series is connected by *and* or *or,* no comma is needed. If a comma is used within any item of a series, a semicolon separates the items.

The chairs, desks, and tables were all refinished.

Attending last week's conference in Williamsburg were David Rice, marketing director; Vicki Fuentos, advertising manager; and John Holmes, sales promotion manager.

P-4-m. A comma should precede and follow *etc.* (unless it closes the sentence).

P-4-n. Two or more adjectives modifying the same noun should be separated by commas if each alone modifies the noun (*simple, well-designed letterhead*). But if the first adjective modifies the combination of the noun and the second adjective, the comma is not used (*fireproof metal container*).

P-4-o. Indicate by a comma the omission of a word or words in a parallel construction.

Model 101 will be available June 1; Model 109, July 1.

P-4-p. Separate repeated words by commas to make the sentence easier to read.

The fire spread very, very quickly.

P-4-q. Use a comma to prevent misreading a sentence.

Soon after, the strike ended.

P-4-r. Use a comma to separate thousands, millions, etc., in numbers of four or more digits, except years, page numbers, addresses, telephone numbers, serial numbers, temperatures, and decimal amounts.

P-4-s. Separate consecutive, unrelated numbers by a comma.

In 1978, 15 new plants were built.

P-4-t. Separate by commas the parts of a date and of an address (*May 5, 1978; 3412 Lincoln Avenue, Riverside, California*).

P-4-u. The name of a state, when it follows the name of the town, is set off by commas.

Our restaurant in Decatur, *Alabama,* burned last week.

P-4-v. A comma follows the complimentary closing of a letter unless open punctuation is used throughout.

P-5. Dash

A dash is used to indicate a stronger break in thought than is shown by a comma. The word or phrase enclosed in dashes is grammatically separate from the sentence and not necessary to the meaning.

P-5-a. A parenthetical expression or an appositive that already contains a comma may be set off by dashes.

All large appliances—refrigerators, ranges, washers, dryers—will be drastically reduced this weekend.

P-5-b. When an introductory word is only implied, a dash is used to set off a following word or phrase.

New inventions are patented every month—hundreds of them.

P-5-c. A dash is used to separate a summarizing word from a preceding enumeration.

Clerks, typists, stenographers—*all* are needed.

P-5-d. No other punctuation is used with a dash. When an expression set off by dashes ends a sentence, omit the closing dash and use the appropriate sentence-end punctuation.

Expansion reached all departments—salary administration, research, and training.

P-6. Semicolon

The semicolon indicates a stronger break in thought than the comma.

P-6-a. Separate the principal clauses of a compound sentence by a semicolon when no connective is used.

Notices of the meeting were sent yesterday; today the agenda was prepared.

P-6-b. When the principal clauses of a compound sentence are connected by a conjunctive adverb (such as *consequently, therefore, however*), use a semicolon.

Budget requests were received late; *therefore,* the preparation of the final budget was delayed.

P-6-c. When either of the principal clauses in a compound sentence contains one or more commas, use a semicolon to separate the clauses if using a comma before the conjunction would cause misreading.

We ordered letterhead stationery, carbon packs, envelopes, and file guides; and plain paper, carbon paper, and file folders were sent to us instead. (The semicolon is necessary to prevent misreading.)

P-6-d. When *for example, that is, namely,* or a similar transitional expression links two independent clauses or introduces words, phrases, or clauses that are added almost as afterthoughts, use a semicolon before the expression and a comma after it.

Mrs. Phillips is a leader in many professional organizations; *for example,* she is president of the National Secretaries Association, a member of the board of directors of the Medical Secretaries Association, and program chairperson of the Business and Professional Women's Club.

P-7. Colon

A colon is the strongest mark of punctuation within the sentence.

P-7-a. A colon introduces an explanation or an amplification following an independent clause.

The company has one objective: to satisfy its customers.

P-7-b. A formal listing or an enumeration is introduced by a colon.

His qualifications are these: honesty, dependability, and sincerity.

P-7-c. If the list or enumeration grammatically completes the sentence, omit the colon.

His qualifications are honesty, dependability, and sincerity.

P-7-d. A colon introduces a quotation of more than one sentence.

Mrs. Evert said: "The fate of Velasco's chemical discharges will be determined by the judge. There are, however, two possible alternatives to the procedure now used."

P-7-e. A colon follows the salutation in a business letter unless open punctuation is being used.

P-7-f. A colon separates hours and minutes (*11:15 a.m.*).

P-7-g. A colon separates the main title of a work from the subtitle (*Africa: Continent in Turmoil*).

P-7-h. At the end of a letter a colon may separate the dictator's initials from the transcriber's (*HWH:me*), or a diagonal may be used (*HWH/me*).

P-8. Parentheses

Within a sentence parentheses set off explanatory words, phrases, and clauses that are not essential to the meaning of the sentence. No punctuation is used preceding an opening parenthesis, but the appropriate punctuation follows the closing parenthesis. If the material enclosed in parentheses requires a question mark or an exclamation point, that punctuation should precede the closing parenthesis.

> Sales have increased (about 20 percent) despite the weather.
>
> He expected to stop overnight in Chicago (or was it Detroit?).

Parentheses also have the following uses:

P-8-a. To cite an authority.

> "Consistency is the hobgoblin of little minds" (Ralph Waldo Emerson).

P-8-b. To give references and directions.

> Insert key at A (see Operating Manual, page 10).

P-8-c. To verify a spelled-out number in legal material.

> The sum of Fifteen Hundred Dollars ($1,500)...

P-8-d. To enclose figures and letters of enumerated items that do not begin on separate lines.

> The reasons are these: (1) rising labor costs, (2) inadequate space, and (3) shortage of personnel.

P-8-e. To indicate subordinate values in an outline.

> 1. Operating procedure
>   a. Open switch A.
>   (1) Hold switch A open and turn valve B.
>   (a) Check flow at nozzle C.

P-9. Brackets

Brackets are seldom used in business letters but are sometimes required in a formal report (1) to enclose material in a quotation that was not in the original; (2) to enclose *sic*, which indicates that an error in quoted material was in the original; (3) to enclose material within a parenthesized statement.

P-10. Quotation Marks

Quotation marks are used to set off direct quotations. A quotation within a quotation is set off by single quotation marks.

P-10-a. Consecutive quoted paragraphs each begin with quotation marks, but only the final paragraph closes with quotation marks.

P-10-b. The comma and period are placed inside closing quotation marks. The colon and the semicolon are placed outside. A question mark or an exclamation point precedes closing quotation marks only if the quoted material is in the form of a question or an exclamation.

P-10-c. Quotation marks also have the following uses: to enclose titles of chapters, parts, sections, etc., of books; titles of speeches, articles, essays, poems, short musical compositions, paintings, and sculpture; and for slogans and mottoes.

P-10-d. Quotation marks are not used for names of books, newspapers, and magazines. In business letters the main words of such titles are usually capitalized and the complete titles are underscored; or the titles may be typed in all capitals as an alternative to underscoring.

P-11. Apostrophe

The apostrophe is used to form the possessive of nouns (see G-1-b). The apostrophe also has the following uses:

P-11-a. To indicate a missing letter or letters in a contraction (*can't, wouldn't*).

P-11-b. To form the plural of letters, figures, and symbols, if its omission would cause misreading (see Sec. G-1-a-15).

P-11-c. To indicate the omission of the first part of a date (*class of '79*).

P-11-d. As a single quotation mark.

CAPITALIZATION

Capitalize parts of business letters as follows:

C-1. Each word of the inside address and the envelope address, including main words of titles of persons.

C-2. The main words in subject and attention lines when these lines are underscored (use all-capital letters when these lines are *not* underscored).

C-3. The first word of the salutation, plus titles.

C-4. The first word of the complimentary closing.

C-5. Main words of titles following the writer's name.

Capitalize the first word of:

C-6. A sentence or a group of words used as a sentence. (*Sales have skyrocketed. No wonder we need help.*)

C-7. Items in an outline.

C-8. Separate-line itemizations.

C-9. A direct quotation. (*Mr. Wheeler said, "Never read your speech to an audience."*)

C-10. Lines of poetry.

C-11. An explanatory statement following a colon if it is a complete sentence that states a formal rule or principle or requires special emphasis. (*He made this point: Build your speech to a climax.*)

C-12. An independent question within a sentence. (The question is, *How much would such a procedure save us?*)

Capitalize the first word and the main words of:

C-13. Titles and subtitles of publications, musical compositions, motion pictures, plays, paintings, sculpture (*Reader's Digest; Official Railway Guide; the play "A Midsummer Night's Dream"*).

C-14. Titles of speeches, lectures, addresses. (He spoke on *"How to Double Your Income."*)

Capitalize the following:

C-15. Proper nouns—names of particular persons, places, and things—and proper adjectives derived from them (*Jefferson, Jeffersonian; Latin America, Latin American; Explorer IV*).

C-16. Descriptive names used in place of proper names (*the Lone Star State*).

C-17. Common nouns when substituted for specific proper nouns (*the Territory, meaning Indian Territory; the Zone, for Canal Zone*).

C-18. Exact titles of courses of study. (*He enrolled in Accounting II and Business Communication.*)

C-19. Titles of persons—business, professional, military, religious, honorary, academic, family—when preceding the name (*President James Jones; Corporal Beatty; Judge Watts; Cousin George*).

C-20. Titles following a name only if they refer to high government officials (*Frank Bates, Associate Justice; but James Adair, mayor of Dundee*).

C-21. Official names of organizations, such as associations, bureaus, clubs, commissions, companies, conventions, departments (*National Sales Executives Association; Dallas Chamber of Commerce*).

C-22. Names of governments and subdivisions of government, whether international, national, state, or local (*Soviet Union; Commonwealth of Australia; the Supreme Court; the Port of New York Authority*).

C-23. Common nouns substituted for a specific organization or for a government agency (*the Company; the Association; the Council; the Department; the Commission*; but *our company; that department*).

C-24. Names of streets, buildings (*Broadway; Chrysler Building*).

C-25. Religious names and pronouns referring to Deity (*the Bible; the Heavenly Father; First Baptist Church*).

C-26. Military services, branches, and divisions (*the Navy; the Armed Forces; the 101st Airborne; the Seventh Regiment*).

C-27. Trademarks, brand names, names of commercial products, proprietary names, and market grades. Manufacturers and advertisers often capitalize the common noun following the trade name (*Xerox; Dictaphone; Coca-Cola, Coke; General Tires*).

C-28. "State" only when it follows the name of the state or is part of an imaginative name (*New York State; Lone Star State*; but *state of New York*); and "States" only when it stands for *United States*.

C-29. A particular geographic area (*Great Plains; the Near East; the West Coast; to visit the South*; but *southern agriculture; drive south two miles; southern Illinois*).

C-30. Days of the week, months, holidays.

C-31. Personifications (*"O Truth, where art thou?"*).

C-32. Races, peoples, languages (*French; Orientals; Spanish*; but *blacks and whites*).

C-33. Historical events and documents (*Vietnamese War; Declaration of Independence*).

C-34. Nouns followed by a number referring to parts, divisions, or sequence (*Column 2; Volume II; Room 17; Car 16788*; but *page 15; paragraph 3; note 2*).

C-35. Every word in a compound title that would be capitalized if standing alone but only the first word of a compound not used as a title (*"UN Aid to Non-Self-Governing Territories"*).

C-36. Certain important words in legal documents such as the name of the document, references to parties, special provisions, and spelled-out amounts of money may appear in initial capitals or all capitals: (*WHEREAS, RESOLVED, THIS AGREEMENT, Notary, SELLER, WITNESS*).

C-37. Emphasized words in sales and advertising material (*Don't miss our famous End-of-the-Year Sale!*).

Do *not* capitalize the following:

C-38. Names derived from proper nouns but no longer identified with them (*diesel engine; india ink; manila envelope*). If in doubt consult the dictionary or a reference manual.

C-39. "The" unless part of the official name (*the Denver Post; the First National Bank;* but *The New York Times*).

C-40. "The" when the name is used as a modifier. (*I find the New York Times foreign news complete and informative.*)

C-41. "City" unless part of a name (*New York City; Sioux City*).

C-42. "Ex," "former," "late" preceding titles (*former President Truman, the late Senator Mann*).

C-43. Names of subjects of study. (*I enjoy psychology more than I do history.*)

C-44. The words *federal, government, nation, union,* and *commonwealth* in ordinary business writing. Capitalize *union* and *commonwealth* only when they refer to a specific government.

NUMBERS

In business correspondence, numbers are more often expressed in figures than in words, both for clarity and for quick reference. The following rules reflect acceptable business practice.

Use words to express the following:

N-1. Exact numbers up to and including ten (*seven sales*).

N-2. Indefinite numbers (*several thousand; few hundred*).

N-3. Ages unless expressed in exact years, months, and days. (*He has a twelve-year-old son; he is 5 years 5 months 11 days old.*)

N-4. A number at the beginning of a sentence. Or, better, recast the sentence. (*Seventy-five more applications were received today.* OR: *We received 75 more applications today.*)

N-5. Informal designations of time. But use figures if exact time is given with *p.m.* or *a.m.* (*The meeting will begin about eleven o'clock. Our hours are from 8:30 a.m. to 4 p.m. daily.*) Use words also to **express periods** of time except in discount and credit **terms and interest** periods (*for the last fifteen years; a 60-day note; 2% 10 days, net 30 days*).

N-6. Ordinals, except dates and street numbers (*his fifteenth anniversary*).

N-7. Fractions used alone (*one-third of the coupons*).

N-8. Numbers in legal documents, usually followed by the amount in figures in parentheses.

N-9. Political and military divisions; sessions of Congress (*Thirty-first Regiment; Eighty-fifth Congress; Thirty-third Congressional District*).

Use figures for the following:

N-10. Numbers above ten when used alone (*450 meals*).

N-11. Exact amounts of money, no matter how large (*an increase of $55,000,000*). For very large amounts the words *millions* or *billions* may be used with figures (*$55 million or 55 million dollars*); be consistent within a piece of writing. In a series repeat the dollar sign before each amount (*$10 to $15 deductions*). Do not use the decimal point or zeros with whole-dollar amounts (*$6; $250*); do use them in tabulations if any of the amounts include cents. Do not use the symbol ¢ except in such technical material as price lists.

N-12. Population figures unless very indefinite. (*Over 50,000 people visited the festival;* but *several hundred thousand are expected next year.*)

N-13. Mixed numbers, including stock quotations (*an average of $5\frac{1}{2}$ errors per page*).

N-14. Numbers in a series of related items (*5 local men, 15 from Nashville, and 20 from out of the state*).

N-15. One of two adjacent related numbers. The first should be in figures unless it is longer and more awkward to write than the second (*fifty 15-cent stamps*).

N-16. Measurements. Use the unit of measure only with the last figure of a series (*6 by 9 by 13 inches; technical style: $2'' \times 3\frac{1}{2}'' \times 4''$*).

N-17. Ratios, proportions, and percentages (*outnumbered 3 to 1; 2 percent*).

N-18. House, street, and ZIP Code numbers (*77 West 11th Street, Los Angeles, California 90017*).

N-19. Highway numbers, pier and track numbers, page numbers, policy and other serial numbers (*Route 75; Pier 88; WA 5-7770*).

N-20. Dates (*May 5, 1979; your order of May 5; shipped on the 7th of June*).

N-21. Decimal amounts (*savings of 0.812 mills; an error of 0.910*).

N-22. Votes (*defeated by a vote of 12 to 5*).

N-23. References to parts of publications (*Figure 17; Chapter 23; Plate VI; Table 41*).

N-24. Statistical material, including ages, time, etc.

ABBREVIATIONS

Abbreviate the following:

A-1. These titles when used with personal names: *Dr., Mr., Messrs.* (plural of *Mr.* and pronounced "messers"), *Mrs., Mme.* (short for *Madame*), *Ms.* (pronounced "mizz"), and *Mses.* or *Mss.* (plural form of *Ms.*). The plural of *Mme.* may either be spelled out (*Mesdames,* pronounced "may-dahm") or abbreviated (*Mmes.*). The titles *Miss* and *Misses* are not abbreviations.

A-2. These titles following personal names: *Esq., Jr., Sr.;* also, academic and honorary degrees such as *M.D., O.D., Ed.D.* (used when *Dr.* does not precede the name).

A-3. Names of government agencies, without periods (*FCC* for *Federal Communications Commission*).

A-4. Names of well-known business organizations, labor unions, societies, and associations. When these abbreviations consist of all-capital initials, they are typed without periods or spaces (*IBM, AT&T, AFL-CIO, NAACP, YMCA*).

A-5. *B.C.* and *A.D.* in dates (*B.C. 350; 440 A.D.*).

A-6. *a.m.* and *p.m.* Designations of time (*6:15 a.m.*).

A-7. *No.* for *number* preceding a figure (*No. 189*).

A-8. Common business terms, according to usage in a particular field (*c.o.d.; f.o.b.; e.o.m.*). Such terms are often capitalized, without periods, on invoices and other business forms.

Do *not* abbreviate the following except as indicated:

A-9. Personal, professional, religious, and military titles when used with a surname only (*Lieutenant Jensen; Vice President Maxon*). When both first name and last name are used, the title may be abbreviated in business correspondence but not in formal usage (*Lt. Col. Robert E. Morris*). *Exception:* The title *Doctor* is usually abbreviated *Dr.*

A-10. Any part of the name of a business firm unless the abbreviated form appears in the firm's letterhead or other official usage (*Sharon Steel Corporation; Koppers Company Inc.*).

A-11. *Honorable* and *Reverend* except in addresses, lists, and notices. And, except in these usages, use "The" preceding the title.

A-12. Names of days and months, except in columnar work if space is limited.

A-13. Geographical names—cities, counties, countries—except for states and possessions of the United States, which may be abbreviated in lists, addresses, and tabulations, according to the forms recommended by the United States Postal Service (see page 8).

A-14. Units of measure except in invoices, lists, and tabulations. Be consistent in using abbreviations in a particular piece of work (*15 inches, or 15 in, or 15″*).

A-15. Metric and customary measurements, such as those shown below. (For a full listing of metric terms and for the proper pronunciation of these terms, consult a dictionary.)

meter (m)	inch (in)
gram (g)	foot, feet (ft)
liter (1)	yard (yd)
decimeter (dm)	mile (mi)
centimeter (cm)	ounce (oz)
milliliter (ml)	pint (pt)
hectogram (hg)	quart (qt)
kilometer (km)	gallon (gal)

A-16. Note that no periods are used in the following: ordinals (*5th*); letters referring to a person or a thing (*Mr. X*); radio and TV station letters and broadcasting systems (*WMCA; CBS*); mathematical symbols (*tan*); chemical symbols (*NaCl*); *IOU, SOS,* which are not abbreviations.

DIVIDING WORDS

Whenever possible, avoid dividing a word at the end of a line. If a word must be divided, insert a hyphen at the point of division, according to the following generally accepted rules.

Divide a word:

D-1. Only if it is more than one syllable, more than five letters, and can be divided so that more than a two-letter syllable is carried over. Divide between syllables (if unsure of syllabication, consult the dictionary) (*knowledge*, NOT: know-ledge; *prod-uct*, NOT: pro-duct; *passed*, NOT: pas-sed; *strength*, NOT: streng-th).

D-2. By retaining a single-vowel syllable preceding the hyphen (*cata-log*).

D-3. Between two one-vowel syllables (*situ-ation*).

D-4. After a prefix or before a suffix (rather than within the root word) (*re-arrangement;* NOT *rear-rangement*). Avoid divisions that could confuse a reader.

D-5. Between double consonants not ending a root word (*remit-tance*), and following other double consonants (*purr-ing*).

D-6. Preceding a suffix that has three or more letters (*compensa-tion*).

D-7. Preferably, only between the elements of a compound word (*bread-winner*).

D-8. Avoid dividing the following: proper nouns; titles with proper names; abbreviations; contractions; numbers, including dates and street addresses.

D-9. Do not divide words at the ends of more than two consecutive lines.

D-10. Do not divide the last word on a page.

NAME _____   DATE _____

A SELECTING APPROPRIATE BUSINESS STATIONERY

Complete each statement below.

1. The appearance of a business letter is important because:

a. _____
_____

b. _____
_____

2. When the stationery to be used by a company for its business letters is being selected, these factors should be given prime consideration:

a. _____

b. _____

c. _____

d. _____

3. The standard size, weight, quality, and color of business stationery are:

a. _____

b. _____

c. _____

d. _____

4. Envelopes and second sheets to be used for business letters should complement the letterheads in:

a. _____

b. _____

c. _____

5. The advantages of a simple, printed letterhead include:

a. _____
_____

b. _____
_____

6. For the reader's convenience, the complete address on a letterhead should usually include:

a. _____

b. _____

c. _____

d. _____

e. _____

7. The company's identification on letterheads, envelopes, and other stationery should match in:

a. _____

b. _____

B DESIGNING A LETTERHEAD

Design a letterhead that you would like to have represent you and the (fictitious) company you work for. Be sure to keep in mind your company's image and the reader's convenience. You may include a logo or symbol.

Sketch your letterhead in the space below. Arrange and type your letterhead neatly on a separate sheet.

THE PARTS OF A LETTER worksheet 2

NAME _____ DATE _____

A ARRANGING LETTER PARTS

Each of the letter parts below is correct in itself, but the order of the lines in each part is incorrect.
Copy each letter part in the answer column, arranging the lines in correct order.

PROBLEM 1: Headings for Letters Without Letterheads

a. ① Charleston, SC 29406
   ② June 18, 19--
   ① 933 Berkeley Avenue

b. ③ January 15, 19--
   ① P.O. Box 1272
   ② Boston, Massachusetts 02104

c. ① Tucson, Arizona 85709
   ② 587 Norton Way
   ③ September 13, 19--

a. *933 Berkeley Avenue*
   Charleston, SC 29406
   June 18, 19 --

b. *P.O. Box 1272*
   Boston, MA 02104
   January 15, 19--

c. *587 Norton Way*
   Tucson, ~~Way~~ AR 85709
   September 13, 19--

PROBLEM 2: Inside Addresses and Salutations

a. ④ ATTENTION MR. JULIAN MOORE
   ② 1751 Walnut Street
   ⑤ Gentlemen
   ① The Finishing Touch
   ③ Jamestown, Ohio 45335

b. ③ Cheyenne, Wyoming 82001
   ② 10047 West 147 Street
   ① Miss Jan Sayers
   ④ Subject: Alumni Fellowships
   ⑤ Dear Jan:

a. _____
   _____
   _____
   _____
   _____

b. *Miss Jan Sayers*
   10047 West 147 Street
   Cheyenne, WY 82001
   Subject: Alumni Fellowships
   Dear Jan:

c. Manager, Accounts Receivable ②
   Preston Hardware, Inc. ③
   8976 Hanna Boulevard ④
   Grand Rapids, Michigan 49502 ⑤
   Mr. James W. Blaney ①
   Dear Mr. Blaney: ⑥

c. *Mr. James W. Blaney*
   8976 Hanna Boulevard
   Grand Rapids, MI 49502

   Dear Mr. Blaney:

PROBLEM 3: Closing and Signature Lines and Special Notations

① a. Sincerely yours,
③   Director of Marketing
② Mr. Mason W. Rawlings
⑤   Enclosure
④   MWR:da

③ b. THE PEABODY CORPORATION
①   Very truly yours,
④   JW/pc
②   Mrs. Jo West, Manager
⑤   cc Mr. John Cook

a. _____

b. *Very Truly Yours,*
   Mrs. Jo West, Manager

B CORRECTING VIOLATIONS OF BUSINESS USAGE

Each of the following excerpts contains *six* errors in correct business-letter usage, as discussed in Unit 2. Underscore the six errors in each excerpt; then write the letter part at the right, making all corrections.

PROBLEM 4: Letter Heading

a. No. 206 East 6th. Street
      ⑤   ④
   Vallejo, Cal., 94590
              ③
   Nov. 3rd, 19--
     ①   ②

b. 906 So. Madison St.
          ③   ④
   Jackson Mis. 39205
          ① ②
   May 30th 19--
      ⑤ ⑥

a. _____

b. *906 South Madison Street*
   Jackson, MS 39205
   May 30, 1900

PROBLEM 5: Inside Addresses and Salutations

a. Personnel Manager

Omega Travel Service, Inc.

Sixteen 9th Street, N.W.

Washington, 20003 D.C.

Dear sir

a. _____

_____

Washington, D.C., 20003

_____

_____

b. Randy Stewart Realty

#646 Loeb Street

Jackson Mississippi. 39205

ATTENTION: MS. MARTHA DONNELLY

Dear Ms. Donnelly; *Company*

b. _____

_____

_____

_____

_____

_____

PROBLEM 6: Closing and Signature Lines and Special Notations

a. Sincerely,

Business World Magazine *ALL CAPS*

(Ms. Anna Mays

fb; AM

CC to Mr. Jack Anderson

Mr. Eli Smith

a. _____

_____

_____

_____

_____

_____

b. Yours Truly,

EATON PRODUCTS

Mr. Neil Simmons, sales mgr

NS/jc

Enclos 3

b. _____

_____

_____

_____

_____

_____

C PREPARING LETTER PARTS

Write the letter parts for each of the situations below.

PROBLEM 7

Prepare the inside address and salutation for a letter to the president of Eugene Supply Corporation, which is located at 987 West Clancy Avenue, Eugene, Oregon 97401. The president of the company is Mark Lambeau.

Mr. Mark Lambeau
Eugene Supply Corporation
987 West Clancy Avenue
Eugene, Oregon 97401
Dear Mr. Lambeau

PROBLEM 8

Prepare the inside address, salutation, and subject line for a letter you are sending to Mrs. Wilma Radford, of the Newton Business Machines Company, 54 Elton Road, Newton, Massachusetts 02159. Mrs. Radford is the sales manager of the company. The subject of the letter concerns leasing terms.

Mrs. Wilma Radford

NAME   DATE

A   CHOOSING AND TYPING LETTER STYLES

1. As you review the basic letter styles described on page 12 and illustrated on pages 14 and 15, decide which style you like best and which you like least.

2. Write two brief paragraphs explaining your decision.

3. Use the two paragraphs you have composed as the body of the letters you are directed to type in Problems 1, 2, and 3 below.

4. Address the messages to your instructor at the school address, and assume you are sending them from your own home or business address.

5. Supply an appropriate salutation, a complimentary closing, and other details as needed.

6. Type a letterhead facsimile for each problem.

7. Set your typewriter margins for a 40-space line (pica margins: 22 and 62), or a 48-space line (elite: 27 and 75).

8. Type today's date on the third line below the last line of the letterhead and leave four lines between the date and the inside address.

PROBLEM 1

Type the letter in the style you prefer, using standard punctuation.

PROBLEM 2

Type the letter in the semiblocked letter style (refer to the illustration on page 14). (If you used the semiblocked style in Problem 1, use the blocked style for this problem.)

PROBLEM 3

Type the letter in any format that you did not use for Problem 1 or 2.

B TYPING A MEMORANDUM

PROBLEM 4

Type the message you composed for Problems 1, 2, and 3 as an interoffice memorandum, using the form below. Set the left margin two spaces to the right of the colon following the longest word in the heading. Set the right margin so that it will be equal to the left margin.

▰▰▰▰ MEMORANDUM ▰▰▰▰

To: From:

Subject: Date:

PROBLEM 5

Type the memorandum above on page 151. Use 1½-inch side margins and a 1-inch top margin. Type the guide words TO:, FROM:, SUBJECT:, and DATE: in all capital letters. Follow the instructions for typing memos on page 13 and the example of a memo typed on plain paper on page 16.

C TYPING A POSTAL CARD

PROBLEM 6

Address the postal card below to Miss Janet Lenari, 4450 Skyview Terrace (use your city, state, and ZIP Code). Use today's date and your return address. Sign your name as manager. The message is:

This card entitles you, as one of our preferred customers, to a 20 percent discount on your next purchase at The Toggery. Come in soon to select your fall wardrobe from our famous-name collection of sportswear and dresses.

CORRECT ENGLISH USAGE

worksheet 4

NAME _S. Newman_   DATE _2-1-82_

A CORRECTING ERRORS IN AGREEMENT

Each sentence below contains an error in agreement. On the lines provided rewrite the italicized part of the sentence to correct each error.

1. The reference section, as well as the appendixes, _were omitted._

was omitted

2. The letters were typed _but not all was signed._

were signed

3. Neither of the applicants _have sales experience._

has sales experience

4. Please make the changes as quickly as possible ~~and~~ the report [have] ~~should be~~ ready by next Tuesday.

The report should be ready by next Tuesday.

5. The nominating committee is responsible for reviewing the qualifications of all candidates _and ~~they will~~ submit a [for submitting] slate of officers._

and it will submit a slate of officers —

6. Everyone thinks that the new policy will pay ~~your~~ [his] _dental bills._

↓sing.   _their dental bills_   _his or her_

7. The automatic typewriter can be operated easily and economically _and ~~you do not~~ need repairs often._ [doesn't]

it does not need repairs often.

8. If we receive your order by December 1, _we ~~might~~ be able to ship the merchandise that same day._ [may]

we may be able to ship the merchandise that same day.

9. The general manager still _~~don't~~ know about the error._ [doesn't]

doesn't know about the error.

10. He is aware of the benefits _that accrues from his policy._

that accrue from his policy

B USING PRONOUNS CORRECTLY

Underline each pronoun error in the following sentences. Then in the answer column write the pronouns that should be substituted for the incorrect words. If a sentence has no errors, write "correct" in the answer column.

1. Responsibility for follow-up letters was divided between him and me.   1. _Correct_

2. My decision to drop the suit was made in anticipation of him filing a countersuit.   2. _his_

3. The papers were signed by Mr. Carson and I.   3. _me_

4. The chairperson commented that everyone did ~~their~~ part well.   4. _his/her_

5. Mr. Fisher sent a memo to his staff stating that Mrs. Robok and himself would discuss the merger next week.   5. _he_

6. She wrote the letter herself.   6. _correct_

7. This job is for someone like ~~yourself~~ who's willing to travel and to work long hours.   7. _you_

C PLACING MODIFIERS EFFECTIVELY

In these sentences underline all modifying words and phrases that are not effectively placed. Then, on the line below, rewrite each sentence, avoiding the use of misplaced or dangling modifiers and other confusing expressions.

1. She hopes ~~tomorrow~~ to finish the assignment, _tomorrow._
   _____

2. You'll praise the quality and dependability that ~~you only get~~ from a Wallen.
   You get only
   _____

3. Having been found innocent, the judge ordered the release of the defendant.
   Having been found innocent, the defendant was released by the judge.

4. In reviewing your case, several questions came to my mind.
   _____

5. Before buying a car, a loan must be obtained usually.
   you must usually obtain a loan.

6. All lights should be turned off before locking the doors. _turn off the lights._
   _____

7. To get the best results, the instructions must be carefully followed.
   you must carefully follow the instructions areful

8. Writing a letter in anger antagonizes not only your customer but loses the sale usually also.
   _____

9. Upon launching the new program, (many objections) faced the Senator. _many obj._
   _____

10. Having been damaged in the fire, we could not inventory ~~all~~ the glassware. _damy in — fire_
    _____

D ELIMINATING INTERRUPTING COMMAS

The following sentences contain essential commas; some also contain nonessential ones. Circle each comma that interrupts or confuses the thought of a sentence. If the sentence is correctly punctuated, write "correct" in the answer column.

1. On March 2, however, I will leave for Ohio State University, where I will be enrolled, for the coming year.

1. _____

2. If you wish to invite Dan, you may call him, at 555-7000, his business number.

2. _____

3. Thank you, Mrs. Kennedy, for the information you sent me, on urban renewal projects, in Chicago.

3. _____

4. In the near future, the speaker said, unemployment figures should decrease."

4. _____

5. Valerie is an enthusiastic worker, and, she is very capable.

5. _____

6. To set realistic goals, for yourself, you must know, what will be expected of you, not only in the job you're aiming for, but also in the positions leading up to it.

6. _____

7. Our plant is operating, at, or very near, capacity, now.

7. _correct_

8. The factors, that contribute most to our success, are budgetary control, and sound accounting practices.

8. _____

9. I am, therefore, grateful to you, and your organization, for the help, which you have given us, during the campaign.

9. _____

10. Although the shipping date is not definite, you will be pleased to know, that work on your order is progressing well, in our plant here, as well as in Rockford.

10. _____

11. Mrs. Jason, asked us to help her prepare the agenda for the conference.

11. _correct_

12. Duplicates must be sent to all supervisors, and managers.

12. _correct_

13. Both of the copies, that were on my desk, must be signed by Mrs. DeGroat.

13. _correct_

14. According to the report, the police found only two people, who were able to give more information.

14. _____

15. We postponed the meeting, but, we were not able to notify everyone, in time.

15. _____

16. Two of the most, interesting speakers, were Mrs. Calhoun and Mr. Stevens.

16. _____

17. Our regional meeting in Youngstown, Ohio, is scheduled for the week of August 12.

17. _Between Courtesy 5th_

18. Before you prepare your report, read this survey, from our research department.

18. _____

19. Brenda Martin, my supervisor, will be on vacation, for two weeks.

19. _____

20. We will meet, on Friday, October 8, if you prefer.

20. _____

E AVOIDING MISCELLANEOUS ERRORS

These sentences will test your ability to avoid errors in basic English or in spelling—errors that are frequently found in business writing. For each pair of terms in parentheses, indicate the correct answer by underlining your choice.

1. My appointment with (Doctor, Dr.) Thompson is for (1, one) o'clock today.

2. I felt (bad, badly) to tell her she had not done (good, well) in the contest.

3. During the past month (there, their) (have, has) been (fewer, less) problems with absenteeism.

4. After (10, ten) (years, years') time, you will be eligible for (4, four) (weeks, weeks') vacation.

5. The (committees', committee's) (reccomendation, recommendation) was accepted by majority vote.

6. The dinner tomorrow at (7, seven) p.m. is in honor of (Prof., Professor) Ann Brantley.

7. Neither you nor I (has, have) the correct answers to the problems.

8. Mr. Lee told the students to (continue on, continue) with the same assignment.

9. The (chairman, Chairman) was (conscious, conscience) of the (disappointing, dissapointing) (affect, effect) that the (President's, president's) message had on all employees.

10. She works for a manufacturer of (women's, womens') clothing.

Now correct any errors in the following sentences. Underline each error, and write the correction in the space provided.

11. The last show starts at nine-thirty p.m.   11. _9:30 pm_

12. Perhaps Mister Stephenson knows, where the original copy was filed.   12. _Mr._

13. The room is only 10 and a half feet long.   13. _10½ feet long_

14. Would you please make 2 copies of this report.   14. _two_

15. These kind of statistics are much more useful.   15. _____

16. Increasing profits always has and always will be the goal of our department.   16. _have   out of context_

17. I think that Lawrence and Paul work good together.   17. _well_

18. Please refer back to page 212 in the procedures manual.   18. ✓

19. Yes, we will try and meet you at exactly 4 p.m.   19. ✓

20. Our new supervisor is very different than our former supervisor.   20. ✓

type of
sorts of
kind of

THE FINAL TOUCHES

worksheet
5

NAME   DATE

PROBLEM 1

The following sentences from business correspondence show what can happen when proofreading is neglected. Underline each error, and in the answer column write its correction.

1. We wish you a happy and <u>preposterous</u> New Year.

2. You'll enjoy an extra measure of comfort and <u>hostility</u> at all our hotels.

avoid 3. Hopefully you will be among the <u>crows</u> visiting our store during our January White Sale.

4. If you care to fly now and pay later, you need pay only 10 percent down and can take as long as 15 <u>minutes</u> to pay the remainder.

5. During the recent storms fierce <u>guests</u> have shoved two new homes off their foundations.

6. On Thanksgiving Day the inmates of the jail are served roast <u>turnkey</u> and all the trimmings.

7. When I think of your interest in <u>boasting</u> and fishing, I'm sure you would enjoy a vacation on Deer Island.

8. We extend the service to all clergymen regardless of <u>donation.</u>

9. The company offers you a number of different policies at low cost and <u>with</u> sales pressure of any kind.

10. At the last meeting we discussed the feasibility of erecting a <u>doomed</u> stadium similar to Houston's.

1. *✗ prosperous*

2. *hospitality*

3. *crowds*

4. *months*

5. *gusts*

6. *turkey*

7. *boating*

8. *denomination*

9. *without*

10. *domed*

PROBLEM 2

The letter on page 158 from Texas Automatic Sprinkler Co. to a customer whose business is now closed contains 33 careless spelling and typing errors. Can you find all of them? Underline each error. Then write the correction just above it.

March 3, 19——

Mr. David Lyons
Folks' Folly
P.O. Box 141
Hudston, Texas 77008

Dear Mr. Lyens;

We are aware that your Restaurant has been closed since
Febuary 27, 19——, and would like to conclude your
contractual relations with Texas Automatic Spinkler Co.

Your contract is in effect until April 3rd, 1982, However,
under the circumstances, we will terminate the contract upon
payment of a short rate termintion differential.

The short rate Termination differential is merly the
difference between the monthly rate you were persently
paying on a full-term contract and the higher rate thas
would have been charged if the Contract had been initialy
written on this much shorter period of time. The total for
the differentail is $363.83, as reflected on the enclosed a
statment. This figure represents the balance on your acount
only through February 27, this year. The remainder has been
waved.

When we recieve your check, which must be in are office by
August 32, 19——, we will prematurely cancell the contract.

Please give this your immediate attention, For your
convience we have enclose a stamped, self-adressed
envelope.

Very Cordially yours

Larry G. Parker

LPG/te

Enclodure

PROBLEM 3

Using the letterheads on pages 159-160, type the corrected letter from Problem 2 in the
semiblocked and blocked letter styles (see the examples on page 14). Place it attractively on the
sheet, single-spaced. Guard against a ragged right margin and the incorrect division of words at the
ends of lines.

TEXAS AUTOMATIC SPRINKLER CO.
121 Homewood Road, Houston, Texas 77028
Tel. (713) 769-8520

AUTOMATIC SPRINKLER CO.
121 Homewood Road, Houston, Texas 77028
Tel. (713) 769-8520

PROBLEM 4

Address the small business envelope below for a letter typed to your instructor. Type your personal return address in the corner. Remember to use the ZIP Code.

PROBLEM 5

Address the large business envelope on page 162 for a letter sent by Charlie's Quick Print to the treasurer of the Des Moines Lions Club, 4060 Ravenswood Avenue, Des Moines, Iowa 50310.

Envelope for Problem 5

Charlie's Quick Print

900 Jefferson Street, Des Moines, Iowa 50314

CHOOSING THE RIGHT WORDS

worksheet 6

NAME _____ DATE _____

PRECISE WORD CHOICES

The following sentences contain complex words, excess words and phrases, trite expressions, inappropriate words, too-general words, incorrect words, and negative words. On the lines below, rewrite the sentences simply and concisely, substituting friendly, conversational expressions. You may assume any information necessary to make your revision clear and direct.

1. We have received and read your communication of March 6 and wish to say that there is truth in each and every statement you make and that we fully understand your position.

   Thank you for your letter of March 6

2. Every effort will be made to expedite delivery as ~~per our agreement.~~ *promised*

   We working hard to speed up delivery as promised

3. We are ~~sorry~~ ~~to have to inform you that~~ it is our policy that we cannot assume responsibility for damages incurred while driving outside our premises.

   We can only assume responsibility etc.

4. If you can loan me the money, please contact me, and I shall come for it immediately ~~irregardless~~ of the time of day.

5. Many people attended our most recent monthly meeting.

6. Since you claim that delivery of your refrigerator was unreasonably slow, ~~I suppose~~ we'll ~~have to~~ investigate and find out the truth about ~~the alleged~~ delay.

7. We note your request and would state that, at our earliest convenience, we will communicate with you further about same.

_____

_____

_____

8. I advise you to except the position by the end of the physical year.

_____

_____

B

USING TIMESAVING WORDS AND PHRASES

Underline excess words and phrases in this letter. Then on the lines below write your own concise, friendly revision in 50 words or less.

Dear Mrs. McCloskey:

We have received and read *Thank you for* your report about the growth and expansion of population in your city during the year of 1978. This report, as you know, is entitled ''Population Growth of San Miguel County in 1978.''

As we read this report, we found ourselves much interested in it, and we want to say here and now that we appreciate your sending it to us.

We also want to add that we are in agreement with each and every recommendation that you make. We feel that a large segment of the people in your community will cooperate with you so that all may unite and work as one in an effort to carry out all these recommendations together.

We hope that hereafter and henceforth you will plan to keep us informed of activities that take place in your community as a result of the interest stimulated by your report on the growth and expansion of its population.

_____

_____

_____

_____

_____

_____

_____

_____

_____

_____

_____

_____

NAME _____   DATE _____

A IMPROVING WEAK SENTENCES

These sentences from business letters are weak and unsatisfactory. Among them are sentence
fragments and awkward, choppy, two-idea, and too-long sentences. Make the necessary revisions.
When you feel all are good, strong sentences, rewrite them on the lines provided.

1. I should appreciate it very much if you would examine the endorsement on that particular check and if possible
forward the check to us and of course we shall return it for your files upon examination.

_____

_____

_____

_____

_____

2. Call me if you need any more help. I am available from 8 a.m. to 5 p.m. daily, from Monday through Friday, here at
the office.

_____

_____

_____

_____

3. In the event your choice has been sold out. Your check or money order will be cheerfully refunded.

_____

_____

_____

_____

4. When you receive our catalog, which should be within the week, you will notice our wide selections and reasonable
prices, which are listed inside the back cover, and we hope you will then talk with Jim Bryce, who represents us in
your area and will help you in every way he can, or send us an order direct, whichever you prefer.

_____

_____

_____

_____

_____

5. I am enclosing the only literature that we have which will be of interest to you, and I have turned your request over to the Chamber of Commerce, which will probably have more literature and booklets which will enable you to complete your project which sounds so worthwhile to all of us who are engaged in this work.

_____

_____

_____

_____

_____

_____

6. You were always a regular customer, and it was a pleasure to check your orders; so now, as you haven't placed an order for quite some time, we're wondering if we did something of which you did not approve, and, if we are to blame, we're sorry to lose your business and we want to begin serving you again.

_____

_____

_____

_____

_____

7. You should use the order forms at the back of the catalog, which we are sending you along with our latest price list, as you requested us to do. Whenever you wish to make a purchase, use these convenient order forms.

_____

_____

_____

_____

_____

B

PARAGRAPHING A LETTER

In the letter below the writer blurred the general effect and destroyed the emphasis by using too many short paragraphs and by omitting needed transitional expressions. Improve both its effect and its emphasis by grouping some of the ideas into longer paragraphs and by adding transitional words and phrases to introduce sentences and paragraphs as needed. Then type your revised letter on a separate sheet, using your favorite letter style. Supply any needed details.

(Today's date)

Dear Mrs. Pratt:

Five little words, ''Add it to my account,'' will now work magic for you at Starr's.

You, as a member of our Easy Payment family, are entitled to a special ''add on'' privilege.

Without a down payment you may order anything we sell and add many items to your account without increasing your monthly payment.

You may increase your balance to $300 and still pay only $10 a month. You will make proportionately higher payments on larger amounts.

Even though you may be short of cash at the moment, you can buy the things you and your family need.

You won't disturb your budget. And you can meet your payments from regular income.

You will find an immense variety of quality merchandise at money-saving prices now in our catalog. You will hear of new items reaching us day by day.

Whatever your needs—wearing apparel, piece goods, toys, appliances, furniture—you can buy them all at Starr's.

You'll enjoy shopping Starr's easy, timesaving catalog way.

Stop in or phone or mail an order soon. Take advantage of the magic of our Easy Payment Plan whenever convenient.

Sincerely yours,

(Your Name)

NAME   DATE

The writers of these messages forgot to plan their opening paragraphs with the reader in mind. Study the problems carefully. Then below each paragraph write your version, improving the tone. Supply any necessary details.

PROBLEM 1

Observe the "we" attitude in this opening paragraph of a letter. You can give your version a more friendly tone by bringing the reader into the picture.

Selfish Tone

> We want you to know that we do appreciate having you as one of our Hansen Equipment catalog customers. We have decided that we can make catalog shopping a lot easier and a lot more convenient by issuing credit cards. With these cards, we can take orders by phone as well as by mail.

Improved Tone

_____

_____

_____

_____

_____

_____

_____

_____

_____

_____

_____

_____

_____

_____

_____

_____

_____

PROBLEM 2

Do you notice a definite lack of interest and a hint of impatience in this reply to a request for information? In your revision show interest in the college student who seeks information from a large department store.

Indifferent Tone

```
Your request is one of many we receive from management
majors asking for data which we are too busy to assemble and
send out. Probably we should use a form letter suggesting
that all you students phone a floor manager for an
appointment to visit the store and see for yourselves how we
handle these matters.
```

Improved Tone

_____

_____

_____

_____

_____

_____

_____

PROBLEM 3

Unconcealed irritation with the customer gives this message an impatient tone. In your revision, you will charge the customer the full price, but you should give her the benefit of the doubt. Perhaps she didn't notice the date.

Critical Tone

```
Did you really think you could get by with a coupon two
weeks out of date? Both the ad and the coupon stated
conspicuously that the half-price offer was good only until
July 31. When you sent your order and check for $3.95 on
August 15, you undoubtedly knew that the price of the
subscription had reverted to the full $6.
```

Improved Tone

_____

_____

_____

_____

_____

_____

_____

PROBLEM 4

Notice the negative-sounding beginning sentence and the overemphasis on money in this opening paragraph of a letter. Does the paragraph make you wonder how much this family vacation is really going to cost and whether the letter is a "gimmick" to draw people to listen to a real estate pitch? You can improve the poor tone by stressing the positive ideas and playing down cost.

Negative Tone

It's a depressing fact that the rising cost of a really good family vacation adds to the strain on today's family budget. Farmington Acres has a solution to this problem. We will give you and your family lodging at reduced rates. In addition, we will provide superb recreational facilities at a nominal charge. And all we ask in return is that you take a personally conducted land sales tour of the area. No gimmicks, no strings, no obligation to purchase a single thing!

Improved Tone

_____
_____
_____
_____
_____
_____
_____
_____
_____
_____
_____
_____
_____
_____
_____
_____
_____
_____
_____
_____
_____
_____

PROBLEM 5

Observe the sarcasm and "don't bother us" attitude in this reply. Write a message that shows interest in this potential customer and tries to keep him interested in your product.

Sarcastic Tone

I am sorry to tell you that the Buzz chain saw Model #511H you asked about is temporarily out of stock in our warehouse, just as Mr. Maccarino of our Lark Avenue store informed you. We should get some in by next month and have them available in the Lark Avenue store, if you can wait that long. Just check back with them in six weeks or so.

Improved Tone

_____

_____

_____

_____

_____

_____

_____

_____

_____

_____

_____

_____

_____

_____

_____

_____

_____

_____

_____

_____

_____

NAME _____ DATE _____

 A **PLANNING TO BUILD GOODWILL IN PROBLEM SITUATIONS**

Study the partial analyses of Problems 1 and 2. Then complete the analyses by giving your opinion of the job you should do in each letter and by writing effective and interesting opening paragraphs for them.

PROBLEM 1

The Background

In January a customer returns several large cartons of Christmas decorations to the store where you are employed as correspondent. You must reply to the angry letter in which she insists that the cartons were delivered on the day before Christmas, too late for her to use them in her home. The store has a delivery slip—signed by the customer and confirmed by the shipping department—that these cartons were delivered to her home on December 16, the delivery date agreed upon at the time of purchase.

The Customer's Request

The customer demands that the store accept the decorations, with a full refund to her.

The Company's Policy

The full refund cannot be approved on this seasonal merchandise after the Christmas buying season is over. The store will, however, refund the January sale price, ½ off the regular price, or will store the decorations without charge until next December.

Your Job When You Write
the Letter

_____
_____
_____
_____
_____
_____
_____
_____

Opening Paragraph

_____
_____
_____
_____
_____
_____

PROBLEM 2

The Background

You work for the Portland (Oregon) Realty Company, whose manager agreed to hold up rental of a penthouse studio for one week to give the client, Hugh Steele, time to make his decision. When the manager didn't hear from Mr. Steele within ten days, he leased the studio to another client. Soon afterward the company learned that a letter from Mr. Steele confirming his decision to lease the studio within the one-week limitation was mistakenly delivered to Portland, Maine.

The Customer's Request

Mr. Steele asserted his right to lease the studio.

The Company's Policy

The lease between the company and the other client was entered into in good faith and is legally binding.

Your Job When You Write the Letter

_____
_____
_____
_____
_____
_____
_____

Opening Paragraph

_____
_____
_____
_____
_____
_____

B IMPROVING POOR LETTERS

Rewrite the following letters using positive language and showing a service attitude.

PROBLEM 3

Poor

> We are very sorry that we failed to send the mirror for your new dresser. We are sending it to you today.
>
> Thank you for your order, and we look forward to serving you in the future.

Improved

_____

_____

_____

_____

_____

_____

_____

_____

PROBLEM 4

Poor

> I am sorry that you had to return a damaged copy of Children's Classics to us recently. It's too bad that several pages were so smeared. The enclosed copy is not damaged, as you will see. Now you and your children can enjoy this wonderful book.

Improved

_____

_____

_____

_____

_____

_____

_____

_____

_____

PROBLEM 5

Poor

Each month our billing department automatically sends
invoices to all people to whom we have provided service
during that month. Therefore, when we sent you a bill for
service, we were merely following our routine billing
procedure.

Of course, because your television is still under warranty,
there is no charge for service. You should have told our service
representative that the set is under warranty. Just disregard
the bill for $35.

We hope that you will get many more years of good service from
your Reliable Television.

Improved

_____

_____

_____

_____

_____

_____

_____

_____

_____

_____

_____

_____

_____

_____

PLANNING AND PREPARING LETTERS

worksheet 10

NAME   DATE

BACKGROUND

As assistant sales manager for Bartlett's Professionals, a placement service for office temporaries, you must answer a request from Mr. Harold Jansen for "more information about Bartlett's services." (Mr. Jansen is office manager of Independent Researchers Inc., 121 Ashley Drive, Fort Worth, Texas 76129.) His request is difficult to answer because Bartlett's offers so many different office services; however, you must write to him.

You decide that your letter should have two purposes: to impress upon Mr. Jansen that he should think of Bartlett's whenever he needs temporary office help and to smooth the way for a representative to call on Mr. Jansen. Thus you decide to explain some of the general services you offer, enclose a brochure describing more services, and tell him that a sales representative (Mona Campbell) will call him.

Here are the jottings you listed for your letter:

Jottings

Mona Campbell will call
Established 1948
Professional help when *you* need it
Clients include conglomerates (example)
Clients include small firms (example)
Well-trained secretaries
Clerical help (filing clerks)
Others (typists, receptionists)
Also accounts receivable help
Data processing help

Telephone survey specialists
Page 4 of brochure (research services)
Wide range—help for one hour or one year
Part-timers are well trained
Sales rep—appointment
Staff is experienced
In business for many years
Research specialists (brochure, p. 4)
Thank you

PROBLEM 1

Revise the above jottings by crossing out any item that is unnecessary or repetitious and joining any items that should be combined. Then number the items in the order in which you decide they should be presented in the letter to Mr. Jansen.

PROBLEM 2

On a separate sheet of paper, rewrite your jottings in the sequence in which you numbered them above. As you do so, make any further revisions that are necessary.

PROBLEM 3

Prepare a rough draft of the message planned in Problem 2.

PROBLEM 4

Edit the rough draft prepared in Problem 3.

PROBLEM 5

From the rough draft edited in Problem 4, prepare a typed, mailable letter. Use an acceptable format, standard punctuation, and the current date. Use your return address, and sign the letter with your name.

WRITING INQUIRIES AND REQUESTS

worksheet 11

NAME _____ DATE _____

 REVISING POOR INQUIRIES

Because they are poorly worded, incomplete, wordy, or ambiguous, the following inquiries are unsatisfactory. In the space provided, rewrite each question, making sure that your revision is concise and that it asks for the exact information needed.

PROBLEM 1

As you revise these excerpts from letters to travel agencies, give special attention to providing the details needed to make each question specific.

1. How much does it cost to fly to California?

_____

_____

_____

2. Could you give me information about renting a car in Europe?

_____

_____

_____

3. What more can you tell me about the Hawaiian Tours you advertised in the paper the other day, particularly with reference to dates, length, and prices?

_____

_____

_____

4. May I take my electric razor and hair styler with me and use them while I'm in Italy?

_____

_____

_____

5. How much should I expect to pay for a good hotel in a coastal resort area?

_____

_____

_____

PROBLEM 2

This rambling letter needs tightening up; and the jumbled questions need to be sorted out, listed one to a paragraph, and numbered for easy identification.

```
Gentlemen:

When I visited a neighbor the other day, I saw her turn-
table, which is a Tone-Master 370, and I liked it. So I
decided I might like to have one of my own. However, since
my neighbor's turntable was a gift, she didn't know anything
about the cost, etc. I'm wondering if you could answer some
of the questions that my neighbor couldn't answer.

I would like to know the cost of the turntable if I ordered
it from you and whether the shipping charges would be extra.
My neighbor's turntable is tan, but I wonder if it comes in
other colors. Also I'd like to know if the case is easily
scuffed and if the tone quality is good at 33⅓ rpm. Could
you tell me whether you carry any turntable accessories?

If you will please answer all these questions, then I can
decide whether to buy or not to buy a Tone-Master.
```

_____

_____

_____

_____

_____

_____

_____

_____

_____

_____

_____

_____

_____

_____

_____

_____

_____

_____

_____

B PLANNING, COMPOSING, AND TYPING INQUIRIES

1. Make a plan for each message on pages 181 and 182. Use the space below each problem for your plan. Follow the suggestions in the Letter Planning Chart, Unit 10, page 57.
2. On a separate sheet, write a rough draft from each plan.
3. Edit each rough draft.
4. Type each letter in good form on a separate sheet. Make up addresses and assume any other information you need to be specific in each inquiry.

PROBLEM 3

Write a letter to *Executive* magazine asking for 20 copies of the free booklet *How to Be a Super Secretary*, which you saw advertised in this month's *Executive*. You plan to use the booklets in night classes for the secretaries in your company. Also, ask that your name be added to *Executive*'s list of subscribers.

_____

_____

_____

_____

_____

PROBLEM 4

Write a letter to Hobbit's Merchandise Co. asking for information about a smoke alarm system which you recently saw advertised.

_____

_____

_____

_____

_____

_____

_____

PROBLEM 5

Make reservations for you and two other executives at the Hotel California for December 5-7. Request three single rooms, and ask the hotel to hold the rooms for late arrival. You also need to know checkout time.

_____

_____

_____

_____

_____

_____

_____

PROBLEM 6

Write this persuasive request as a representative of Santa's Helpers, an association that is trying to make sure that every child in the community receives a toy at Christmas. Address the request to a club or another organization and ask that group to "adopt" a child for Christmas. The club may select its child from descriptive (though anonymous) lists prepared by Santa's Helpers, who will distribute the gifts that are donated by those adopting the children.

1. Remember the joy of Christmas?

2. trying to make sure every child in the community receives a toy at Christmas.

3. benefit — to make a child happy

4. Thank you.

PROBLEM 7

As chairperson of the Assembly Committee of your school, write a persuasive request to Dr. Louis Cowan (345 Heite Lane, Chicago, Illinois 60617), noted lecturer and author of *The Right to Choose Your Job*. Ask Dr. Cowan to address an assembly to be held on the third Wednesday of next month on the topic of "A Student's Responsibility in Choosing a Vocation." You can pay travel and hotel expenses but no fee.

PROBLEM 8

As a member of the Office Employees' Club at Cameron Products Company, write a letter to persuade the merchants of your town to donate prizes to be awarded for the best entries in each category of a hobby show. The purpose of the show is to raise money to send underprivileged boys and girls to a summer camp.

WRITING REPLIES TO INQUIRIES AND REQUESTS

NAME _____   DATE _____

A REVISING A POOR REPLY TO AN INQUIRY

PROBLEM 1

On the lines below, write an improved reply to a prospective customer's letter.

> Referring to your letter of December 10, I am sorry to tell you that the electronic Pong game about which you inquired is currently out of stock and will not be available until the first of January. We deeply regret that you cannot receive the game in time for Christmas, but perhaps you would like to try ordering some of our other games. You will find several in our current catalog.

_____

_____

_____

_____

_____

_____

_____

B PLANNING, COMPOSING, AND TYPING REPLIES TO INQUIRIES

1. Make a plan for each message. Follow the suggestions in the Letter Planning Chart, Unit 10, page 57.
2. Write a rough draft from each plan.
3. Edit each rough draft.
4. Type each letter in good form on a separate sheet. Make up addresses and assume any other information you need to be specific in each inquiry. For background information, refer to the Worksheet problems for Unit 11.

PROBLEM 2

Prepare an effective reply to your revised draft of the multiple-question inquiry of Problem 2, Unit 11. Organize, paragraph, and number the answers in this reply to best accomplish the objectives of the reply.

PROBLEM 3

Reply to the request in Problem 3, Unit 11. You are sending the booklets in a separate envelope. The letter was given to someone in the subscription department who will confirm the inquirer's second request.

PROBLEM 4

Write the affirmative reply that, as secretary of the Shasta Club, you might write to Santa's Helpers (Problem 6, Unit 11).

PROBLEM 5

Write the reply that, as secretary of the Shasta Club, you might write to Santa's Helpers (Problem 6, Unit 11) if the organization has very good reasons for not adopting a child this Christmas. Be gracious and helpful even though you must say "no."

PROBLEM 6

Write the letter in which Dr. Cowan might reply affirmatively to your request (Problem 7, Unit 11). Make the acceptance specific as well as cordial.

PROBLEM 7

Write the letter in which Dr. Cowan might explain his reasons for not complying with your request (Problem 7, Unit 11) and in which he would suggest several alternatives. Make both the reasons and the alternatives relevant and practical.

PROBLEM 8

Write the affirmative reply that the manager of the Variety Store might make to the persuasive request written for Problem 8, Unit 11.

PROBLEM 9

Write the cover letter for the brochure you are enclosing about the auto mechanics training program offered by Ryder's Technical School. RTS has a one-year program that covers tune-up, wheel alignment, fuel systems, and so on. You are answering the general request for information on the program from Jim Bailey, 293 Steeplechase, Yorktown, Massachusetts 06125.

Enclosed is the brochure you requested avh

I am enclosing the brochure about the auto mechanics training program offered by Ryder's Technical School. Our one-year program covers you will find

NAME   DATE

 WRITING GOOD ORDER LETTERS

Apply the techniques you studied in Unit 13 as you revise the poor order letter in Problem 1 and compose a good order letter in Problem 2.

PROBLEM 1

On the lines below, rewrite the following poor order letter. Assume any information you need to make your letter clear and specific.

> I am interested in obtaining some merchandise from you for use in my office. I need about 2 dozen black typewriter ribbons, 5 packages of bond paper, 5 boxes of envelopes, and 1 box of carbon paper.
>
> Will you please send these items as soon as possible. If you need more information to fill this order, please do not hesitate to contact me.

_____

_____

_____

_____

_____

_____

PROBLEM 2

On the lines provided, write the body of the following order letter which you are to compose.

Order the Tone-Master about which you inquired (Unit 11, Problem 2). (Remember also that your inquiry was answered—see Unit 12, Problem 2.) Use the information from these two letters to make your order specific and complete.

_____

_____

_____

_____

_____

_____

B PLANNING, COMPOSING, AND TYPING REPLIES TO ORDERS

1. Make a plan for each message. Follow the suggestions in the Letter Planning Chart, Unit 10, page 57.

2. Write a rough draft from each plan.

3. Edit each rough draft.

4. Type each letter in good form on a separate sheet. Make up addresses and assume any other information you need to be specific in each inquiry.

Background Facts

Who is writing the letter?

An employee of Shelby Products Co.
4017 Fulton Ave.
Northbrook, Illinois 60062

To whom is the letter written?

A customer of Shelby Products Co.

What is the purpose of the letter?

To tell the customer what is being done about the order and to build goodwill and encourage future business

PROBLEM 3

You received today a customer's order for three gallons of white waterproofing paint. The order was accompanied by a check. In your acknowledgment you could include these positive ideas: quality and effectiveness of paint, details of shipment, our prompt, efficient service, appreciation for order and check, should receive paint Friday. Make the message direct, specific, and concise.

PROBLEM 4

Now assume that you will not be able to send the paint (Problem 3) immediately. Explain the reason for the delay (make up the reason) and tell the customer when delivery may be expected. Your purpose is to retain the order. Remember to start with a pleasant but indirect approach. Show that you are interested in serving the customer.

PROBLEM 5

Reply to a customer's order, with payment, for three boxes of personalized golf balls. The customer forgot to give the names to be imprinted on the balls. You can send the balls in a *few* days, *after* the customer tells you the exact lettering desired for each box of balls. Build goodwill—don't risk losing the order.

WRITING GOODWILL LETTERS

worksheet
14

NAME   DATE

Prepare friendly messages that will build goodwill and that are appropriate to the following situations. If you need specific directions, refer to the worksheet for Unit 13, section B, page 186. Supply needed details to make your letters cordial and interesting.

PROBLEM 1

As a member of the Office Employees' Club at Cameron Products Company (Unit 11, Problem 8, page 182), write one of these two appreciation letters. Try to substitute a more original approach for the usual "thank-you-for" opening.

a. Thank the manager of the Variety Store for the prizes (identify them) she donated for your hobby show.

b. Thank the editor of *The Hometown News* for the excellent publicity that the newspaper gave to your hobby show.

PROBLEM 2

As chairman of the Assembly Committee, write a letter to Dr. Louis Cowan (Unit 11, Problem 7, page 182) to express appreciation for the inspiring talk he gave at your school assembly yesterday.

PROBLEM 3

Write one of these two welcoming letters, in which you encourage a feeling of loyalty to the company you represent.

a. As president of Grand Manufacturing Company, welcome Malcolm Greer, proprietor of Greer Stereo Systems and Accessories (of your town) as a dealer. He has just entered into an agreement to handle Grand products in his (also your) community.

b. You are an employee of Grand Manufacturing Company and president of the Secretarial Club (the Accounting Club or the Sales Club) there. Welcome one of your classmates, who has accepted a job as secretary (accountant or sales representative) at Grand, to membership in the Club.

PROBLEM 4

Write one of these two letters of congratulations.

a. Write to one of your former English instructors whose new novel (you name it) has just appeared on *The New York Times* list of best-sellers.

b. As mayor of your town, write a congratulatory letter to the Southern Manufacturing Company as it celebrates the fiftieth anniversary of the opening of its facility in your town.

PROBLEM 5

Write one of these two form announcements, in which you will promote goodwill toward the organization.

a. Write the letter to go along with the brochure your college is sending to guidance counselors in the high schools throughout your state. The pamphlet *Choosing a College* is not slanted in favor of any college or type of college, but the letter may include a bit of low-pressure selling of your own school.

b. Write the letter announcing a two-day Open House at Southern Manufacturing Company early next month in commemoration of fifty years in business. In the letter you will invite customers and friends on tours of the plant to see how Southern operates and will mention refreshments and other plans for showing your hospitality.

PROBLEM 6

As president of Cooper Business Machines, Inc., write a letter to the publisher of *The Hometown News*, which was broken into and vandalized last night. Express your sympathy for their business trouble and offer to help.

WRITING SALES LETTERS

NAME   DATE

Plan and prepare sales promotion letters that will present the products described below to prospective buyers in terms of their needs. Select products that you know and prospects who, in your opinion, could buy and use the products advantageously. Supply sufficient specific details to make each letter an effective sales message.

PROBLEM 1

Your product is a subscription to a newspaper or magazine. Your prospective buyers are students at schools similar to your school. Select a newspaper or magazine that you like to read regularly, and try to persuade your readers that they will find it as enjoyable and as worthwhile as you do.

PROBLEM 2

Clip a picture of a small appliance or a transistor radio (cost not over $25) from a newspaper, magazine, or catalog. Choose a friend or an acquaintance (possibly a neighbor) who you think does not now use the article but might like it if he or she tried it. Write the letter that you think would convince your friend or acquaintance that he or she wants and needs the article pictured. Attach the picture to the letter when you hand it in.

PROBLEM 3

Plan and write a form letter that would make a life insurance policy appealing to young executives. Get the reader sufficiently interested to send in the reply card for further information (after which a sales representative will call on him or her).

PROBLEM 4

As a representative for a shopper's service, write a sales letter promoting Rainbow Luggage. The three-piece vinyl set comes in six fashionable colors. The cost is $89.97, payable in installments.

PROBLEM 5

Write a letter to convince the readers of your monthly magazine to buy a special publication featuring ten great mystery stories. The reader receives a free bonus gift but may return the mystery book within seven days if not satisfied. The hardbound volume consists of 931 pages and 61 full-color illustrations. It costs $10.98, payable in three monthly installments of $3.66 (plus postage) with no interest or charge for credit or handling.

PROBLEM 6

As a representative of a large mail-order house, one of your direct-mail jobs is to write a letter to promote Macho boots. Made of water-resistant leather, they are ideal for work or sport. They come in men's sizes 7-12D and sell for $42.99. They also have a one-year warranty: If a leak occurs because of defects in material or workmanship, the boots will be replaced. You are enclosing an order form. Payment may be made by check, charge card, or C.O.D.

PROBLEM 7

Plan and write a letter in which you try to sell at least 100 pocket record books (for the coming year) to a retailer for Christmas stock. They make good-looking gifts at a price that the dealer's customers will appreciate—and a markup which the dealer will like. Be sure to describe the book's features and uses as the customers will see them. You are enclosing an order form. The retail price is $2.97; the dealer's cost is $.99 each—or $.89 each for an order of 100 or more.

NAME   DATE

Plan and prepare letters appropriate to the following situations. Besides you, the following firms are involved in the correspondence: Sully's Catalog Service, 1505 Hendrix Street, Spokane, Washington 99202; Cole Manufacturing Company, 539 Jefferson Avenue, Naples, Florida 33940; and Redfield Games, 616 Marshall Avenue, Providence, Rhode Island 02909. Supply specific details as needed.

PROBLEM 1

You bought a doughnut machine—guaranteed against *defects in material and workmanship only* for one year—from Sully's two months ago. Now you return the doughnut machine because it is not working and ask for a replacement or free repair. Write the letter you will send with the doughnut machine.

PROBLEM 2

Write the reply Sully's might make to the claim letter you prepared for Problem 1 if an examination reveals an apparent defect in the heating element of the doughnut machine. Prompt replacement of the doughnut machine at no charge to the customer is, of course, the adjustment planned.

PROBLEM 3

Write the reply Sully's might make to the claim letter prepared for Problem 1 if an examination reveals that the heating element of the doughnut machine was damaged when the doughnut machine was dropped, had some heavy object dropped on it, or otherwise received a serious jolt. Since the damage is not due to defective material or workmanship, Sully's does not offer replacement or free repair but is willing to repair the doughnut machine at the cost of these repairs to the company—a cost considerably less than you would pay elsewhere.

PROBLEM 4

Write the claim letter that Mr. R. F. Bruce, manager of Redfield Games, might send to Cole Manufacturing Company asking for an adjustment on two dozen Speedway Tele-Games received too late for Christmas merchandise. Cole's sales representative promised delivery by December 10. Instead, the games arrived on December 24, causing financial loss, overstocking, and jammed storage space. Mr. Bruce would like to return the unopened cartons of Speedway Tele-Games at Cole's expense.

PROBLEM 5

Write the reply Cole might make to the claim letter prepared for Problem 4 if the Speedway Tele-Games were held up in transit because of a trucking strike. While agreeing to accept return of the games and to make the necessary adjustments in the store's account, Cole also suggests an alternative. If Redfield will keep the games, Cole will credit the store's account for a 10 percent discount—with the idea of less bother and more sales for both companies.

WRITING CREDIT LETTERS

worksheet 17

NAME   DATE

Plan and prepare friendly letters that will stimulate credit buying and that are appropriate to the following situations. Make any reasonable assumptions or supply additional details if needed.

PROBLEM 1

In January, Mrs. Linda Stafford applied for a credit account at Chaney's Interiors, 443 Shelby Drive East, Grand Junction, Colorado 81501. She wished to buy on credit two Tiffany-style lamps costing a total of $182.

After checking her credit standing and finding it highly satisfactory, the store opened an installment account for her. Mrs. Stafford agreed to pay $22 down and $20 on the 15th of each of the next eight months.

Write the credit approval letter which Chaney's might write to welcome Mrs. Stafford as a new credit customer.

PROBLEM 2

As credit manager of Shale Automotive Parts Company, 2710 Nesbitt, New Orleans, Louisiana 70183, write to acknowledge the credit application and first order of James P. Westerman, owner of Westerman's Service Station, 3301 Ridgeway Road, Lincoln, Nebraska 68510. His order for batteries, along with an invoice, is being shipped today on 2/10, n/30 terms.

The investigation showed that Westerman has been 30 to 60 days late in paying his recent creditors. Because the good battery-selling season is approaching, you have decided to extend credit to him. You must, however, set a tentative credit limit of $300.

In the letter to Westerman, welcome him as a new credit customer and explain clearly the terms, limits, and conditions stated above. Also tell him about some services, sales helps, and other merchandise which Shale has to offer.

PROBLEM 3

Reply to Ms. Rose Tutwiler's application for a charge account at Donna's Boutique, 3291 Austin Peay Highway, Hartford, Connecticut 06501.

Donna's checked Ms. Tutwiler's credit record and found that she had charge accounts in eight other stores in the city—each with an unpaid balance. Ms. Tutwiler's credit history during the last few years was one of irresponsible buying, of continued difficulty in making payments, and of numerous past-due accounts.

Write the message that Donna's might send her, a letter that should keep her goodwill while making it clear that the store would not open an installment account for her at this time.

PROBLEM 4

Write the letter of appreciation that Weaver's House of Fashion, 2793 Darlington Avenue, Raleigh, North Carolina 27613, might write to Miss Carol Damron, a customer who has been making charge account purchases regularly and paying promptly for ten years. Make any reasonable assumptions you care to about the nature of her purchases and payments.

WRITING COLLECTION LETTERS

worksheet
18

NAME   DATE

A WRITING COLLECTION LETTERS

Prepare friendly messages that are appropriate to the following situations. Supply specific details as needed.

PROBLEM 1

On your installment account at Karney's, a local store, you paid $20 on February 15, $20 on March 15, and $20 on April 15. In May you find yourself drastically short of funds because of emergency repairs on your car. Write a letter to the store explaining the situation. Ask that the May payment be deferred, and promise to continue the regular payments in June.

PROBLEM 2

Assume that Karney's accepts your explanation (Problem 1) and agrees to defer the May payment. On June 15 you miss another payment. You make no reply to the statements the store sends you as reminders on June 25 and July 10, and you miss the payment due on July 15. Write the letter (an impersonal gentle reminder) that Karney's might send you on July 20.

PROBLEM 3

Write the next collection message (a request for explanation) that Karney's (Problem 2) might send you on August 5 if you had made no payment on your account since April 15 and had not replied to the three reminders sent to you.

PROBLEM 4

Write the fifth collection message (a firm appeal) that Karney's might send you on August 20 if you did not reply to the request for explanation (Problem 3) and still had made no payment on your account since April 15.

PROBLEM 5

Write the ultimatum Karney's might send you on September 5, after you had missed four payments and had not responded to the five collection messages.

B MINIMIZING COLLECTION PROBLEMS

In the space below, itemize some of the ways in which credit people help to minimize collection problems.

_____

_____

_____

_____

_____

_____

_____

_____

_____

_____

HANDLING ROUTINE CORRESPONDENCE

worksheet 19

NAME   DATE

A PREPARING ROUTINE COMMUNICATIONS

Using separate sheets of paper, plan, prepare, and type letters and memos to fit the situations described in the following problems.

You are secretary to Mrs. Katherine Dante, a vice president of the Campbell Textiles Company. The office address is 303 Beale Street, Canyon City, Oregon 97820. Today is Monday, February 4.

PROBLEM 1

Mrs. Dante asks you to prepare a memo answering "yes" to an invitation to attend a "welcome back" party for the president of Campbell Textiles upon his return from a business trip abroad. The party is to be held in the Banquet Room at 8 p.m. on Friday, February 8.

PROBLEM 2

Mrs. Dante has previously accepted an invitation to speak at the March meeting of the Spokane (Washington) Chapter of Associated Travel Agents. Now she asks you to send a data sheet to Mr. Derek Bronson, president of the chapter, 5355 Hemingway Court, Spokane, Washington 99219.

PROBLEM 3

Mrs. Dante asks you to answer a letter just received from Mr. Benjamin Soule, 615 Lake Street, Salem, Oregon 97308. A representative of McCormick-Perrine Interiors, Inc., Soule refers to the enclosed estimates for the renovation of the executive offices of Campbell. However, the estimates were not in the envelope. Write a tactful follow-up message to Mr. Soule.

PROBLEM 4

Acknowledge the renovation estimates received a few hours after you mailed the letter to Mr. Soule (Problem 3). Be sure to tell him to disregard your earlier message.

B WRITING TRANSMITTAL LETTERS

Using separate sheets of paper, write transmittal letters and memos for each of the following situations.

You are secretary to Mr. Benjamin J. Curde, Marketing Director, Plum Electronics Corporation, Youngstown, Ohio 44485.

PROBLEM 5

Mr. Curde asks you to send a copy of the new Plum Catalog to Ms. Alicia Fenway, Manager, Radio Headquarters, 12 Grand Street, Boston, Massachusetts 02151.

PROBLEM 6

Mr. Curde asks you to send a copy of the June sales report to Morton L. Ball, manager of product development. Use a memo form to transmit the report to Mr. Ball.

NAME   DATE

A EXAMINING YOUR JOB MARKET AND YOURSELF

Use ruled or typing paper for Problems 1, 2, and 3. Do not hand in these sheets. They are for your own use in studying your job market, in analyzing your personal traits and abilities in reference to a prospective job, and in discovering some "evidence" that you may adapt in the application letters you will write.

PROBLEM 1

On the first page, list the following items:

1. *The vocation* you plan to enter. (If you have not yet decided on one particular vocation, list two or three vocational choices.)

2. *Two or more specific jobs* which could provide the first step in the realization of one of the vocational choices listed under item 1 and into which you might fit upon completion of your formal education.

3. *A number of the duties* that a person holding one of the jobs listed under item 2 would presumably be expected to perform.

4. *Several companies* in your community (or in other communities in which you would like to live and work) that employ persons in the job detailed under item 3.

PROBLEM 2

After drawing a vertical line the length of the page, slightly to the left of center, on the second page, continue your analysis:

1. In the column at the left *list a number of your personal traits* (not physical features) that could help you in carrying out the duties listed under item 3 of Problem 1. Use concrete adjectives, such as "dependable, neat, cheerful, tactful."

2. In the column at the right, opposite each trait listed, *jot down any evidence* you can think of to show that you have the trait. For example, as evidence that you are *punctual*, you might write "get to classes on time and turn in assigned work when it is due." And as evidence that you are *intelligent and industrious*, you might write "have record of continued good grades along with participation in out-of-class leadership activities."

PROBLEM 3

After drawing a vertical line the length of the page, slightly to the left of center, on the third page, continue your analysis:

1. In the column to the left *list a number of your abilities* (things you can do well) that could help you in carrying out the duties listed under item 3 of Problem 1. Be specific—for instance, ability to write computer programs in COBOL, prepare financial statements, compose effective business letters.

2. In the column to the right, opposite each ability listed, *jot down any evidence* you can think of to show that you have that ability. For example, as evidence that you *can take dictation,* you might write "have passed tests in which I took dictation at 100 words a minute and transcribed mailable letters at 25 words a minute" or "have worked in an office where I took dictation at 80 words a minute and transcribed as many as 20 letters a day."

B WRITING LETTERS ABOUT EMPLOYMENT

Plan and prepare each of these letters, the résumé, and the application form thoughtfully and edit them carefully. Make them your very best—models that you can adapt quickly to actual situations when you have limited time to write and mail your own letters about employment. Use appropriate stationery.

PROBLEM 4

Prepare the comprehensive résumé that you might mail with the application letter you will write for Problem 5. Make it an attractive, easy-reference summary of your qualifications for the job you want.

PROBLEM 5

Prepare an invited application letter in reply to a pertinent ad clipped from a newspaper or a magazine. Hand the ad in with your letter. Address the letter to the appropriate person in the company, if you can find out his or her name and official title or position. Otherwise, address it to the Personnel Manager or the Personnel Department of that company. Assume that you will send the résumé prepared for Problem 4 with the letter.

PROBLEM 6

Assume that your application letter (Problem 5) won you a personal interview, in which you had interesting meetings with the personnel director and others and an exciting look into the work of the company. Although you were told that you made a good impression and that you would hear more later, the company made no job offer. Write the letter of appreciation you might send to the personnel director the day following the interview. You are enclosing your completed application blank (Problem 7).

PROBLEM 7

Complete the application blank on pages 201 to 203. Be sure to include part-time jobs and summer employment. You may type the data or write in longhand (using a pen); in either case do it neatly, carefully, and correctly—as though you were actually applying for a job. Assume that the company is the same one to which you applied in the preceding problems.

Ernest and Fast Associates
Employment Application

An Equal Opportunity Employer
Ernest and Fast Policy and Federal Law Forbid Discrimination Because of Race, Religion, Age, Sex, Marital Status, Disability, or National Origin.

Date_____

Personal Data

Applying for position as _____ Salary required_____ Date available_____

Name: _____
　　　　　　(Last)　　　　　　　　　(First)　　　　　　　　　(Middle)　　　　　　　　　(Maiden)

Present address _____
　　　　　　　　　(Street)　　　　　　　(City)　　　　　　(State)　　　　(Zip)　　(How long at this address)

Permanent address _____
　　　　　　　　　　(Street)　　　　　　(City)　　　　　　(State)　　　　(Zip)　　(How long at this address)

Telephone number _____ Social Security number _____
　　　　　　　　(Area code)

Are you a U.S. citizen? ☐ Yes ☐ No　　　If non-citizen, give Alien Registration No. _____

Check appropriate box for age: Under 16 ☐, 16 or 17 ☐, 18 through 64 ☐, 65 or over ☐

Person to be notified in case of emergency:

　Name_____ Telephone_____

　Address_____

Relatives employed by Ernest and Fast:　　Name_____Department_____

　　　　　　　　　　　　　　　　　　　　　　Name_____Department_____

Will you consider relocation? Yes ☐　No ☐　　　Domestic　Yes ☐　No ☐　　　International　Yes ☐　No ☐

Have you ever been employed by Ernest and Fast or its subsidiaries?　　Yes ☐　No ☐

If "Yes", indicate department, publication or company _____ Dates_____

Have you previously applied for employment with Ernest and Fast?_____ If "Yes", when?_____

How were you referred to Ernest and Fast?　☐ Agency　☐ School　☐ Advertisement　☐ Direct contact　☐ **Ernest and Fast employee**　☐ Other

Name of referral source above:_____

Military Data

Have you ever served in the Military Service of the United States? _____

Branch of Service _____ From _____ To _____ Rank _____

Give details of Service duties which might apply to civilian occupations _____

Educational Data

Schools	Print Name, Number and Street, City, State, and Zip Code for each School Listing	Dates	Type of Course or Major	Graduated?	Degree Received
Grade School		From_____ To	////////		////////
High School		From_____ To			////////
College		From_____ To			
Graduate School		From_____ To			
Trade, Bus., Night, or Corres.		From_____ To			
Other		From_____ To			

Approximate scholastic average: High school _____ College _____ Class rank: High school _____ College _____

Percent of college expenses earned _____ How earned? _____

Activities

Do not name organizations that will reveal race, religion, age, sex or national origin.

School and college activities _____

Special interests outside 1. _____   Indicate the amount of 1. _____
of business.   2. _____   time devoted to each.   2. _____
                    3. _____   .3. _____

List any activity that might represent a conflict of interest with Ernest and Fast. _____

Skills

List any special skills you may have _____

	□ Speak	□ Speak	□ Speak
What foreign languages do you:	□ Read _____	□ Read _____	□ Read _____
	□ Write	□ Write	□ Write

Business machines you can operate _____

Typing speed _____ words per minute   □ Electric
                                         □ Manual   Steno speed _____ words per minute   Method _____

Employment Data
Begin with most recent employer. List all full-time, part-time, temporary, or self-employment.

		Mo-Yr	Mo-Yr
Company name		Employed from	To
Street address		Salary or earnings Start	Finish
City State Zip code		Telephone (Area code)	
Name and title of immediate supervisor		Your title	

Description of duties

Reason for terminating or considering a change

		Mo-Yr	Mo-Yr
Company name		Employed from	To
Street address		Salary or earnings Start	Finish
City State Zip code		Telephone (Area code)	
Name and title of immediate supervisor		Your title	

Description of duties

Reason for terminating

		Mo-Yr	Mo-Yr
Company name		Employed from	To
Street address		Salary or earnings Start	Finish
City State Zip code		Telephone (Area code)	
Name and title of immediate supervisor		Your title	

Description of duties

Reason for terminating

		Mo-Yr	Mo-Yr
Company name		Employed from	To
Street address		Salary or earnings Start	Finish
City State Zip code		Telephone (Area code)	
Name and title of immediate supervisor		Your title	

Description of duties

Reason for terminating

PROBLEM 8

Assume that you had a second interview with the company last week, and the job was offered to you. The next day you wrote a letter thanking the person for the interview and telling him or her that you will let him or her know within two weeks whether or not you will accept the job.

This morning another company offered you a job that (for any reason or reasons you wish to assume) you have decided to accept. Write a letter declining the offer for the job you were offered first.

PROBLEM 9

You have just started to work, and you are enjoying your new job very much. In the final interview, you were told that one of the former employers (or teachers) you gave as a reference had given you an excellent recommendation. This recommendation was a strong factor in the decision to offer you the job.

Write a letter to your former employer (or teacher) thanking him or her for helping you get the job.

NAME _____   DATE _____

In each of the following problems, you are asked to assume a specific role. For each problem, much of the information needed has been gathered for you, but you must organize the information into a meaningful report. As you do so, you may make up and add any details that will help make your report complete and effective. Use the space provided to organize and outline each report, then draft the report on a separate sheet of paper.

PROBLEM 1

You are the Assistant Sales Manager for Worldwide Films Corporation, a movie distribution company. Three months ago, you suggested to your boss, Ms. Wendy Ann Jordan, that Worldwide would probably do very well to rerelease some of its older films because of the nostalgia fever among so many people. You suggested testing the idea by rereleasing only three movies in selected markets: New York, Boston, and Atlanta.

The results of the test proved that you were right: In the past two months, one movie, "The Last Roundup," grossed $1.2 million in New York, $1.34 million in Boston, and $1.1 million in Atlanta. The second movie, "Inside City Hall," grossed $1.43 million in New York, $1.62 million in Boston, and $1.54 million in Atlanta. The third movie, "The Witness," grossed $850,000 in New

York, $945,000 in Boston, and $1.25 million in Atlanta. Because you are confident that these results prove that Worldwide's other older films can be rereleased very profitably, you decide to prepare a memo in which you will (1) summarize the results of rereleasing these films and (2) suggest other films that could be just as successful.

Write the memo. (Hint: In your memo, prepare a chart showing the gross sales for each film by city. Use the discussion of the success of these three films to convince your boss that she should approve the rerelease of other films. Also include another chart of estimated sales for the other films you suggest for rerelease. Make up the names of films and the estimated gross receipts for each.)

_____
_____
_____
_____
_____
_____
_____
_____
_____
_____
_____
_____
_____
_____

PROBLEM 2

You are Assistant Warehouse Manager for Durable Plastics Inc., a middle-sized manufacturer of miscellaneous plastic products. The main office and the warehouse for this company are located in Los Angeles, California. About two years ago, Durable opened its first branch office, a sales office in New York, where four full-time sales representatives sell Durable products on the East Coast. These four men and women have developed annual sales on the East Coast of approximately $3.56 million—a growth of about $3 million in only two years! In the same period, Durable's West Coast business has grown from about $12.2 million to $17.6 million. To meet the tremendous increase in the demand for its products, Durable expanded its manufacturing facilities last year, but its warehouse space has remained the same.

Everyone in the company (including you and your boss, Mr. Harvey Winkel, Warehouse Manager) is aware of the obvious need for more warehouse space. In addition, everyone agrees that Durable should lease a new warehouse (rather than expand its present warehouse or build a new warehouse)—but where? Most people in the company have assumed that Durable should lease another warehouse in the Los Angeles area, but you are convinced that this is not the best solution.

Having studied the problem carefully, you are ready to recommend that Durable should lease a warehouse in New Jersey, not in Los Angeles. Among your reasons are the following: The Los Angeles warehouse is spacious enough to handle all of Durable's West Coast business for many years. Although business has grown in recent years, company analysts agree that sales on the West Coast are now at about the maximum level; they do not expect West Coast sales to increase substantially in the next ten years. Everyone agrees that future growth will come from New York, Pennsylvania, Massachusetts, and Connecticut. A warehouse in the New Jersey area would be able to handle orders for these states faster than a Los Angeles warehouse; in addition, shipping would be cheaper from a New Jersey warehouse. The space available in the present Los Angeles warehouse would be sufficient to take care of all West Coast business; and the New Jersey warehouse could then take care of all East Coast business.

Through a real estate broker, you have found three suitable sites in New Jersey; in Trenton, Somerville, and in Secaucus. Each site has more than 200,000 square feet of space available, and each is available for long-term leasing at reasonable rents. You plan to enclose with your memo to Mr. Winkel a description of the three warehouses that the real estate broker supplied.

Write the report to Mr. Winkel.

_____

_____

_____

_____

_____

_____

_____

_____

_____

_____

_____

_____

_____

_____

_____

_____

_____

_____